THE JIVE 95

An Oral History of America's Greatest Underground Rock Radio Station KSAN San Francisco

HANK ROSENFELD

Essex, Connecticut

An imprint of Globe Pequot, the trade division of
The Rowman & Littlefield Publishing Group, Inc.
4501 Forbes Blvd., Ste. 200
Lanham, MD 20706
www.rowman.com

Distributed by NATIONAL BOOK NETWORK

British Library Cataloguing in Publication Information Available

Library of Congress Cataloging-in-Publication Data

Names: Rosenfeld, Hank, author.
Title: The Jive 95 : an oral history of America's greatest underground rock radio station KSAN San Francisco / Hank Rosenfeld.
Description: Essex, Connecticut : Backbeat, 2023. | Includes bibliographical references. | Summary: "The Jive 95: An Oral History of America's Greatest Underground Rock Radio Station KSAN San Francisco is an oral history of America's first hippie underground FM on the dial that broadcasted the countercultural consciousness of the '60s and '70s to a new generation" — Provided by publisher.
Identifiers: LCCN 2022054120 (print) | LCCN 2022054121 (ebook) | ISBN 9781493070862 (cloth) | ISBN 9781493070879 (epub)
Subjects: LCSH: KSAN (Radio station : San Francisco, Calif.) | Alternative radio broadcasting—California—San Francisco—History—20th century. | Counterculture—California—San Francisco—History—20th century. | Rock music—California—San Francisco—1961-1970—History and criticism. | Rock music—California—San Francisco—1971-1980—History and criticism. | Radio broadcasters—California—San Francisco—Interviews. | Rock musicians—Interviews. | LCGFT: Oral histories.
Classification: LCC ML3534.3 .R675 2023 (print) | LCC ML3534.3 (ebook) | DDC 781.6609794/61—dc23/eng/20221228
LC record available at https://lccn.loc.gov/2022054120
LC ebook record available at https://lccn.loc.gov/2022054121

∞™ The paper used in this publication meets the minimum requirements of American National Standard for Information Sciences—Permanence of Paper for Printed Library Materials, ANSI/NISO Z39.48-1992.

You are everywhere you're supposed to be
And I can get your station
When I need rejuvenation

—Van Morrison, "Wavelength," written for KSAN creator Tom Donahue

What if all of life is a show?

—Philip Roth

I mean, anybody, who has seen the vision of what has to be, knows that he either has to do, what has to be done, to bring about what has to be or, he is fucking off.

—Ken Kesey

DEDICATION

This book is dedicated to Jeff House, who was not able to complete his narrative, *To Live Outside the Law You Must Be Honest*, for which he interviewed some of our storytellers. To every hung-up person in the whole wide universe—and especially to Norman Davis, who established the Jive 95 website, from which some of these stories have been taped together.

CONTENTS

FOREWORD

Robin Menken

The most revolutionary things about radio in the 1960s were:

Wolfman Jack outing R & B on XERF-AM in Ciudad Acuña, Mexico, blasting across the United States.

KWKH's Louisiana Hayride outing C & W and rockabilly, including Elvis. Both helped break down racial barriers.

Motown's commercial success, leading to a generation of kids of all colors dancing together.

The British Invasion launching a world of music and American musicians and songwriters, coming from folk music, jug band, country and urban blues, jazz and classical training, morphing into folk-rock bands and original sounds, played on KMPX and KSAN.

The scene, riding on a wave of weed, shrooms, and LSD, was in San Francisco, with free Panhandle concerts, Victorian ballrooms (sprung wood floors), dedicated to the infinite variety of hippie-garbed, dropped out, turned on—historicized in exquisite psychedelic posters. Even the Stones and Beatles wandered up and down Haight Street, inspired to take back the San Francisco sound and the LSD, trying to top the other band's last album.

And none of this would have mattered without a station that played whole album sides (the concept albums!) that spread a culture borne by music across the world. No honchos were telling DJs what to play in rotation.

We were the weirdos, the arty kids expressing ourselves; our clothes were our silks, our heraldry, how we recognized each other, the weirder the better—our emotional trips taken on music heard over our station, the soundtrack to these movies we were starring in . . . the movies of our lives. It was the opposite of selfies. We weren't logging evidence of us fitting in, being liked. Monetizing. We were inventing a world and leaving no trace. Let the world catch up.

Robin Menken was in the Family Dog and Second City. She was a DMT shaman, hippie queen, and cover designer of two LPs that KMPX DJ Howard Hesseman (under the name Don Sturdy) art directed: Country Joe McDonald's *War War War* and *Hold On It's Coming*. Robin co-produced the latter album for her husband, Joe. She was once on the cover of *Rolling Stone*.

INTRODUCTION

I come from a long line of radio listeners. My parents had WJR 760 on all day, broadcasting "from the Golden Tower of the Fisher Building"—Detroit Tiger games, brilliantly-skilled morning hosts, and the school-closing announcements after overnight snowstorms. My sisters Jill and Nancy dug WKNR "Keener 13," and "The Big 8" CKLW which came from across the river in Canada—stations blasting Motown soul and teeny-bopper Top 40 pop. In 1967, I had my own radio station: my pal Shel and I bought a "transmitter kit" we saw in the back of a Daredevil comic book—by attaching it to a nine-volt transistor radio, we could reach homes half a block away. (Our programming on WSHR—ShelHankRadio—centered on announcing, "If you are within the sound of our voices, call!")

In 1978, my father warned me about moving to California, reciting a line from a poem by Alfred Lord Tennyson about "the lotus eaters" out there. Soon I was driving a taxicab in San Francisco. And when I heard the greatest radio station ever—KSAN—come over the Plymouth Fury radio, I knew I had to work there. KSAN was "The Jive 95.

On April 7, 1967, its prototype, KMPX, took the air as the first FM underground rock 'n roll radio station. And the rest is legendary. (Much of it myth.)

This book is about one specific broadcast outlet, in one specific city, that happened to spark a nationwide movement and rock the world. Our hero of this happening is a hip genius named Tom Donahue. They called him "Big Daddy" because he went six foot five and "four hundred pounds of solid sounds." Quitting his rule as DJ king of what he called "the rotting corpse" of Top 40 AM radio, Tom took over a low-powered FM station and turned it into the voice of a counterculture. This vast, weird, new community of young people, tuning in to KSAN

Tom Donahue emcees a Jive 95 rock show; t-shirt designed by friend Dan O'Neill.
COURTESY BOB SIMMONS

to get turned on to new, inventive ways of making connections with one another. Jive 95 "Gnus" man, Wes "Scoop" Nisker calls it, "tribal radio. The main message was always music. But KSAN began to function as a communications center for the antiwar movement. Being radical became part of my job description." Being radical became part of my job description. And the main message was always the music." 1967 was the first time the kids could catch on their radios the same bands they danced to at the Avalon and Fillmore ballrooms: Santana, the Grateful Dead, Jefferson Airplane, Quicksilver Messenger Service, Country Joe and the Fish, Janis Joplin with Big Brother & the Holding Company.

How did Donahue blow open the medium in the late 1960s? Who were the Jive 95? And how does a state-of-the-edge mix tape of mind-expanding music, crazy funny news, and the sounds of revolution get appropriated by fat-cat corporate culture? Beat poet and '60s avatar Allen Ginsberg called it "Moloch"—a force of death and ruin sucking KSAN into a late '70s wasteland where, as Elvis Costello sang, the radio is in the hands of such a lot of fools trying to anesthetize the way that you feel . . .

I came aboard in 1979. My only experience had been on WESU, a college radio station in Middletown, Connecticut. All of sudden, every day working in San Francisco radio was the time of my life. Being alive and live in the radio moment, what Scoop called, being in "the Here and Wow!" felt part of KSAN's last heyday of free expression. We were still a mouthpiece for the mobilization of . . . something. Something never heard before? And I'd always wanted to know how Tom Donahue created something out of nothing. I wanted to feel that flash from the early days, the spirited beginnings of *underground radio*. How was a troupe of twenty-somethings able to *get it together* and become what John Coltrane referred to as "a force for real good"? For three years, I've been corresponding with some of those original "heads" and "freaks," and "straights," too; it's been so gratifying discovering a KSAN network of enlightened, gifted people, who continued doing great things. Teachers, filmmakers, journalists, editors, authors, activists, pranksters, and the hippest of parental units. Now approaching geezerhood, they remember (!) a time when, if their timing was right, how much outrageousness one could fit into sixty-seconds of airtime. "First of all," station sage Bonnie Simmons explains, "we were really young. And second, we were in the hippest city in very interesting times."

I've come from a long line of radio stations since 1979, and been canned from many of them (radio is volatile!)—from New York to Minneapolis, Los Angeles to "somewhere in the Mediterranean Sea." But return with me now to those most thrilling day trippers of yesteryear! Where music was their weapon and comedy their kiss! When they followed a mighty avatar able to leap tall corporations in a single sound! And where, using his super powers to alter minds, told other humans terrestrially-bound (but paying attention): "Listen man, radio waves are one of our most important, permanent creations. Somewhere past Alpha Centauri, your show is still headed out into the universe."

Note: For a modern reading experience: audio of DJs, concerts, commercials, and other goodie oldies are accessible via QR codes. Visit jive95.com for additional stories and audio, more tales to astonish that couldn't fit between these covers, including *Where are they now?* info, plus assorted *mishigoss* like you wouldn't believe. This book draws on Jeff House's unpublished interviews and includes quotes based on materials gleaned from books—especially Milan Melvin's autobiography, *Highlights of a Low Life*, edited by Peter Laufer. Some material has been edited for clarity.

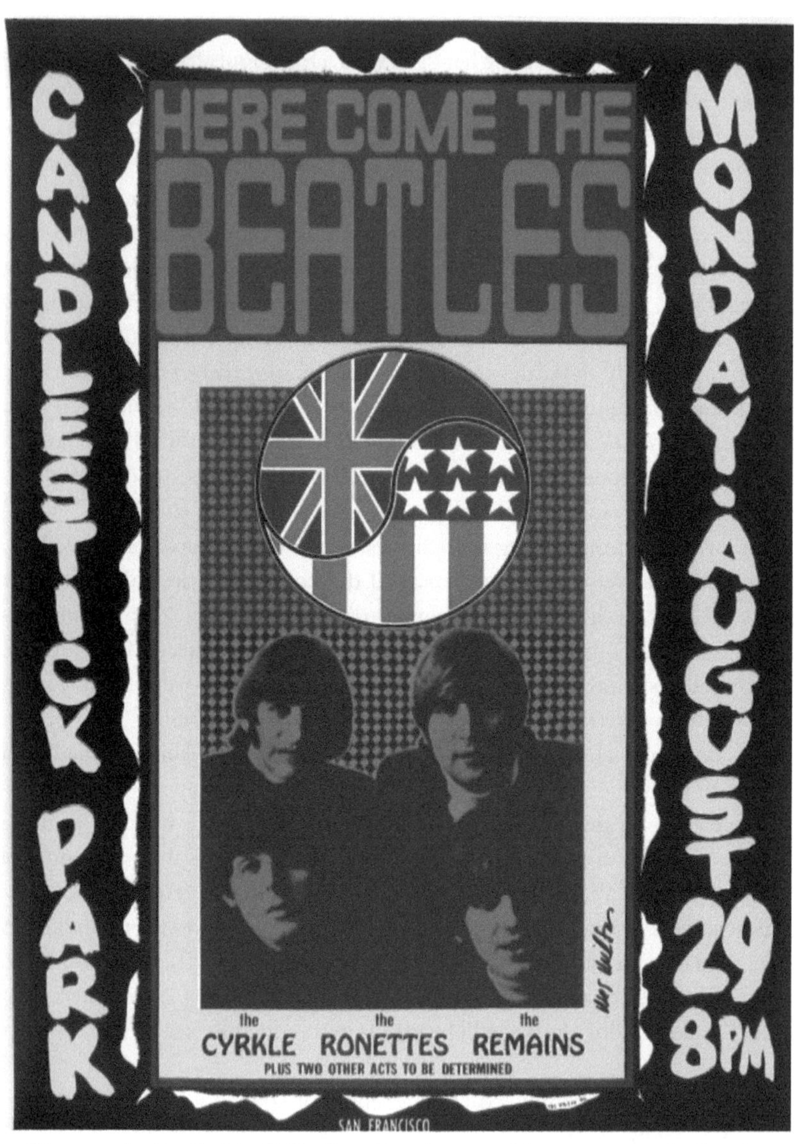

There go the Beatles! In 1966, Tom Donahue put this concert on, the last the Beatles ever gave in the United States. POSTER BY WES WILSON

1

BEATLES!

Hank Rosenfeld: Our first speaker admired Tom Donahue and was his friend. Joel Selvin, author of more than a dozen books, including *Summer of Love: The Inside Story of LSD, Rock & Roll, Free Love and High Times in the Wild West* and *Altamont: The Rolling Stones, the Hells Angels, and the Inside Story of Rock's Darkest Day*, spent decades as a reporter and music columnist at for the *San Francisco Chronicle.*

JOEL SELVIN It starts with Tom Donahue, a six foot five inch, 450-pound giant who virtually invented underground FM radio in 1967. A bear of a man; not unlike a young Orson Welles. He came to San Francisco in 1961 after being chased out of Philadelphia by a payola scandal.

Next, Ben Fong-Torres, who came to DJ at KSAN while he was editor at *Rolling Stone* magazine, is the author of many books, including *The Rice Room*, and *The Hits Just Keep on Coming: The History of Top 40 Radio*, The *San Francisco Chronicle* called Ben the "keeper of the story of rock, a walking, talking rock 'n roll encyclopedia."

BEN FONG-TORRES For teenagers in the early '60s, there was Top 40, a rock 'n roll hit parade hosted by screaming DJs who also showed up at high schools for sock hops, at teen fairs, or at local TV dance shows hoping for the big time. By then, Tom Donahue was a Top 40 DJ in San Francisco, opening his show with a rumbling but somehow friendly warning: "This is Big Daddy

Tom Donahue, here to clear up your face and mess up your mind." He also produced concerts. Like the Beatles in '66—their last show ever in the U.S.

Everything starts with the Beatles, in my book at least. My sisters saw them in Detroit at Cobo Hall and at the Olympia hockey barn. The Beatles' final American appearance was August 29, 1966, in San Francisco's baseball stadium, Candlestick Park. There, six months before Tom Donahue began his great adventures in stereo, the entire Family Donahue helped out to put on the Beatles show, including his partner, Raechel, and tween daughter Buzzy. (Both became DJs.)

RAECHEL DONAHUE The only reason we produced the Beatles' 1966 San Francisco show in the first place was because of the contract. They hated America so much by now, they were going to break the contract, but Tom put a clause in there that basically said, "Either do the freakin' show or give us ten thousand dollars." That was a lot of money. So they chose to do the show. They would have left the country otherwise.

The Beatles arrived in an armored truck to protect them from the crazy crowds.

JOEL SELVIN It was about to begin. But the head groundskeeper said he was not about to let these longhaired Mop Tops ruin his freshly mown ballfield.

RAECHEL DONAHUE The Beatles were in their armored car coming through ballplayers' tunnel. But this groundskeeper was hanging on his gate going, "No! We have a pennant race going on here!" Tom's partner, Bob Mitchell, started digging his foot into the Giants infield grass, laughing, "And there's another bad bounce for the home team!"

JOEL SELVIN Donahue was on it, like always. He said to the guy, "Okay, you win. Now go out there and tell those kids there ain't gonna be a show." The Beatles performed eleven songs in thirty minutes. On a high stage surrounded by a fence, the Beatles performed eleven songs in thirty minutes, none from their new LP, *Revolver*.

Dan Hicks—he'd go on to front Dan Hicks & His Hot Licks—was at Candlestick Park.

DAN HICKS We were told the Beatles' playing was always drowned out by girls screaming, but we could hear them. How were they? The Beatles were fine.

RAECHEL DONAHUE The Beatles sang totally flat. I'm right in front of the stage as they start into "Love Me Do"—I know they couldn't hear themselves—gawd, they're singing in the key of R.

BUZZY DONAHUE I got to go backstage. I was lucky enough to meet everybody. And the great photographer Jim Marshall took a photo of me with John Lennon. Yeah, I had my Beatle haircut.

RACHAEL DONAHUE When it was finally all done, we just barely broke even.

BEN FONG-TORRES Tom had quit his job as Top 40 top dog at KYA in '65.

JOEL SELVIN He said a man can only play so many Herman's Hermits records and still feel good about himself. He dreamed of playing longer cuts; the longest thing he played on KYA was Marty Robbins' "El Paso." That was the one you went to the bathroom on.

BEN FONG-TORRES Now he was on the alert for the next radio revolution. If only there was a way to perform the magic of the medium, without playlists and pimple cream commercials . . .

2

SECRETS OF THE RED DOG SALOON

And I live like an outlaw
An' I'm always on the run
An' I'm always getting busted
And I got to take a stand
I believe the revolution
Must be mighty close at hand . . .
I smoke marijuana
But I can't get behind your wars.
And most of what I do believe
Is against most of your laws
Oh . . . oh what you gonna do about meeee?
Oh . . . oh what you gonna do about meeee?

—Quicksilver Messenger Service, "What about Me?"

Let there be dancing in the streets,
drinking in the saloons,
and necking in the parlor!

—Groucho Marx

In 1965, Quicksilver Messenger Service was among the first to play the heady mix of folk-rock, jazz, and classical that was called "psychedelic" music. That year is crucial to understanding how Tom Donahue rewrote the radio playbook to include, "What About Me," and other questions for the authorities behind war, discrimination and the many injustices killing the country that decade. Two amazing characters from Donahue's original radio gang—Milan Melvin and Chandler Laughlin—were wild-eyed *companeros* cooking up new ideas in an old saloon 250 miles from San Francisco.

JOEL SELVIN Virginia City, Nevada, was a silver-mining town south of Reno. Newspaperman Mark Twain worked there as city editor of the *Virginia City Territorial Enterprise* in the 1860s.

Jump ahead a hundred years later to an evolutionary leap in consciousness, described by Dennis McNally, author of *A Long Strange Trip: The Inside History of the Grateful Dead* and other other biographies of San Francisco heroes like Jack Kerouac.

DENNIS MCNALLY In a snowbound Sierra cabin in 1965, Chandler Laughlin and a couple of friends are playing Risk on LSD when a notion crossed their minds: the old, broken-down Red Dog Saloon could be the *cool place* for friends to come dance and play.

Chandler invited some new friends, artists from San Francisco State forming a folk-rock band called The Charlatans, to come play Virginia City.

JOEL SELVIN Chan Laughlin inspired the Charlatan's look: they wore string ties and three-piece suits from the 1800s. The Red Dog Saloon looked like the Wild West, with one additional element: LSD.

CHAN LAUGHLIN The only ground rules were, "You're in a western movie. Play it!"

PETER RICHARDSON, author of *No Simple Highway: A Cultural History of the Grateful Dead* No one suspected the Red Dog experience would have far-reaching consequences for the San Francisco scene two hundred miles west.

CHAN LAUGHLIN Everyone was on acid that first show—the band, the Red Dog employees. Everyone. The Charlatans hadn't actually rehearsed as a band much. When they started trading instruments during "Wabash Cannonball," things got disorganized.

Ralph J. Gleason renowned jazz columnist at the *Chronicle* and an early advocate of rock 'n roll, visited Virginia City to write up the scene.

"Mining camp desperado . . . riverboat gambler . . . I. Magnin beatnik . . . India import exotic. Variations on every dance of the past decade: the hitchhike, the jerk, the hully-gully, all improved on and individually performed for self-expression . . . eyes all shining with the light of LSD."

DAN HICKS, the Charlatans, author of *I Scare Myself: A Memoir* I met Milan Melvin at the Red Dog, a cool cat, tall, thin, good-looking biker guy. One of those guys who'd traded with Indians and had belts with old turquoise and buffalo nickels. Later became a DJ at KMPX.

MILAN MELVIN The Red Dog, to me, was an outlaw enclave. It was revolutionaries and hustlers, anarchists and beatniks, musicians and Indians. You know, quality people. People you could trust at that time.

DAN HICKS There was a contingency of townsfolk who didn't like the hippies being there. We found a tombstone on stage with "CHARLATANS" etched into it. It was left by the Clampers.

MIKE FERGUSON, the Charlatans They were some a-hole lodge, red shirts type thing. "E Clampus Vitus!"

DAN HICKS Whenever they saw us they went ape shit.

MIKE FERGUSON We went to San Francisco that fall to get away from them.

MARK TWAIN, in *Roughing It* "He dropped his ears, set up his tail, and left for San Francisco at a speed which can only be described as a flash and a vanish! Long after he was out of sight we could hear him whiz."

From the Red Dog Saloon to the City by the Bay, as author Chuck Klosterman writes in Sex, Drugs, and Cocoa Puffs, *"In the realm of rock & roll, the cool kids rule!"*
POSTER BY ALTON KELLY

3

THE HAIGHT-FULL GREAT

After discovering it was some of Donahue's crew that helped start the scene in Virginia City, I followed the trail of the Charlatans (early steampunks?) who high-tailed it to Frisco in '66. In "The City," a couple of Red Dog irregulars, Chan Laughlin and Jack Towle (another future Donahue hire), seeking their next creative concoction, moved in with the Family Dog.

CHAN LAUGHLIN The San Francisco rock 'n roll scene was invented by the Charlatans and the Family Dog.

DENNIS MCNALLY The Family Dog were hard-core hipsters not yet called hippies.

CHAN LAUGHLIN All we really wanted to do was throw a big dance to raise money to buy land in Arizona to run a mail-order pet cemetery.

JOEL SELVIN They had a lot of dogs, many of which were run over in traffic in front of their Victorian.

A young Texan named Chet Helms co-founded the collective.

JOEL SELVIN Chet Helms approached the new community with a missionary zeal. A pot dealer and a dumpster diver, he threw parties visited by many of the rapidly expanding households of young people who were growing their hair, smoking marijuana, taking LSD, and thinking about things in a different way.

Luria Castell, activist with the Family Dog (and go-go dancer pal of Chan's at the Red Dog), explained to Ralph Gleason of the *Chronicle* what was happening: "Music is the most beautiful way to communicate, it's the way we're going to change things. Letting it come out in a positive way with the simple health of dancing, getting crazy once a month or so."

JOEL SELVIN The Family Dog's first big dance concert was called "A Tribute to Dr. Strange."

STEPHEN GASKIN, author of *Haight Ashbury Flashbacks* That title because a lot of pop philosophy was in Marvel comic books and their characters. Doc Strange had to do a lot of self-conquering. The battles he fought were not something that could be done with a superhero kick: he had to get to himself *inside*. People used metaphors from the books on trips; they'd talk about how this was like when Thor happened across the bridge in Valhalla.

JOEL SELVIN "A Tribute to Dr. Strange" was a happening. Suddenly, almost everyone at Longshoreman's Hall that night thought: *I had no idea there were so many of us.*

BEN FONG-TORRES There were two old ballrooms. Chet Helms and the Family Dog put on shows at the Avalon. Bill Graham, a New York transplant, began staging concerts at the Fillmore. We'd pay our two dollars and walk into a new world: light shows where artists swirled colored oils, and gels projected patterns, pulsing in time with the music. Loops of cartoons with old film clips mixed in. Strobe lights made it seem like anyone moving was in an old-time movie. Black lights gave any white object, from clothing to teeth, a glowing violet. People got high and danced—some, with no need for a partner, dancing endlessly.

Chan Laughlin and Milan Melvin combined forces with Bay Area artists, psychedelic posterizers like Alton Kelley and his spacey chums. They produced the illustrations announcing ballroom rock shows—posters that are now archetypal pieces from that period—and also some far-out work for KMPX and KSAN.

ALTON KELLY Everybody knew everybody. It was a long-running party for that short period of time.

4

HIS SECRET IDENTITY

Big Daddy: a man massive as media; aurally fixated on casting wide as worlds. Possessor of a sense of timing, of space, a sense of the connectedness of all things—his sense of segue. For a clearer picture, let's go to *Rolling Stone*'s Ben Fong-Torres, the one and only Raechel Donahue, beloved DJ Bob McClay, and true blue compañero Milan Melvin.

MILAN MELVIN Tom was older than the rest of us at the station by at least ten years—he was thirty-eight when he began KMPX—and eons ahead of us in experience. From army intelligence in the Philippines and ambitions to join the CIA in the mid-'50s. I saw a photo of him then: a tall, dark-haired man at the microphone with an Adam's apple the size of Alcatraz. And cool? All of us would learn plenty from Tom about cool.

BOB MCCLAY Donahue's presence in North Beach made a long-lasting impact on its cultural life—he befriended poets, artists, musicians, hanging out at Enrico's or New Joe's.

JOEL SELVIN And taking tons of LSD!

MILAN MELVIN I don't think Tom did anything that wasn't fun. Ever. That guy was one of the most well-qualified people to live I ever met. I mean he had all the desires for everything, and he had taste in everything. A man of insatiable appetites for fine food, dangerous drugs, and mind-bending music. He loved to live in a grandiose manner. With his own court, and we were so many fools.

CHAPTER 4

Let's hear from two of the famous foils who sat at the feed of Big Daddy at Enrico's sidewalk café, 504 Broadway west of Columbus in North Beach.

DAVID STEINBERG, director/comedian I had great delight being with him. He had a pedantic knowledge of humor as well as a sense of humor.

TOM SMOTHERS, Dick Smother's brother Many times he and David Steinberg and I ended up laughing and crying. He never repeated a story and was also the most gracious host I'd ever known.

DAVID STEINBERG That patriarchal image; he loved it, and he played it well.

BEN FONG-TORRES Both of his parents were journalists. His name was Thomas Coman, born May 21, 1928, in South Bend, Indiana.

RAECHEL DONAHUE Tom Coman Sr. was in the Harry S. Truman administration in the '50s. He was on the United States' first federal labor board. President John F. Kennedy asked his father to be his secretary of labor. Turned it down; the family lineage, if you go back, back, back—you'll find one Martha Ball: wife of George Washington, our very first president!

As a youth, Tom Jr. owned a boxer named Socrates Dionysus and was a member of several kennel clubs. He learned to perform, and directed productions for the Levittown Players of Bucks County, Pennsylvania. His first radio gig?

BEN FONG-TORRES His first job was in 1949 at WTIP in Charleston, West Virginia, doing a show and cleaning the bathroom for fifty dollars a week. Donahue eventually became a top-rated DJ at WIBG, Philadelphia. Once, he was in college, thinking of a career as a butcher—now he was injecting Black music into Wibbage's menu of pop.

RAECHEL DONAHUE His parents about had a fuckin' heart attack that their son was a DJ at what was called, "a race and blues" station.

BOB MCCLAY Then came the payola scandal. Tom was encouraged to leave town by his partner-in-crime and future business partner, Bob Mitchell who was already in San Francisco. The Federal Communications Commission was making a lot of announcers sweat.

Corruption investigators in Philly found Big Daddy to be a dangerous East Coast radio personality. He was not only bigger and smarter than they were—he was already gone. Split the scene.

BOB MCCLAY When I got to San Francisco, he was a DJ on KYA, probably the most successful AM station in the country. Top-rated? Out of a hundred people listening to their radios, forty were tuned to KYA—that left thirty-nine competitors to split the rest of the San Francisco Bay Area. And the finest of their top-flight DJs was Donahue.

5

BIG DADDY, SLY STONE, AND THE ONE-HIT WONDERS AT THE COW PALACE

I've been making extra money playing high school sock hops.
I'm a big-time guest mc.
You should hear me talking to the little children.
And listen what they say to me.

—Harry Chapin, "WOLD"

Bay Area all-star favorite, Terry McGovern, says Donahue and Mitchell were real idea men in a fertile San Francisco environment.

TERRY MCGOVERN It sounds corny, but revolution, change, all that stuff you hear about, was in the air. Here are two young AM jocks; they love radio but they don't like corporate—same old story—who decide to try something else. Except their backdrop for the dream was The City of San Francisco. So their wild ideas started paying off.

Between '62 and '67, they grew a mini-empire that included, Autumn Records (music is happening, people are dancing in the streets: why not start up a label?); Cougar Productions, for management and booking; Danton Inc. for concert production; and the very popular, "Tipsheet" from Tempo Productions. The Tipsheet went to small stations all over the West: a countdown list of 45s Donahue thought were the cool ones to play—he also included funny lines for the DJs to use if they wanted to sound intelligent. Eric Christiansen was one of Donahue's first employees at Tempo.

ERIC CHRISTIANSEN I mean, he would slide me some money—I wasn't on the payroll. I stuffed envelopes with promo 45s and sent them off. But I had a ground-floor view of a rising company. Donahue treated everyone like kids, so I fit right in. And I went home with lots of free records—great pay when you're twelve!

Buzzy Donahue saw her dad's shows at the Cow Palace show when she was eleven.

BUZZY DONAHUE Thirty acts on the bill, in front of eighteen thousand people. The Cow Palace was where white audiences saw Black acts for the first time. Ray Charles, Chubby Checker, the Ronettes; the energy in there was amazing. Bands doing their one hit song, giving 110 percent—like Bobby Freeman's "The Swim"—and being hustled offstage to make room for the next group. The house band included Sly Stone.

Sly was nineteen, and a fledgling co-producer at Autumn Records with Donahue. Dan Hicks remembers when the Charlatans were invited there to do a demo.

DAN HICKS Tom Donahue had a few things going with some pop bands, maybe the Beau Brummels, having some success with these local long-haired bands. He wanted to see if the Charlatans were gonna be one of them, so during that Red Dog summer of '65, we took the train down from Reno. Tom picked out songs that he thought could be hits—I think "Leavin' on a Jet Plane" was one. These were the first recordings of the Charlatans. I remember Sly Stone running around from one instrument to the next, showing us how versatile he was and that he could play all the instruments. I got the impression he was trying to impress, like, *dig me.* It was kind of rinky-dink.

ERIC CHRISTENSEN I got to watch Sly lay down a bass line for Harper's Bizarre's cover of Simon and Garfunkel's "Feeling Groovy." I watched him produce psychedelic bands like the Mojo Men and Vejtables, faux Beatle bands like the Tikis, and record and play behind teeny bopper bands like the Spearmints. Tom saw it all in Sly Stewart right away: a hipster from Vallejo in the East Bay far ahead of his time.

BEN FONG-TORRES Sly wanted to follow Donahue and Mitchell. He hosted shows on KDIA and KSOL in Oakland, playing Dylan, the Beatles, Lord Buckley . . . he brought a piano into the studio and sang happy birthday to listeners. Sometimes he sang the commercials. He said, otherwise, it'd be boring.

DAN HICKS Sly had a pretty cool radio show. He was kind of sexy and he'd get girls on the phone, and he was good with the writing thing.

BEN FONG-TORRES When the show ended he would go play with his band, Sly and the Stoners. By '67, he had formed the Family Stone and left radio for good.

ERIC CHRISTENSEN Nobody'd heard music like Sly's. Sly broke through for a ton of Black rock and funk bands to follow. Arthur Lee of Love and Sly were the first Black musicians I remember embracing psychedelia. Tom bought him a purple XKE. Custom-painted.

SIDE TRIP

Grace Slick and the Great Society, and Donahue's North Beach Club

One psychedelic group Sly Stone produced at Autumn was called the Great Society (see Lyndon Johnson). Donahue was impressed with their lead vocalist. "She had the all-time freakiest voice I'd ever heard," he said. "I was so fed up with happy little girls with too many petticoats and dimples in their knees singing dumb songs that didn't mean anything. And I kept saying listen, man, the first person that comes along and puts words in

a chick's mouth, who gives her some balls, who makes you think she's a human being, instead of another species, will really have something that can cut it. When I heard Grace Slick that day, I knew well that's really where the chick is at."

JESSE BLOCK, director KSAN documentary, *Something In The Air* The Great Society was unbelievably bad. They told Tom they'd been playing together six weeks, so he knew it was probably three, referring to an old story: A promotion man tells everybody, "My record's a smash," and a guy says, "Yeah? Call the factory, let's see how many you've sold." Guy at the factory says, "We've sold two." Promotion man hangs up and he says, "It sold four."

Donahue said, "This voice you gotta check out." Marty Balin and Paul Kantner heard Grace sing at the Matrix, a club Marty'd opened in order to showcase his folk-rock group. Slick took on Signe Wilkerson's vocals for the Jefferson Airplane.

MILAN MELVIN Tom created his own club, Mother's, on Broadway. Said he wanted to duplicate the acid experience, and indeed, the people who designed it put a whole environment on your head. Tom wanted a *feel* to it; he wanted it to be like a *womb*.

ERIC CHRISTENSEN Tom opened Mother's with a week of one of my all-time favorite bands, the Lovin' Spoonful. I was there every night.

RAECHEL DONAHUE Lovin' Spoonful's drummer turned in our neighbor Howard Hesseman for selling pot. That ended the Spoonful. (We stopped playing them on KMPX.)

Actor Howard Hesseman, known as Don Sturdy, was a member of the San Francisco was a member of the satirical troupe The Committee in San Francisco. He spent ninety days in the county jail for selling an ounce of marijuana—a conviction later thrown out for entrapment.

HOWARD HESSEMAN Tom and I met on the street right after I came out of jail. Meeting Tom Donahue the first time was much better than the first time I got laid.

SIDE TRIP

Busted

And you'll be amazed on the gaze of their faces
as they sentence you.

—Blood, Sweat, and Tears, "Smiling Phases"

JESSE JARNOW, author of *Heads: A Biography of Psychedelic America* By 1967, it seems every band was busted for marijuana. They would appear in court, and if the judge thought blue jeans were inappropriate, any spectator he wanted he had the bailiff throw out.

JOEL SELVIN When Albert Goldman signed Big Brother and the Holding Company, the famous manager added one thing to the agreement: "No *schmeeze*." The band hadn't heard the Yiddish word for junk before. But everybody nodded. Goldman said three of them were already lying.

6

SHE'S SO RAECHEL

Don't you ever listen to the radio
When the big bad beat comes on?
I know you gotta dig it.

—Bob Seger, "Heavy Music"

In '64, as Tom Donahue was turning on teens tuned to KYA, Raechel Hamilton was finishing high school. To learn how Rae helped Tom make KMPX happen, we'll hear her describe her journey, which began in National City, California, by the Mexican border. Her father left before her first birthday, and she moved with her mother to live with relatives up north.

RAECHEL DONAHUE Uncle Homer had built his house into a hillside in this tiny mining town, Grass Valley, eighty miles from Sacramento. I spent a lot of time learning how to fire a gun, shoot an arrow, skin a deer, cut the heads off chickens, and smoke behind the barn. My mother, Mary Hamilton, was a beautiful woman, but she was one selfish lady. She sent me to charm school because she wanted me to be Shirley Temple—I learned to ballroom dance and twirl a green umbrella while warbling "Give My Regards to Broadway." Uncle Homer hauled logs and took me on truck runs to Los Angeles, and Aunt Verona taught me to form letters using toothpicks, which was great for capitals—I used the same method with my son Jesse, using pipe cleaners instead of toothpicks, so now the letters could be bent into lowercase. I knew I wanted to be a writer by the time I was five. I read the dictionary; I read every *True* magazine. My grandmother had a bookshelf nine feet tall, and she gave me her collection of James Joyce, Herman Melville, and Henry Miller. All adult stuff. I think I read every banned book in America.

Remarried, Mary, and her remarkable little Rae, left Grass Valley for Riverside County, east of LA, where the youngster would not/could not be corralled.

RAECHEL DONAHUE Immediately I began formulating an escape plan. I couldn't relate; I was nine and already light-years ahead of the other kids. I wrote a play about women who were on the wrong planet, the gist being that women could run their own world. The teachers found me precocious; the performance by my fellow fourth graders, so-so. I turned in a book report on *Ulysses*, and the teachers thought, *we've got one of them.* I was reading the Beats, darkened my long hair, and was ready to graduate at sixteen and leave for San Francisco—they said I needed PE credits. In '63, with money I made selling magazines door-to-door, I bought a '58 Thunderbird, packed $125, and my mother gave me her silverware—she said I would need it at some point. I don't know why. I made my boyfriend take my virginity my last night in Riverside, and I actually said, "That's it?" I was surprised when I got to San Francisco and there was no beach in North Beach. I found a room in the Haight, in a rooming house run by Willie Chu, a beatnik poet who was writing "Cheezit, it's the cops!" in Chinese characters on his front window when I showed up. I fashioned a new name for myself: Raechel Steele. I learned the lingo: *juice* was liquor, *bread* was money, and *drift* meant get away from me. I went to San Francisco State and cooked for a fraternity. Bell Telephone wouldn't hire someone seventeen—jailbait—so Willie forged documents and all of a sudden I was twenty-one! I got a job dancing in a bar in North Beach, owned by a cop who put me on the late shift, which meant I was to both go-go and clean up. I danced in a fringed minidress for voyeurs, but growing up in the country, I had no fear. One night after closing, the owner told me we were going upstairs to have sex. He said he knew I wasn't twenty-one. I said I knew cops weren't supposed to own bars. North Beach had a lot of open secrets. One night I watched a bearded guy, about six foot four, I thought around three hundred pounds, smoking a cigar, watching me.

"You dance good."

"I dance *well*, asshole. Drift."

At that time it seemed all the clubs north of Broadway were going topless. A cook taught me how to belly dance; it was a *thing*, like limbo. This wasn't a career move, so when I heard about a job at a small record company, I dressed like Tuesday Weld, in Mary Janes, white stockings, and a headband, and went down to Potrero Hill. As I walked up the stairs to the office, there was a girl running down in tears. I thought, *this ought to be good.* Inside was the enormous guy from the club that night. Another guy, sort of wacky doodle, was up on a desk swearing, jumping side to side like Yosemite Sam. (Bob Mitchell had Tourette syndrome. He said he "made Lenny Bruce sound like a pussy.") I sat down, crossed my little legs, took out my pencil, flipped open my steno pad, and said, "Would you like me to take that down in a letter?" The fat man looked at him. "Hire her, man." I started as their secretary the next day. Every day at one o'clock they split for the track. They had horses at Golden Gate Fields across the bay.

JOEL SELVIN Tom was fantastic at the track.

RAECHEL DONAHUE I finally went with them and I was enamored. I learned everything: read the racing forms, collected data, and bet discriminately. I never made enough to pay off a mortgage, but I could pick a top-three winner in nine races, and Tom and Bob admired my skills. A tiny blonde in her teens looking all Alice in Wonderland, prancing up to the window with a stack of hundreds. "And I want, um, this much?" These guys had knowledge I didn't have.

VICKY CUNNINGHAM, Donahue's assistant, KSAN Tom would treat groups of listeners to Golden Gate Fields. He claimed it was a public affairs thing, examining race relations at the race track.

RAECHEL DONAHUE I became an honorary member of Tom's inner circle. He told me, "Inside this 350-pound frame, there's a 95-pound jockey dying for a mount."

KMPX ad in the first issue of Rolling Stone *magazine in San Francisco, 1967.*
© GREGORY IRONS / COURTESY GREGORY IRONS ESTATE

7

"TOP 40 RADIO IS DEAD AND ITS ROTTING CORPSE IS STINKING UP THE AIRWAVES," SAYS TOM DONAHUE IN *ROLLING STONE*, 1967

https://www.youtube.com/watch?v=HkB_By6y6gE
Tom Donahue show highlights, 70 minutes.

BEN FONG-TORRES In 1967, *Rolling Stone* was San Francisco's new music and culture magazine. Tom Donahue laid down his epitaph for AM pop music in their second issue: "Somewhere in the dim, misty days of yore, some radio station statistician decided that regardless of chronological age, the average mental age of the audience was twelve-and-a-half, and Top 40 AM radio aimed its message directly at the lowest common denominator. . . . The disc jockeys have become robots. They are performing their inanities at the direction of programmers who have succeeded in totally squeezing the human element out of their sound, and reducing it to a series of blips and bleeps, and happy, oh yes, always happy-sounding cretins, who are poured from bottles every three hours. They have succeeded in making everyone on the station sound the same: asinine."

JOEL SELVIN He said, "A man can only play so many Herman's Hermits records and still feel good about himself."

BEN FONG-TORRES If only there was a way to perform the magic of radio, without playlists and pimple cream commercials.

Tom and Raechel lived on Telegraph Hill in a rented house on Alta Street, high above North Beach.

RAECHEL DONAHUE One night Ken Kesey made an entrance by fire escape. "Oh, hi!" "What are you doing here?" "Running from the cops." "Oh, hi!"

Radio friends like Bobby Dale came over to play records not allowed on their stations. Bobby's wife, Norma, remembers those nights.

NORMA DALE We listened to Who's Afraid of Virginia Woolf on vinyl, and Lenny Bruce. I learned in their house what books to read like, Edgar Allan Poe, Shaw's Don Juan in Hell. And cards! Whist, gin, euchre, five hundred. Tom was formidable. Raechel unbeatable. Rae could roll a joint with one hand while shuffling with the other like you couldn't believe. And she made a big meal for everyone.

RAECHEL DONAHUE Never trust a woman who brings her grandfather's poker chips to a game.

NORMA DALE Rae could roll a joint with one hand while shuffling with the other like you couldn't believe. She made dinner for everyone.

RAECHEL DONAHUE The neighborhood was my victim. My father said my mother could burn watermelon, so I never learned to cook. Tom bought me volumes of *The Gourmet Cookbook.*

NORMA DALE Voco was their neighbor, he was always there. He was a DJ and musicologist and had *extreme* knowledge. He turned me onto Lord Buckley.

> *LORD BUCKLEY*
> *Have you ever swung around a beautiful country road, with a gleam of sweet life in the air, groovy with gold in your pocket, riding a wild set o' wheels at an easy pace [he makes sound of car passing]. Are You There? Everything is cool and smooth . . . You're driving along and ya feel the sun and the radio's swinging a beautiful crazy wild tune. And ya feel so good you—Ah!—if you're right in there tight! And ya feel it. And suddenly your mind—frrr!—goes over to Hippieville. You start thinking about a beautiful girl you met there five years ago. What a gasser she was. Take me now!*

VOCO "Laughter is truly religious," said his Lordship. He said, "When a person is laughing, he's illuminated the full beauty of a human being . . . you're thinking love, you're vibrating love. It's prayer. It's a beautiful thing." I love that cat!

NORMA DALE I loved that cat—everyone loved Voco. And mostly, always we had music.

RAECHEL DONAHUE It's Tom's birthday: our neighbors are all smashed. We're struggling to play cards, high as we are. Tom says, "Do you realize we sit here every night and smoke dope and play records for each other," wondering why nobody'd done this on radio.

HOWARD HESSEMAN Tom all along talked about the idea of a station that would resemble the experience of being in the living room of a friend who had an astonishing stereo system, a great record collection, and some really great weed. What more do you need?

RAECHEL DONAHUE Voco had a test record from Elektra, an acetate test pressing—white label, nothing else—and he put it on the turntable. "Father, I'm going to kill you!" Tom turns around, says, "—the fuck is that?" "I dunno, man, it's some record I brought from work. 'Elektra 4695.'" Whatever. It was apparent this was not music that was going to be played on Top 40. The next morning, too early for people who had taken acid the night before, I found Tom leafing through the phone book.

BEN FONG-TORRES Down the hill lay KMPX, an unsullied little station at 50 Green Street, bartering time to foreign language and religious groups who bought her by the hour.

RAECHEL DONAHUE I remember the first time we went down there, there was the owner, Leon Crosby, sitting in his office with his head in his hands. He was crying. Tom goes, "This is the one." We persuaded Crosby to let us take over, I think it was the Portuguese hour. So we already had a built-in audience because San Francisco had so many different cultures, each listening to this station. And since nobody changes the station *before* they turn on the radio—say, the night before, their parents have been listening to their hour or two—and when they turn it on again it's, "Father, I'm going to kill you!"

MILAN MELVIN At first, it was only Tom and Rae, six to ten. Tom convinced Leon Crosby that if his programming idea was successful, he could bring in the people he wanted. Take over the operation, in other words. Buy out the other programming and make ourselves twenty-four hours.

In January '67, the station already had a cool DJ. But since Donahue didn't have goddamn FM, he didn't get Larry Miller midnights to six. Larry had done radio and fronted a rock band in Detroit before heading west to become KMPX 106.9's "First Freak."

BEN FONG-TORRES Larry Miller played whatever the heck he wanted.

JOEL SELVIN Larry basically started underground FM.

BEN FONG-TORRES He invented the term "folk rock."

LARRY MILLER I think of the folk-rock fusion that Dylan started and had been picked up on by former folkies like the Byrds and the Mamas and Papas. That to me was probably the most important thing going on in music in those days. Along with the British Invasion. It's one thing to see Hot Tuna play—it's another thing to know where they came from and what that culture was. Without any appreciation for the roots of where the music comes from, there's a tendency for pop music to be somewhat shallow to start with.

Greil Marcus grew up in San Francisco. The author of many books on music and culture, Marcus dedicated *The Doors: A Lifetime of Listening to Five Mean Years* to Larry.

GREIL MARCUS When we discovered Larry Miller's late-night show on this foreign-language station, we'd stay up all night to hear music we'd just danced to at the Fillmore or the Avalon ballrooms. Just for the thrill of hearing it on the radio, to hear it as public culture, public language, wondering who else was listening.

February '67 Larry Miller Show.

> *LARRY MILLER*
> *That started it all off . . . the Beatles and some of their earlier things like, uh, "I Saw Her Standing There," one two three four my heart went boom, and things like that, heh heh. Well, it's a nice innocent, naive, absolutely unloaded lyric, ya know, and I believe that. Also a word from Columbia Records about a new album from Marshall McLuhan called "The Medium is the Massage," which is worth a try . . . it's a very far-out record, a very good thing to listen to in a dark room with your eyes all bandaged andyour head all spinning from the demon weed. Eleven minutes before one in the morning. Larry Miller here. How about "Wild Thing" by the Troggs?*
>
> *All right, girls, spit out your gum there and calm down. A new group from England called Traffic, been hearing a lot of it around here, been released on the Atco label, the song is called "Paper Sun." This is KMPX, heck of a radio station, the mighty X! The super X! The incredible radio station here which is soon to explode wide open with all sorts of beauty and great sounds and wonderfulness, right on top of your tree there. You ready for that? KMPX is at 107 FM stereo, San Francisco. Tell your friends, uh, where it's at and, uh, join the fun. This is Mrs. Tunji's little boy Ola, Olatunji and the "Drums of Passion."*

MILAN MELVIN Larry read ads on the air for places like Larry Blake's in Berkeley where he ate and drank before coming to work. But he wasn't generating much income for the station. His worst sin was probably that he wasn't in tune with the drug culture. In other words, the bulk of our audience. He could put interesting music segues together, but more often than that he created a mood with an Indian raga, instead of whipping the audience upside the head with a fucking barn burner by Spike Jones. Listeners were coming down from their acid trips at like 4 a.m., so he was out of sync with them.

LARRY MILLER KMPX became a beta. We didn't really know what to do. I think the best stuff I ever did was educational—turning people on to stuff. Playing "Crossroads" by Robert Johnson and then "Crossroads" by Cream. I did an interview with Cream producer Felix Pappalardi—later of Mountain. He brought in tapes of *Disraeli Gears*, and I was the first DJ in America to play "Sunshine of Your Love." Two in the morning, Felix goes home, leaving the tapes. He left *Disraeli Gears*! He got in trouble with Atco Records. "You left the tapes in this hippie radio station?" Record companies had to time the release of a single: every pop station got it at noon on Friday. But then, when it did hit the streets, the album sold thousands—it was out of stock and had to be back-ordered. "Say, as soon as that album comes out I want a copy, I just heard it on the radio." Atco congratulated Felix Pappalardi on his brilliant marketing strategy getting the album to move.

MILAN MELVIN Some said Larry was a juicer, not a pot smoker like the rest of us. He was pissed off from the get-go when Donahue came on board. I think Larry felt Big Daddy was a Top 40 reject and knew little about free form as Larry envisioned it. And he let this eat away at him, or something else ate away at him all night long, midnight to 6 a.m. All I knew was, he was one grumpy motherfucker when he came into work and was even worse when he left.

At twenty-four, Larry Miller was part of FM radio's avant-garde. Later, he got a master's in education and taught college in Boston. He called himself "the old hippie DJ" and died in 2016 at 75. After playing Tower of Power's "What is Hip?" he said: "The working definition of 'what is hip,' is the search for the authentic experience."

8

A BEAUTIFUL JAILBREAK FROM EVERYWHERE

http://www.jive95.com/airchecks.htm
Assorted KMPX/KSAN DJs and tunes.

We get more about the little radio shop on Green Street in North Beach not far from the Ferry Building at the end of Market from a host of KMPX/KSAN characters: Thom O'Hair, Norman Davis, Bob McClay, Fred Greene, Bob Simmons, and Howard Hesseman. And Chet Helms of the Family Dog weighs in. First, though: Roger Steffens, archivist, DJ, and author of books, including *So Much Things to Say: The Oral History of Bob Marley*.

ROGER STEFFENS It is hard to imagine now, but except for a few effete hi-fi snobs and opera and classical music lovers, hardly anyone listened to FM back then. It cost too much to have an FM set. There were hardly any stations. And what there were were invariably uptight. Straight. Then you had this revolution.

THOM O'HAIR What was happening was that the medium was being discovered. Stereo was the new hot property, but records were produced in mono. Stereo became essential, really influential in FM, anytime after the Beatles' *Sgt. Pepper* and Jimi Hendrix's *Are You Experienced.* The artists led as always, and radio—I mean, it was like going from black and white to color. Underground stuff had really started on late-night radio in the mid-'50s. It started on the border blasters, the X stations in Mexico. Tom Donahue managed to be the *lens* that focused all this wonderful energy together, and he was the right guy at the right place. And he was tied into the recording industry, and he was tied into the performance industry. And Bill Graham and Chet Helms were doing things, and Stanley Mouse and Victor Moscoso were doing posters that were blowing people's minds, and that whole scene was just taking off, and that was also happening in New York, and it was just . . . what a time! I mean, what a time!

NORMAN DAVIS Tom Donahue and his crew of underground radio freaks had taken over!

THOM O'HAIR A beautiful jailbreak from everywhere, from decades-long pop drool singles. That's what gave it its edge: protesting an unjust war and world, fighting for freedom from oppression, and doing your own thing, whatever that might be. It provided a Morse code you could dance to. And more importantly, it scared the shit out of your parents.

HOWARD HESSEMAN I think Donahue nailed it.

BEN FONG-TORRES Tom Donahue is considered the father of free form. It's a myth. He was one of the parents, ultimately its godfather and by far its more articulate spokesman. But he wasn't the first to do what he later called "freak-freely" radio. In 1966, WOR-FM in New York was playing rock album cuts and assorted other music. Pete Fornatale on WFUV, Fordham U in NYC, was mixing cuts into thematic sets, quietly breaking new ground.

BOB MCCLAY Whenever somebody asked him if he was the creator of FM rock radio, Tom said, "Let everybody else be first. I'll be happy to be second."

FRED GREENE It wasn't the first free form, but it was the one that made it a success.

CHET HELMS I love Tom Donahue; he was a great mentor and a great friend. But I get tired of the continual thing of "Tom Donahue started underground radio." That's simply not true, historically or any other way. This goes back to this kind of Dionysian and democratic level of association among people at that time. It wasn't any big deal to be a DJ on that station, you know? You were just a guy that everybody knew on the street, a guy you sat and smoked a joint with and listened to records with at home. A guy at the party—that kind of level of access. The first free-form station around San Francisco was KPFA. And basically the only way you could get it was to send in thirty-five dollars, and KPFA sent you a one-station tuner and an antenna kit, okay? That's the way you got FM radio initially.

BOB SIMMONS From April 7, 1967, the new kind of people—the flowering counterculture—had a radio station of their own.

RAECHEL DONAHUE The most common phone calls we'd get were, "Hello? Is this really happening?" Swan and Juju were our first visitors—they brought incense, pot brownies, acid, fringe, feathers, bells.

JOEL SELVIN Swan and Juju decorated Tom's studio with flowers, posters, a Viet Cong banner, beads, and buttons. Listeners camped in the lobby with looks of amazement at something listening to *them*. Donahue said there was one point where he found the seriousness about it insane, that it was like reaching the Shrine of Lourdes or something.

MILAN MELVIN Spring '67 in North Beach. I remember the night clearly. My roommate Carl Gottlieb, a member of The Committee, heard backstage about a new radio station. He said it was a station "for us." Whatever that meant. The context is important: there was Top 40 radio, which was a "flash from the past!" and big voices, pimple creams and Pepsi jingles. Tunes that didn't last longer than two minutes and ten seconds. He rolled the FM dial to 106.9, cranked up the volume, and what I heard changed my life. This rumbling voice you could almost see coming out of the speakers, rattling the glassware. The voice wasn't screaming. This was from the bottom end of a baritone saxophone, speaking in tones clearly mellowed by marijuana. Like it came from a friend sharing a park bench with you in Golden Gate Park. The music came on—an ethereal twelve-minute instrumental, a raga by Ravi Shankar. Which segued into a gospel choir, seamlessly, then into B. B. King, followed by long tracks from the Stones. The pimple commercial was nowhere to be heard. In fact, no commercials aired! And it was in stereo, amazing on its own then. KMPX. Carl and I could not believe our ears. Three hours and six joints later, I knew I needed in on this action. The next afternoon, I went to meet Tom Donahue. Where to begin? Here was the man to match that voice. Damn near four hundred pounds of him.

CHAPTER 8

RAECHEL DONAHUE Bill Graham said Tom had a voice like Zeus.

BOB SIMMONS The man had a voice that came from down in a barrel, a voice so authoritative that when he gave you the time and temperature, the time and temperature would adjust to what Tom said it was.

JOEL SELVIN Tom had a vision. He understood what communications was about. But more than that, he knew what life was about. He really got it.

9

CARL GOTTLIEB, HOWARD HESSEMAN, AND THE COMMITTEE

The 1967 scene: George Harrison lollygags along Haight Street in heart-shaped sunglasses. Paul McCartney arrives in Frank Sinatra's plane, meets and greets the Jefferson Airplane; they turn him on to the hallucinogen DMT, he turns them on to "A Day in the Life."

JOEL SELVIN KMPX was a staff full of stoned hippies and crazed idealists.

NORMAN DAVIS They were given the freedom to say anything they wanted, encouraged to do weird things on the air.

RAECHEL DONAHUE First thing we did was get Voco, Howard Hesseman, Carl Gottlieb, Milan Melvin—our neighbors, basically—to bring their LPs and 45s to the station. (In case it didn't work out, we had colored stickers so we could get our music back.) Tom decided we would play all kinds of music, without barriers of style or length; DJs chose what they liked.

MILAN MELVIN I remember the night clearly. Spring '67 in North Beach. My roommate Carl Gottlieb, a member of The Committee troupe, heard backstage about a new radio station. He said it was a station "for us." Whatever that meant. The context is important: there was Top 40 radio, which was a "flash from the past!" and big voices, pimple creams and Pepsi jingles. Tunes that didn't last longer than two minutes and ten seconds. He rolled the FM dial to 106.9, cranked up the volume, and what I heard changed my life. This rumbling voice you could almost see coming out of the speakers, rattling the glassware. The voice wasn't screaming. This was from the bottom end of a baritone saxophone, speaking in tones clearly mellowed by marijuana. Like it came from a friend sharing a park bench with you in Golden Gate Park. The music came on—an ethereal twelve-minute instrumental, a raga by Ravi Shankar. Which segued into a gospel choir, seamlessly, then into B. B. King, followed by long tracks from the Stones. The pimple commercial was nowhere to be heard. In fact, no commercials aired! And it was in stereo, amazing on its own then. KMPX. Carl and I could not believe our ears. Three hours and six joints later, I knew I needed in on this action. The next afternoon, I went to meet Tom Donahue. Where to begin? Here was the man to match that voice. Damn near four hundred pounds of him.

CARL GOTTLIEB, screenwriter, *Jaws* The station was so young! I got on the air, Sundays noon to six, I think. There were still holdovers from this previous incarnation as an ethnic FM station that sold tours to Yugoslavia. At noon, the station changed its clothes and came back as first-time-in-history-hippie-underground-FM-free-form-radio! It was great to be on the ground floor of that kind of a revolution.

HOWARD HESSEMAN Like Carl, I was doing six nights a week at The Committee and moonlighting at KMPX for ten bucks a shift as weekend on-air anti-personality. I followed several hours of classic Chinese opera, or the Top 10 Polka Review and the Latvian Antler-Dance Show, changing the mood a little with Miles Davis *Sketches of Spain*, or long improvisatory pieces by Albert Ayler and Ornette Coleman. I always thought of myself as having come up in the '50s, my tastes more defined by then than by the '60s, certainly in terms of jazz, poetry, literature in general. And life. I never saw myself as a hippie, but I was going with the flow.

CARL GOTTLIEB I'd open with the Beatles' "Good Morning" at noon. That's when most of our listeners were just shaking the cobwebs. Then came whatever I wanted: here's Ma Rainey, here's Janis Joplin, Blind Boy Slim. Walter Winchell narrating the capture of Lepke Buchalter and the end of Murder Incorporated—one side of an LP. On AM you had to play 45 singles in mono. On FM you could play 33 1/3 rpm in stereo, of anything that could be recorded! A lot of stuff that was finding its way onto these big vinyl discs was rare and worthwhile. Greenwich Village folkies Dave Van Ronk, Len Chandler, Karen Dalton—wonderful artists nobody'd heard of then. My friend Judy Henske had a big belting voice. The Jefferson Airplane was happening, so I went on and said, "Here's Judy Henske . . . she makes Grace Slick sound like Mary Poppins."

HOWARD HESSEMAN Tom, for all the emphasis he put on freedom for the disk jockey, could get out of line when his overall concept of the station was challenged. I was playing Coltrane to exhibit drummer Elvin Jones—his chops versus those of Ginger Baker with Cream. Ten minutes into their tracks, the phone rang. Tom said, "How much John Coltrane are we gonna hear?" I said, another five minutes. "That's five minutes too much. You've gotta play something else, man." That's the only time I can remember Tom stepping down with any force on somebody's choice of what to play. And he did it kiddingly, you know? I think it was educating an audience to what had come before, and then variations of a form that they were embracing. The sources of that form, rock 'n roll, come out of gospel and honky-tonk music combined, both of which deal with experiences common to the audience in terms of lyric content. You don't know where you're going if you don't know where you come from. And you hardly know where you are.

SIDE TRIP

Voco

Voco was the wizard. He grew up in Detroit as Abe Kesheshian, turned Donahue onto the Doors, and, at KMPX and KSAN, Voco called his pioneering show *Lights Out.*

VOCO *Lights Out* was a magic carpet ride of music for the most beautiful audience on the planet. My opening was, "It's midnight, lights out, clothes off, candles glowing, incense is fading away, don't need no electricity, baby, I'll be your amplifier, 'cause we can boogie in the dark!" Our journey might take us to B. B. King's "Hold That Train, Conductor," followed by Richard Strauss's "Also Sprach Zarathustra" and Buffalo Springfield's "Broken Arrow." We're talking new music, electronic, Middle East, jazz, pop, classic, blues . . .

JOEL SELVIN Voco was huge—his *Lights Out* show was another world!

DUSTY STREET When you find an individual whose heartbeat is music, if you're like me, you listen.

A *Lights Out* LP was put together, featuring Voco and Dusty and their favorites, including Tower of Power from Oakland.

VOCO I literally begged and haunted record companies to give me the opportunity to record a concept album. The answer was always the same: "Concept albums do not sell because we can't put them on the road." Meaning, *they can't own the act.*

Blue Thumb Records released *Lights Out San Francisco (Voco Presents the Soul of the Bay Area)* in '72.

EDDY GOLDBERG, KMPX Engineer One day in '68, Abe came in, chain-smoking his Philip Morris Commanders—they had the highest nicotine and tar content—and he said, "Eddy, wait until you hear this!" Edwin Hawkins, pianist at a church in Berkeley, had done an arrangement of a song called "Oh

Happy Day" with his Northern California Youth Choir. They recorded it on the cheap, pressed in five hundred copies to sell in churches to fund the choir's participation in some kind of competition. Voco discovered one of the 45s and played it for me and the listeners—the next few days the station was flooded with requests, and "Oh Happy Day" started to get airplay on local soul stations like KSOL and KDIA. And the rest is international fluke hit history! I don't think Abe ever really got the credit he deserved. And he was only forty-five when he died of a heart attack.

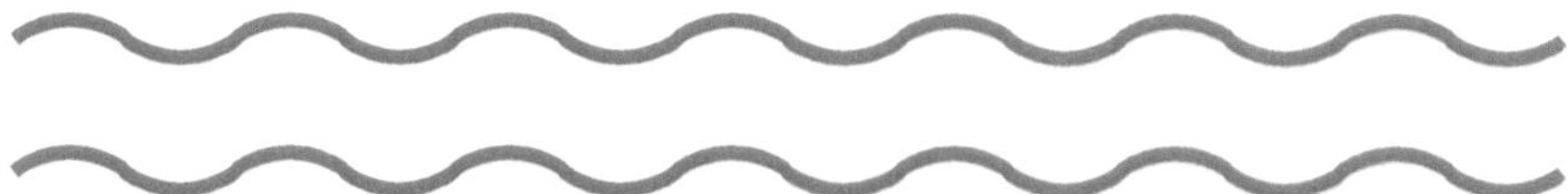

SIDE TRIP

Local Bands

The music you listen to becomes the soundtrack of your life. It may be the first music you made love to or got high to or went through your adolescence to or whatever poignant times in your life—well, that music's gonna mean a lot to you. It's gonna take on much more import than just the sound of the notes. It's become the background track for your existence.

—Michael Bloomfield

Two innovative Bay Area bands who got on Donahue's wavelength were the Youngbloods and Creedence Clearwater Revival. Sal Valentino of the Beau Brummels (see chapter 5) and Quicksilver Messenger Service (see chapter 2), wrote and performed "Get Together" ("Come on people now, smile on your brother . . . "), but it was Jesse Colin Young and the Youngbloods who made it a folk-rock anthem.

JESSE COLIN YOUNG Musicians realized that, because of Tom, maybe we didn't have to keep making hit records to get some visibility. We made "Ridgetop"—and I mean "Ridgetop" was seven or eight minutes long—and we knew because of Tom Donahue there was a place for this kind of music to be heard. What I loved was, I could listen to the radio station at any time and learn things. It seemed like nobody sounded like anybody else.

JOEL SELVIN There was a bunch of longtime frat party rockers out of the East Bay. By 1968, their lead vocalist had listened to enough KMPX to devise a tape expressly created for airplay. He took the Dale Hawkins three-minute rockabilly classic from 1957, "Suzie Q," and expanded it to an eight-minute psychedelicized version—complete with extended guitar solo.

MILAN MELVIN Tom thought the song was great. But the name of the band was the Gollywogs. Tom advised changing it, and minutes later, John Fogerty came into the station with a label that was still warm, saying "Creedence Clearwater Revival." And Tom played their song.

JOEL SELVIN Airplay on KMPX made the difference between the quartet plugging away in front of a few desultory dancers at Dino & Carlo's in North Beach and headlining at the Fillmore. A version edited down from the eight minutes went on to become a nationwide AM/FM hit for Fantasy, a jazz label in Oakland.

The first album from Country Joe and the Fish was called *Electric Music for the Mind and Body*. Country Joe tells how he once heard it at Janis Joplin's apartment in the Haight.

COUNTRY JOE MCDONALD I remember Janis had an apartment on Lyons Street. That's where I spent a lot of time. KMPX was a very tiny station then. The DJs were Tom Donahue and Larry Miller. And Janis and I, we'd be lying in bed, listening to the radio to hear ourselves. And they would play a Big Brother track and we'd go *Ahh! Wowwww! So cool, man!* Then, they'd play Country Joe and the Fish. *Wowwww!* It was like too much, you know? Because they had an EP. We had an EP. I was like, *There's something in this, really*. I mean, if you took Tupac Shakur's platinum whatever and the influence he had, and compare it to Janis and me in that flat—you can't even see us! Who was listening to that radio station? Us and a hundred people.

10

MILAN MELVIN, DAN O'NEILL, AND THE UNDERGROUND COMIX RADIO ANTENNA

Buzzy Donahue was fourteen when she started coming down to her father's radio station after classes at Galileo High. Buzzy and Katie Johnson (see chapter 11 on KMPX's exploding of engineer gender roles) describe how, before there was an internet, interlinkage was tight between listener and station.

BUZZY DONAHUE I was at the front desk when this kid called and said he'd been busted in Oakland for marijuana. He was given one phone call, so he called KMPX. He knew we could find him a lawyer.

KATIE JOHNSON A lot of phone calls came in from kids spaced out on drugs, wanting someone from the station to talk them down from bad trips.

BUZZY DONAHUE This is how the community feels about you and brings you into their scene. Community radio stations do that today.

But it was not easy for them to reach their community.

BUZZY DONAHUE We had a terrible signal, and were always going off the air. I remember Hendrix was at the station and we went off the air; he knew it might be a couple hours before we were back up, so he just hung out looking at records in our library.

MILAN MELVIN Dig: You couldn't listen if you didn't live in North Beach or in the signal shadow behind assorted San Francisco hills. I'd go into head shops that had AM/FM receivers and have them tune it to 106.9—just static and shop owners giving me amused looks. I was perhaps the most hopeful that we'd be able to synthesize Tom's revolutionary concept in radio and make a living at it, too. When I started, Donahue said he was working for free, and if I volunteered, I could choose any position I wanted. I thought the best thing I could do was generate some money for this new thing. But nobody could get our signal! So, back to the drawing board.

Bob Postle and Paul Boucher came to Tom's rescue, with a dipole antenna: a simple TV antenna cable split in two to make a T-shape. If it was held perpendicular to the station's signal, voila! Tom and Larry Miller hit the airwaves offering a diagram of it on a postcard, drawn by cartoonist Dan O'Neill. Then it was like all hell broke loose for us—the lobby packed with freaks looking for the antenna, and every store in town with any interest in the hipster subculture—like Don Weir's Music City—was playing our station. First sponsor I brought in was the Family Dog's Avalon Ballroom Family Dog's Avalon Ballroom and Bill Graham's Fillmore jumped on board early. I was selling so much time, I brought on guys to help me: Whitney Harris, our "straight" salesman; Jack Towle, original member of the Family Dog; and my old pal from Red Dog days, Chandler Laughlin.

CHAN LAUGHLIN I was in jail in Contra Costa County for a marijuana offense. My dear friend Milan recommended me as a potential employee, and Tom Donahue wrote a letter to the judge: "If you let him out of jail, I'll put him to work." Donahue told me, if I could sell pot, I could sell ads.

MILAN MELVIN Together, we came up with a simple concept:

1. Identify the audience. The few hundred of us dancing to each other's music. Selling each other drugs. Fucking ourselves flat. And laughing ourselves silly. Those of us who half hoped the whole world would catch on and enjoy the fun, while at the same time hoping word would not get out and blow our cover.

: Larry Lightbulb helps you get even better reception. Or any. Dan O'Neill, 1967.
© DAN O'NEILL

2. Play the music to the audience that it was playing to itself, only provide a broader spectrum of it than any one individual had mastered, in stereo.
3. Advertise only products and services that we were consuming, like the dance halls, head shops, the music equipment stores. Produce the spots (ads) ourselves so they fit the sound and are more like a recommendation from a friend than a harangue from a guy selling you. Ads from "middle class" agencies weren't even to be considered.

CHAN LAUGHLIN As new people came on board, Tom broadened his vision to incorporate our ideas. Or he would wing it until he could verbalize it back to us.

MILAN MELVIN He was our Big Daddy, and we were the Pied Piper of the Summer of Love in San Francisco! Once those T-antennas got around, the sound was everywhere. You could walk down the street in the Haight-Ashbury or Polk Gulch or Castro and pop in and out of shops, or pass by groups of people sitting in parks, and only hear KMPX.

1967 staff. Standing from top l–r: Howard Hesseman, Kathy Lerner, Paul Boucher, Dusty Street, Ed Hepp, Morgan Upton, Carl Gottlieb, Bob McClay, unknown, Milan Melvin, Linda Bacon, Larry Miller, Buzzy Donahue, and Katie Johnson. Seated l–r: unknown, Raechel Donahue, Tom Donahue, Chandler Laughin, and Bob Prescott. Seated: Cosmo Donahue, Jack Towle, Voco, Candy Culkin, Michael Chechik, Sue Henderson, and Jane Oliver. Photo by Baron Wolman. (Identities courtesy of Raechel and Edward Bear)

PHOTO BY BARON WOLMAN COLLECTION/ROCK & ROLL HALL OF FAME/GETTY IMAGES

Terry McGovern: "KSAN in a jukebox, radio personalities in compartments. All around them, dreamy images of Hendrix and Dylan and Beatles and the Stones. Like, 'We're in the jukebox serving these artists.'" By Norman Orr, 1968.
COURTESY NORMAN ORR

B105

KSAN

METROMEDIA STEREO 95

SAN FRANCISCO / OAKLAND

FREE FORM PROGRAM SCHEDULE

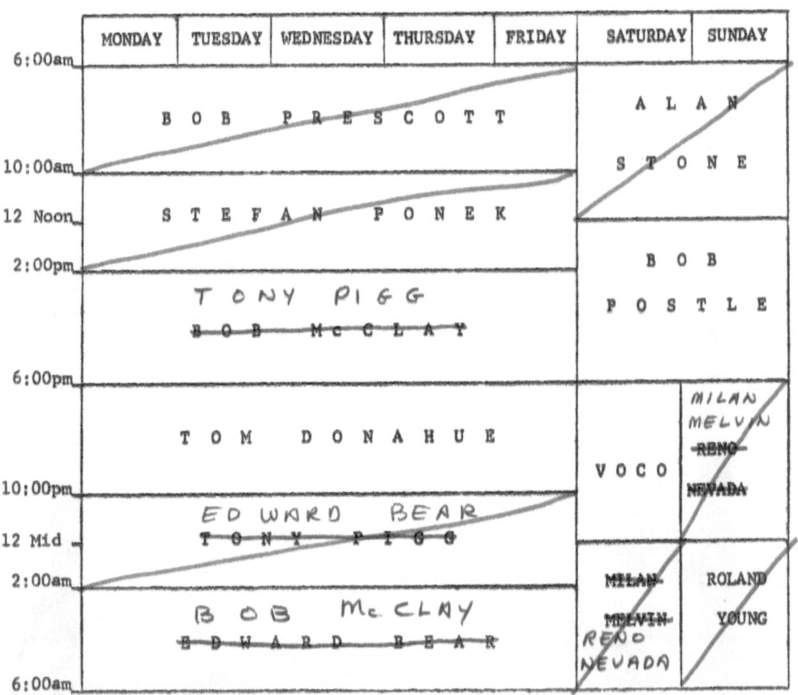

	MONDAY	TUESDAY	WEDNESDAY	THURSDAY	FRIDAY	SATURDAY	SUNDAY
6:00am	BOB PRESCOTT					ALAN STONE	
10:00am	STEFAN PONEK						
12 Noon						BOB POSTLE	
2:00pm	TONY PIGG ~~BOB McCLAY~~						
6:00pm	TOM DONAHUE					VOCO	MILAN MELVIN ~~RENO~~ ~~NEVADA~~
10:00pm	EDWARD BEAR ~~TONY PIGG~~						
12 Mid						~~MILAN~~ ~~MELVIN~~ RENO NEVADA	ROLAND YOUNG
2:00am	BOB McCLAY ~~EDWARD BEAR~~						
6:00am							

Effective: August 12, 1968

211 SUTTER STREET • SAN FRANCISCO, CALIFORNIA 94108 • 986-2825

Fluid DJ shifts, 1968.
COURTESY BOB SIMMONS

Siddhartha Boutique spot, 1968

Are you wearing clothes? Or are you just standing there, nude? You're probably wearing clothes. Look at them. Think about those clothes you're wearing. Are they just covering you up? Would you rather go nude? If you have to wear clothes, take a look at clothes that turn you on when you put them on. Slip into [echoes] Siddharthaaaaa. Move into world-exotic clothing.

MILAN MELVIN When Tom and I hit some established ad agencies, we'd laugh about our impact on the personnel. He is six foot three and over 350 pounds by now, shoulder-length black hair, a massive black beard, black sport coat over black pants and black turtleneck. I am the same height and literally weighing in at less than half of him, dark hair that hangs straight to my waist, and fitted into a mod suit with tie. We walk through these agency typing pools to the accompaniment of stifled gasps and whispers.

JOEL SELVIN Milan was often in a purple cape, carrying a violin case for his briefcase.

CARL GOTTLIEB I met him through a friend at Hamburger Hamlet on the Sunset Strip. If you had hair as long as Milan's in '66, you had to have started growing it in '64, which made you an original and trustworthy. He was losing his apartment in San Francisco, and I offered him my place near Ghiradelli Square. If someone smoked dope in '67, you gave them the keys to your house. Women followed Milan home like lost kitties, providing a bounteous overflow of opportunities.

DUSTY STREET Milan Morell Melvin the Third. Tall drink of water. Long dark hair. Fu Manchu mustache and he rode a Harley-Davidson. What was not to love, right?

11

THE CHICK ENGINEERS

Here's how music radio was done in 1967: DJs introduced and back-announced the songs. In a separate booth, engineers cued up the records on turntables and played them. And all engineers were men.

RAECHEL DONAHUE Tom, who liked women a lot, thought it shouldn't be only men who were allowed to play in this radio game.

VOCO Being a triple Gemini, his head constantly cooking, he came up with the greatest innovation ever in radio!

RAECHEL DONAHUE The soon-to-be-legendary "chick engineers." Bless his heart.

VOCO Blessings be upon you, Katie, Dusty, and Suzie Sweetsmiles! The ladies were the basis for our success from the start. They never allowed us to bring our bummers into the show. They have been and always will be the unknown pulse of underground radio.

MILAN MELVIN Katie Johnson had experience at KPFA Pacifica in Berkeley, and Dusty Street I recruited from SF State.

DUSTY STREET We met in film class. I quit and I went to Mexico for eight months because I'm silly, came back, and we were sitting in Enrico's; I was bemoaning the fact that I didn't want to go back to school or become a telephone operator. Milan said, "I've just gone to work for this guy Tom Donahue who started a radio station. He's looking for female engineers!" I went down to 50 Green Street, and Donahue asked me if I had a license and I said I did—of course. I didn't even know what one was. I went and failed the broadcast part of the FCC test; all I qualified myself for was Western Union operator. Thank God everybody at the station was either too stoned or involved in their own stuff to recognize I didn't have the license—I worked there six months until somebody figured it out. By then I knew enough about the equipment to pass the test. My first day had been so bad, the DJ sent me home. I thought my new career ended the day it started. Why Tom Donahue hired me is still a mystery.

KATIE JOHNSON I didn't know anything about him, and I was stunned walking into this little tiny studio that was completely full of Tom Donahue. Ha! It seemed very—I mean, it was very dreamy. We had my interview while he was doing his show.

DUSTY STREET Tom created *The Chicks Show*, giving us a few hours Sunday nights to do our own thing. I was Dusty "Superchick" Street! It was on that show that I found my voice.

SIDE TRIP

Donahue's Top Three From '67

San Francisco was where the missing children were gathering and calling themselves "hippies." When I first went there, I did not even know what I wanted to find out, and so I just stayed around a while and made a few friends.

—Joan Didion, *Slouching towards Bethlehem*

Tom Donahue: "'67 was a time of a lot of fun in San Francisco, and some paranoia, because the media had discovered the Haight-Ashbury. If you checked the average living room in the Haight, it would contain at least three people working for advanced degrees in psychology, another three preparing articles, 'I Was a Hippie in the Haight-Ashbury,' and at least two undercover agents."

*Goldie and Bear (with bear costume), Voco and Dusty,
Steve Ponek and family, Stinson Beach 1969.*
COURTESY BOB SIMMONS

BEAR

Bear—Edward Bear—was a big city cat. Steven Hirsch was his given name. In New York in '66, he had a late night gig at classical WNCN, and a day job managing Café Figaro in the Village.

EDWARD BEAR Bob Prescott, a guy I worked with at Café Figaro, split for San Francisco. About a year later, I arrived swinging in a hammock in the back of an orange hearse my friend Charlie drove. I'd been invited west to be writer-photographer for Ralph Metzner's incarnation of *The Psychedelic Review*, a political, erotic literary magazine. I thought, *Well, that sounds good.* I heard this station, call letters KMPX, and I went, *Whoa, that sounds good, look at that!* The morning DJ, Bob Prescott, introduces me to Tom Donahue. How about that? I said, "Forgive me, but I'm probably the best programmer you ever encountered." Something like that, coming from New York, program director at WNCN, a classical, jazz, blues, rock background. "I feel them all." He said, "Okay, wise ass, prove it." That very midnight, I made an audition tape, first three to four minutes a sound exploration-explanation of the history of mankind, starting with, you know, space, water, reptiles, mammals, human. Out of the human came the sound of the Maharishi—he was doing something like, "Life flows on the ocean of love," on and on . . . and ba-da-boom! I explained that I was a bear recently out of the mountains, with some observations about humankind. Left it on his desk. Got the job. Another thing that made me feel like a bear was, a bear doesn't want to get angry, but would if made angry. I did not like to be messed with. And I couldn't stand the scent of most people.

MILAN MELVIN Bear was the perfect guy to hear from midnight to dawn in the Summer of Love. Bear had an excellent ear for the segue and tirelessly promoted peace and love. His girlfriend, Goldie, was the ultimate flower child.

Promo, 1968. COURTESY EDWARD BEAR.

SIDE TRIP

Trouble in Pasadena

From 1967 to 1975, Ronald Reagan was governor of California. He described the hippie like this: "Someone who dresses like Tarzan, has hair like Jane, and smells like Cheetah."

CHRIS DARROW Nitty Gritty Dirt Band Our station was KPPC in Pasadena. They'd often play an album from beginning to end with no break. I was friends with the DJ, B. Mitchel Reed. I went to Mitch's house in Laurel Canyon and listened to a fourth generation pre-release bootleg cassette of *Sergeant Pepper's Lonely Hearts Club Band.*

FRANK ZAPPA The station in Los Angeles decided they'd made a lot of money and that they didn't need Tom anymore. So they fired him. Do you know what happened? The disk jockeys grabbed all the records and just walked out of the damn station, and the bands in town picketed the station. The only people who would service them with records was Liberty Records. Just one day after playing the weirdest underground stuff they could get their hands on, the station was playing, "Let It Be Him," by Vicki Carr, because that's the only kind of record they could get. A whole movement was there trying to keep Donahue on the station.

CHRIS DARROW Underground radio all the way!

KMPX staff walkout in spring of 1968, the first "hippie strike."
PHOTO BY JERRY TELFER/SAN FRANCISCO CHRONICLE VIA GETTY IMAGES

13

HIPPIES ON STRIKE, 1968

In March of '68, after less than a year on the air, Donahue's KMPX was number-one in the Bay Area. Also that month, he was fired. Station owner, Leon Crosby said, no—Donahue had quit. The staff walked out.

AAFIFMWW
The Amalgamated American Federation of International
FM Workers of the World Limited
North Beach Local No. 1

RAECHEL DONAHUE This was our union for America's first hippie strike. It all happened because we became a success. Leon Crosby said, "It's time for you to wear suits and ties; we're going to have some structure here. What we're going to do is bring in some of my people." We said, "No we're not," and formed the Amalgamated American Federation of International FM Workers of the World and got ourselves a union lawyer.

Michael J. Kramer, author of *The Republic of Rock: Music and Citizenship in the Sixties Counterculture,* offers his perspective on the job action.

MICHAEL J. KRAMER The KMPX strike is a good example of how the counterculture was never merely about stoned hedonists. AAFIFMWW was a name at once ridiculous and rich with historical reference to the Wobblies and their more anarchic, bohemian tradition of unionizing.

EDWARD BEAR This was a clear conflict between straight management and hip air staff.

BUZZY DONAHUE Even though the situation called for patience, by early spring everyone had run out of it.

EDWARD BEAR Leon Crosby was sweet, misguided, and really out of it.

MILAN MELVIN Leon Crosby was a nervous, mousy little character with a pencil-thin mustache, who wore a cheap rug and dyed his protruding tufts to match. He seemed terrified of longhairs.

EDWARD BEAR He was scared of "hippie chaos" and wanted us to follow a dress code. He didn't quite understand how talent worked. He was a square.

SUE HENDERSON, engineer Crosby was living in a different dimensional field than we were. I had hip huggers with seams up the front and back. Yellow. Black velvet, a twenties flapper dress. Really cool lace socks. I don't think I owned a bra then, actually. I was comfortable walking down the street in a lace top with not much underneath it. I'd come to work a little out there, but that's what I wore. Dusty too, certainly.

MILAN MELVIN The underground was happening on all levels. We were the most popular sound among the emerging subculture, and to everyone's surprise the ratings were strong. Ad space was almost entirely sold out.

The San Francisco *Chronicle* called KMPX "the Voice of the West," and "the Bay Area's only turned-on broadcasters." One reporter was particularly tickled by the "acid drolleries of long-haired Larry Miller." Another paper praised the "acid drolleries of long-haired Larry Miller."

MILAN MELVIN We were part of the community. Crosby didn't give a rat's ass about that—if we'd been hippos farting underwater while broadcasting, that would've been fine as long as it brought him cash. We dealt more with his general manager, Ron Hunt, indistinguishable from tens of thousands of other middle-class midwesterners. Not a bad guy, but he just didn't have a clue about what was whirling around him. He saw money pouring in, and he knew he had nothing to do with the success, so he stayed in the wings. But it wasn't just our music that brought us notoriety and support. KMPX's sound was personality driven; the people who put the music together had vast knowledge and honest enthusiasm. But when our arguments against running establishment ads surfaced, Hunt and Crosby freaked out. That we would even remotely *not* run a Pepsi jingle, not accept all the money that came with it. Like Leon was in control! Sales had gone through the roof because of the staff's unfettered creative control policy.

Susan Krieger is a scholar whose 1979 book *Hip Capitalism* captured the turmoil at the station.

SUSAN KRIEGER As soon as the controversial Pepsi ad aired—KMPX's first nationally produced jingle—a meeting was called. Bear found it abhorrent. McClay was beside himself. They went around the room, and Voco stood up. "Well, I drink the stuff," he said. They all did.

Pepsi spot

ANNOUNCER: Let's join the Pepsi Generation!

YOGI: [South Asian appropriation] This is Yogi Hananda speaking. Whenever I finish working a hard day of meditation, I find a tall, cool Pepsi-Cola is so refreshing. It refreshes your mind and your body. But most important, it fills your psyche with little dancing bubbles. Whenever friends drop in at the ashram, it is always a party when I bring out the Pepsi-Colas! [enhanced shimmering of hippie crash pad curtain beads]

Journalist Sandy Darlington responded in the underground *San Francisco Express-Times*: "There used to be this word 'hippie.' I'm still fond of it, but it doesn't serve like it used to. So I'll call us the Community. In a society that seems to be breaking into Establishment White vs. Black, Lyndon Johnson vs. Stokely Carmichael, we are emerging as the Third Force . . . what you might call the mostly white alternative. In a world of KFRC vs. KDIA, we are KMPX, complete with all the contradictions of people who advertise Peace & Freedom, Record City, Pepsi-Cola, and the highway patrol on the same station."

BEN FONG-TORRES In the fall of 1968, Tom Donahue duplicated his KMPX format four hundred miles south at another tiny FM losing money running religious and foreign programming.

JOEL SELVIN KPPC broadcast from the basement of Pasadena Presbyterian Church, hence the call letters. Tom wanted to change to KHIP. The church was not amused. But Tom could now hold forth nightly in both the LA Basin and San Francisco Bay Area, through the magic of audio tape recording!

MILAN MELVIN We were soon flying back and forth from Burbank almost every day. He felt there were all these people down there hearing KPPC for the first time and loving it. KMPX folks were brought down to do special shows. I was setting up a sales department. Katie Johnson set up the engineering.

KATIE JOHNSON I made several trips to help out. There were no good engineers in Pasadena.

SUSAN KRIEGER Big Daddy was spending a lot of time in LA trying to get his sister station off the ground, and not at KMPX.

KATIE JOHNSON At the start of '68, KMPX raised their rates by as much as 60 percent. The national minimum wage went up to $1.60 and we got raises to $2. But things began to get out of hand. I was angry at Crosby. The station was making money, and we were still using pieces of home equipment we'd had since we went on the air! The money had to be going somewhere. I switched from engineer to payroll and discovered the account at Wells Fargo was always low. After checks bounced, I went to the National Labor Relations Board. Crosby turned that into a personal offense; I had hurt his feelings! I found out he was putting money into his wife's house up in Marin and subsidizing a girlfriend's wig shop over in Fremont. It gets worse. Records were disappearing. And equipment. One morning, Crosby accused another engineer and me of being late. He didn't know the other woman's only reason for being there at all was that she was a groupie.

Steppenwolf's song "The Pusher" incensed Crosby and Hunt. They said playing it was against the law because it had "God damn" (the Pusher man) in there thirteen times.

KATIE JOHNSON Then came the memo: *Anybody playing dope lyrics will be fired.*

SUSAN KRIEGER *Employees are asked to be cautious in making loud noises and swearing in the station. Employees are to cut down on personal and* *long-distance calls. That goes for incoming calls, too. Employees will be paid every two weeks now.* Crosby called Milan a subversive, that he just wanted to play profane records—and here they'd sent him down to Pasadena in good faith.

MILAN MELVIN Here's a story. Early on, when we went twenty-four hours a day and revenue stopped coming in from foreign programs, the entire burden of KMPX's financial survival was placed on my shoulders. Crosby and Hunt slapped a bill for our transmitter on my desk: three thousand dollars. Seventy-two hours to pay it off or our signal goes off—meaning certain death to our underground radio newborn baby. I spent two days pleading with sponsors for advances on what they owed us. Bill Graham, building his empire like a maniac—too tight to come up with a nickel before it was due. Chet Helms, way too disorganized to do anything about money. The local retailers, the head shops, clothing, records, and instrument stores, said our advertising had helped sell so much product, they'd reinvested the cash into more inventory! I damn near broke down. Deadline day, I walked into Tom's office and told him I was the reason the station was fucked. Tom began to roll a joint, contemplating. I said I'd handled lots of problems around the station, but this one was beyond me: "I'm out of strokes, Tom. I'm sorry." I'd let the station down. He leaned across his desk, handed me the joint, and from somewhere deep inside that baritone sax came, "Milan, I'll take care of everything. Don't worry." I'd never felt such relief in my life. Big Daddy would find a way. I went back to my office, lit the joint, and kicked back to enjoy the pleasant ride. Loaded and loving it—out of the crosshairs!—loving all the dope dealers in town who brought fists of fine weed into the station, giving it in appreciation of the good music we were giving them. *Dope dealers couldn't advertise!* I phoned a fellow I'd grown up with. He said he would go out back and dig it up. He blew my mind. "Why didn't you ask sooner?" This is an hour before they were gonna pull the plug. Donahue said they'd made payroll with dried mud money. My friend kept his cash in a buried coffee can.

Katie Johnson discovered thirty-three thousand dollars had gone missing at KPPC.

KATIE JOHNSON The sales manager had been stealing. And Lee Crosby was not supporting his girlfriend's wig shop; she'd been supporting *him* for three years. He also accepted loans from his wife and sister. Crosby was not a marginal businessman managing to stay alive; he was a marginal businessman getting away with murder. Me, I'd had enough. I was tired of coming in and getting yelled at *by Leon Crosby.*

CHAPTER 13

SUSAN KRIEGER Donahue met with Crosby at KMPX. Crosby told him he could keep his position as program director at one of the stations, but not both. Donahue walked out. The next day, Donahue went back to pick up his things. People were walking around stunned. Crosby told the press he'd given Tom a choice of stations but never got an answer.

RAECHEL DONAHUE Leon, like most bean counters who don't know anything about the art we were doing, decided he could do it without Tom; he could bring in some schlep, pay him half as much, and it'd be great. What he didn't understand was our loyalty. Tom had given all of us our breaks. That's why when Leon Crosby said, "Tom quit," we went, "We don't think so."

MILAN MELVIN The straw that broke the camel's back? The length of my hair. Leon wanted me more presentable to ad agencies. There were some nasty meetings. He ordered me to "straighten out." A minor issue. But on March 14, I joined the conspiracy to strike.

Sunday, March 17, Ron Hunt begged Donahue: "We can settle today!" But even if Donahue called off a strike at midnight, the air staff was already beginning to celebrate. On Sunday nights, when an engineer came in to do maintenance, the station went off the air from midnight to six a.m. Monday.

DJ PHIL HAMMOND
Good evening. The moon is in Scorpio. The great sphinx looks with scorn upon our station. To his mighty disgust white sheep have been sacrificed to our sponsors with averted face, and hordes of black scorpions overrun our controls. Tonight Pluto, the god of death dripping crimson, stands atop our broadcast tower to signal our redemption. The great sphinx stirs at his coming. He knows death is near, and his giant wings, unused for centuries, begin to throb and tingle with anticipation. Soon he will fly in the sunlight.</ext>

Bear, the station's highest-paid DJ—$125 a week, far below Top 40 announcers—led off at the microphone for Team AAFIFMWW.

BEAR *Hello, this is Edward Bear, and, as you know, we've been talking of splitting, and that is indeed what we're doing; the entire staff, from secretarial help on through everybody, is going out on strike at three o'clock this morning. It's kind of apparent that the ability to have creative growth here has been so limited to the point that the foreseeable future is grim. This does not mean the present is that* *awful! You have, we have all been enjoying a groovy thing. I'm sure most know that Tom Donahue, more responsible than anybody for the existence of KMPX, quit last week. The entire strike has to do with that. This is in sympathy with Tom. My head is in a strange place because I really feel sad, and at the same time rather hopeful. . . . We're called the Amalgamated American Federation of International FM Workers of the World, Limited, North Beach Local No. 1. Yeah, it's crazy. Voco, did the Dead say they're definitely coming?*

VOCO *Right.*

BEAR *Anybody else?*

VOCO *The Dead will be here. Allman Joy will be here.*

BEAR *Anyway, there's going to be a dance.*

VOCO *The cops are going to crash.*

BEAR *I don't think we're gonna get a hassle from the heat because they're aware that something's going to happen. There have been announcements in the Fillmore and the Carousel and the Avalon, for people if they want to come for support, hang out at about three o'clock. There will be music. There will be all of us picketing. If somebody would like to bring some barrels or firewood, that'll really be a groove and we could have some fires out there maybe.*

VOCO *Well, I'll tell you what. Now I've got to give an ID. We're not that gone! This is KMPX Stereo, San Francisco, at 107. This is Voco and Dusty. Ed Bear's here. And if you don't believe we're leaving, you can count the days we're gone. Ooh! I must have stolen that from B. B. King! Long time ago. The whole staff here is splitting. And we're going to have a little picket party out front. We're going to do a little rockin'. Listen. KMPX will probably still be on the air—maybe Buffalo Bill will be one of the announcers, I don't know. So don't help me out.* Help me in.

BOB MCCLAY *This is Bob McClay, and I'm up way past my bedtime. Only a very heavy moment would bring me in at a time like this. We feel that KMPX has been, up to this moment, probably the best radio station that any of us have had the pleasure of working for.*

VOCO *Amen. Amen. Hey, make it here, 50 Green Street. We're gonna make a joyful noise you can dance to. There's a light show going on downstairs. The groovy people from the Family Dog, the Avalon Ballroom, brought their light show. The Ace of Cups are here, missing one Ace. Denise, if you're near abouts and you'd like to fall on by, the girls are here and they'd dig to play! Yeah. This is Voco. And if you want to hear me anymore, it won't be here on KMPX for a while. But I'll be on KPFA tomorrow night at midnight, on the King Biscuit West. I think that's the name of the show. I'll be there at midnight. I gotta play the blues* somewhere, *baby.*

BOB MCCLAY *They're here! They just walked in with their cannons.*

VOCO *Beautiful, man, come on in. We're going to split downstairs. The Grateful Dead are here. Ace of Cups are here. The light show from the Family Dog. We're all here. Hurrah! [voices whooping] Dusty, I got you a gig tomorrow at Mr. Bimbo's in the fish tank.*

PHIL HAMMOND *The time has come again for KMPX to take a brief rest while our team of technical tinkerers tear away at our tiny transistors. KMPX broadcasts on an assigned carrier frequency of 106.9 megacycles, with eighty thousand watts of power authorized by the Federal Communications Commission. We will return to the air at 6 a.m. with a reading from the I-Ching. [Song: Little Milton's "Feel So Bad": "I shake my head and walk away . . ."]*

A VOICE *This is Radio Free San Francisco. Everybody is free to do as they please. [hammering noises] Let's go. [The sound of a needle sticking . . . then a click.]*

***Chronicle* reporter George Gilbert, who had gone undercover, embedded in the underground scene, described what he saw in the studio.**

GEORGE GILBERT "Voco, his black beard brushing the microphone, told an astonished audience that the staff was striking. Everybody, despite the crisis, was grooving to James Brown. Rocking on the balls of his feet and staring at the groovy chicks dancing in the studio was Augustus Owsley Stanley III, the Henry Ford of LSD. The Grateful Dead arrived and offered their help. Ten or fifteen hippies wandered about with sad, lost faces. Five hundred more waited outside. At five minutes after three o'clock in the morning the amplifiers were plugged in and the Creedence Clearwater band came alive. So did a lot of people on Telegraph Hill, only a few decibels west."

JOEL SELVIN When the DJs came out, there were huge cheers.

MICHAEL J. KRAMER Creedence Clearwater Revival, the Grateful Dead, and Blue Cheer performed in the street outside the studios as a light show swirled through the San Francisco fog.

JOEL SELVIN Stevie Winwood and Jim Capaldi of Traffic arrived—their first time in America—at midnight. Just after that, Owsley fed them LSD—also their first time.

DUSTY STREET Stevie Winwood played on a flatbed truck. Blue Cheer hit about three notes and the cops descended on us, man. I mean, if you don't know who Blue Cheer was, this was three guys that had more Marshall amplifiers than the five top rock bands of the time. Needless to say, that was a large sound.

Blue Cheer claimed to be the first power trio; Voco produced their version of "Summertime Blues." The band was always worth checking out, Donahue said, "even if you didn't particularly dig the kind of music they played. They were three incredible animals and they all had hair down to their ankles. So you knew they at least had a commitment to hair for a while."

GEORGE GILBERT "The cops arrived and told the throng to turn it down. Creedence Clearwater frowned. So did everybody else. The two cops left quickly, and everybody cheered. But the cops returned in a little while with two sergeants. And the dance on Green Street was over. "Everybody come over to Pier 10," somebody shouted from the makeshift bandstand. "We'll resume there." Everybody did, but somebody forgot the amps and five hundred disgruntled hippies went home for the night."

JOEL SELVIN Later that morning, a letter of support arrived from the Rolling Stones. The Beatles sent a wire.

RAECHEL DONAHUE Bill Graham sent a truck full of food. Listeners brought their buckets of brown rice with vegetables. Even the longshoremen, who'd wanted to kill us when we first went on the air, came to help us guard the line. They'd grown to love us so much! And we'd made ridiculous demands. We asked for summer solstice off, various other weird days.

CHAN LAUGHLIN Lynn Hughes came down from the Red Dog [his girlfriend; she sang with the Charlatans], and we scheduled the staff and volunteers to walk the picket line seven days a week, twenty-four hours a day. We organized everything in my Chevy van. That's where we distributed benefit checks, pamphlets, food.

Meanwhile, Leon Crosby, who once ran a broadcasting school out of KMPX, rushed to San Francisco State, Fremont College, and College of St. Mary's to recruit new on-air talent. *Chronicle* columnist Ralph Gleason described what happened next: "Immediately, four of the furthest-out strikers (led by the truculent Chan Laughlin and crazy Katie Johnson) sped out to CSM where Chan says, 'We literally blitzed the place. We ripped down every announcement posted on campus.'"

MILAN MELVIN We tried to explain our side of the situation—students might not have realized what the strike meant. Or that it was even on. But when the scabs were hired, it was the first time I thought they showed we were replaceable. The scabs claimed the music was more important than a certain bunch of people's jobs and that Donahue and the rest of us were on an ego trip—it was all a power play. They, the scabs, were the ones keeping the station alive.

RAECHEL DONAHUE There's always the ones who are gonna cross the line. "Yeah, I could be a disc jockey; all I have to do is piss off a whole lot of people!"

SUSAN KRIEGER Ron Hunt slept on his KMPX office floor. The picketers had made it so bad he couldn't leave the building. Crosby had to sell time to an Italian-language program again.

DUSTY STREET There were a lot of people, including Larry Miller, who crossed the picket line. I don't think they understood the power of the group of people that made KMPX, because KMPX was not an individual. We were the sum of our parts. We all had our own focus. Mine was blues, Tom was very much into rock 'n roll, Voco had his eclectic taste, and Bob McClay's was whatever Bob McClay's was.

SUSAN KRIEGER One release described, *"a tribe of people" who had brought new music to the cities of San Francisco and Los Angeles: "When these two stations were teetering on the brink of collapse, management had been content to have long-haired, barefoot, and beaded employees. But when they were successful, management had seen fit to remove some of them. We love these stations, not as a collection* *of chairs, desks, tubes, and turntables, but as the living idea of a loving group of people. We love our work and only wish to be allowed to do it as we have in the past. For the present, KMPX and KPPC are on the air. The idea is on the street.*

MILAN MELVIN We'd gone door-to-door asking advertisers to stay off the air until we settled—we didn't expect to be off more than a week. Thirty sponsors formed a committee in support. Bands who would've been coming in for interviews on the air were now playing benefits! Chet Helms at the Avalon, Ron Rakow at Carousel, and Bill Graham at his Fillmore/Winterland ballrooms gave us stage time between musical sets to explain our case. Everything was going for us.

Strike Benefit drew 3,000 and included Blue Cheer, Creedence, Ace of Cups, Charlie Musselwhite, Black Swan, Frumious Bandersnatch, and Jeremy & The Satyrs. Winterland, April 1968.

Reggie Williams ran the Straight Theater, a Haight Street favorite near the Stanyan Street entrance to Golden Gate Park. He and his crew organized a different kind of benefit, with a little boost from the Beatles.

REGGIE WILLIAMS We always had a strong connection to KMPX at the Straight. We put on an all-night event for the station called the "Second Annual Grope For Peace," sponsored by the Psychic Research Foundation, who were Family Dog and Red Dog Saloon folks, also known as the Psychedelic Cattlemen's Association. As another benefit, we presented the "Northern Hemisphere Premiere" of the Beatles' newest release, a television movie called *Magical Mystery Tour*. I sent Milan Melvin to SFO, where he fought to get what authorities were calling a "dirty" flick through customs. He showed up at three a.m. with the reels, two thousand fans outside the theater waiting their turn to get in and see it. We ran it for twenty-four hours.

Another event that went down was on Bay Area Channel 2. Reporter Claude Mann is on the scene. (I'm looking at black-and-white footage found on the San Francisco State Archives website. The vertical hold is out of whack because the tape is a few video generations beyond, what, fifty-five years?) Mann stands in the 50 Green Street parking lot, his black suit in front of the white VW Beetle. A small circle of laidback activists, singing songs and carrying signs, photos or drawings of DJs held high. A Beat character smoking. A picketer with a body length God's eye of colorful (one assumes) yarn. A strumming folk singer, and a hippie jump-dancing around—he could be one of those groovy listeners who dig what KMPX really stands for: "KillerMaryjanePotX." Claude Mann, a TV man from 1968, seems down with the zeitgeist.

https://diva.sfsu.edu/collections/sfbatv/bundles/232777
KTVU coverage of strike.

CLAUDE MANN This isn't the opening of a new North Beach night spot, as you might surmise from a casual glance. Actually, this is a strike. But it's a strike by union members of something called the Amalgamated American Federation of International FM Workers of the World, Limited North Beach Local No. 1. These are the thirty employees of KMPX.

We see (thanks to the SF State Archives site) black and white footage (vertical hold alert!) of people singing songs and a-carrying signs. Here's a child holding up a giant God's eye. A folksinger strumming, a hippie dancing, and some beat character smokes. Claude Mann pulls Jack Towle from the picket line A Family Dog member who got his KMPX job through the Chan Laughlin/Milan Melvin connection, Jack is another radio outlaw to Mr. and Mrs. 1968 America watching at home.

CLAUDE MANN Jack, you're a member of the negotiating committee.

JACK TOWLE Yes, I am.

CLAUDE MANN What's going on here? What's the beef?

JACK TOWLE Well, we're on strike today. And we're trying to get our program director back, and we would also like to get some control of the sales department that we don't seem to have right now. The child that we've created here is being taken by a stranglehold, which if something isn't done about it, will kill it. And the time to act is now, while there are still enough of us here at one time to act together!

"Come a cow ki-yicky-yicky-yeah," sings the folkie (from "When I Was a Cowboy," by Huddie Ledbetter, Alan and John Lomax.) Not identified (no chyron at KTVU?), she looks like Stephen Stills' rock 'n roll woman from his eponymous Buffalo Springfield song. *She's a joy to knowwww.* How do I know? Check the archives! Tap that QR code, gentle viewer!

CLAUDE MANN I understand the entertainment we're getting today is nothing at all to what you had last night.

ROCK 'N ROLL WOMAN Oh, that was beautiful, yeah. Clear Light was here and several other bands.

CLAUDE MANN Four hundred people dancing in the street?

ROCK 'N ROLL WOMAN Yeah, it was beautiful.

CLAUDE MANN And you've got something else lined up, too.

ROCK 'N ROLL WOMAN We have a benefit at the Avalon Ballroom, Wednesday.

CLAUDE MANN Are you optimistic all these tactics are going to gain your objectives for you?

ROCK 'N ROLL WOMAN Oh yes, because we're really out front. We're really telling it like it is.

Pretty-eyed, pirate smile. She's a flower child speaking truth to power, etc.

CLAUDE MANN Well, it's a picket line unlike anything that's ever been seen on the labor front before, but the thirty former employees of the radio station say they feel they have a loyal audience and a loyal group of sponsors and they *shall*, with these tactics, overcome. This is Claude Mann, reporting from North Beach.

(Brother Claude, down with the zeitgeist!) Straight salesperson, Whitney Harris, wrote a letter to the *Chronicle*, thanking associates and bands for their benefit concerts. "This is folk music," he said. "And we are folk." The *Chronicle*'s Ralph Gleason described strikers as "workers seizing the tools." (When reporters at his newspaper walked off their jobs a couple months earlier, he walked over to KMPX and read his thrice-weekly "Lone Ranger" column on the air.) As the strike continued into May, a "letter to the world" appeared in the *San Francisco Express-Times* underground weekly.

> It is too bad and sad to bear, that we will never have KMPX again. It doesn't matter who "wins" the strike—the way and the light are lost. You see, it was not the programming which really got it—it was and always has been the strong loving, even blessing, intent of those who played the platters which made your ex-station a way to live in and with. But now you people hate too much. I shan't again believe your recorded words of love. You are bitter exiles, the scabs are inept creeps, and the listeners (I am one, hello) turn off their radios and learn to live alone. God bless us all and may we yet find all the love we need. Catessa

SUSAN KRIEGER Katie Johnson abandoned the strike line during the sixth week. She thought the group was doing horrible things they were not conscious of. She thought they'd all changed during the strike, but none of them would admit it. She never came back.

Ad in National Lampoon *by Gilbert Shelton, known for* The Fabulous Furry Freak Brothers, Wonder Wart-Hog, *and other underground graphix.*
CARTOON BY GILBERT SHELTON

14

THE JIVE 95!

This isn't brain surgery. It's only rock 'n roll.

—Tom Donahue

HANK LONDON, producer The strike ended after eight weeks. It was never really settled.

MILAN MELVIN We voted overwhelmingly to move off the streets. There was no chain of command, but I was virtually second in command after Donahue. I met with Stefan Ponek, DJ and sales manager at KSFR, a classical station owned by Metromedia. Stefan asked if I thought striking KMPX staffers would come over. His bosses knew I had the keys to a vault of advertisers who had stuck with us and were eager to get back on the air. It sounded like a lifesaver to me. But there was some fine print. And a deal breaker: Tom Donahue was not invited. I told Stefan I'd communicate the proposal—but I was positive nobody would consider going anywhere without Tom. It was all of us or none, take it or leave it! Tom began negotiating for us. There was some fine print, but soon I was making sure there was a smooth transition from the street back to the air for everyone.

Tom Donahue and Bob McClay were out searching for a new station in which to sell the products of their minds. ABC Radio in Chicago was a possibility. Milan Melvin, second in command, stayed in San Francisco.

MICHAEL J. KRAMER Donahue, who was accused of using the strike to wrest control of KMPX, persuaded the staff to follow him to a new station. Things went precisely in the opposite direction from what the strikers and supporters had hoped: away from a liberated community, toward corporate control. Nevertheless, at KSAN, the KMPX crew carried on the initial spirit of the 1968 strike. Now members of a very traditional trade union, the International Brotherhood of Electrical Workers, the staff still engaged in labor activism on its own terms.

EDWARD BEAR Metromedia saw an opportunity for a format that sparkled.

BUZZY DONAHUE Metromedia had lots of shiny stuff. Nice equipment. But it was a challenge.

MILAN MELVIN Not all of us walked into our new station crying tears of joy. I felt it was the beginning of the end. How could you use "underground" and "Metromedia Incorporated" in the same sentence?

EDWARD BEAR And Big Daddy wouldn't take me along! Stefan Ponek from the leftover staff—he did a weekend KSFR show called *Underground Sunshine*—took my shift. While I had the best numbers of everybody, Donahue had trouble with me. I am a free spirit, and we were all supposed to be free! I'm from New York and have an attitude. So, there it is. But here ya go: the rest of the crew wouldn't allow it; they said, "No! Bear is too important to the whole thing." So Donahue tossed me a bone—the night shift. I resented it. I was middays on KMPX. And then I came to fall in love: all night offers greater freedom, tons of empty space in which to provide a soundtrack for San Francisco. KSAN took to the air on Tom Donahue's fortieth birthday, May 21. Eight days before my thirtieth. With Bob McClay as the first DJ on the air: the spirit of KMPX, resurrected in a new package! May '68! Google "Paris," and what else was happening on the planet then!

DUSTY STREET I went from KMPX to KSAN as an engineer because Voco didn't know how to run a board. Voco was kind of *anti-magnetic*. It had been the combo operation at KMPX, but at KSAN everyone was running their own board. The other chick engineers were kind of left by the wayside.

EDWARD BEAR Moving down the dial from 106.9 megahertz to 94.9 megahertz was the easy part.

DUSTY STREET Here we all come in, and Stefan really didn't know what was going on.

STEFAN PONEK The first day was madness. Here was KSFR, the quiet failing classical station, and in comes this bunch of hippies with bells, see-through blouses, filling the station with flowers everywhere. And truckload after truckload of records. It was beautiful. For the first couple months, you never knew what would happen next.

BUZZY DONAHUE Tom's ideas scared them. He'd come to board meetings, hair tied in a long braid, tie-dyed T-shirt, all 350 pounds of him. They would take one look and not know what to do.

DUSTY STREET Poor Stefan. We were mean; he went through years of abuse. I would have hated to be one of the out crowd.

STEFAN PONEK The acceptance thing was very heavy.

DUSTY STREET What really made KSAN unique in the beginning was we were the only one. I think what we did at KSAN was we expanded what KMPX was. We became a little more professional, we were paid a lot more—we were such stars at KSAN.

HOW WACHSPRESS, engineer They were prima donnas. There was a lot in the music business then. Minor celebrities, but they were bigger than movie stars.

DUSTY STREET Metromedia came galloping to the rescue of KMPX and took us in because they knew a good thing when they heard it.

STEFAN PONEK I could go into KSAN on a sunny day, smoking a joint across the Golden Gate Bridge, put on Vivaldi's "Spring Concerto," segue to a bluegrass fiddler, come out into something by Cream, and it would work. And because we could do that and other people did not know how to do that, we were pretty cherished by the community.

> *Stefan Ponek . . . 94.9 Metromedia Stereo . . . KSAN . . . the Jive 95 . . . Good way to just spend the day, stretch out by the pool, imbibe what you imbibe, and just kinda lay there till it gets hot . . . and roll in . . . ker-splash*

> *. . . then crawl out again and do it again. . . . That's "Sunny Afternoon," by the Kinks . . . before that was Traffic with "Paper Sun"; Aretha, "Hello Sunshine"; Chicago Transit Authority with "Wake Up Sunshine"; and Moby Grape doing "Beautiful Day Today." If you're crazy, too . . . "Triad" by the Airplane. . . . The moon is still in Leo; we'll be going into Virgo about what, 2:02 this afternoon, something like that . . . for a couple of fine days. . . . Here's a nice new flower here in the booth . . . that should help the whole thing all day long. [reads spot] "Evelyn Wood Reading Dynamics" . . . the late President Kennedy took Evelyn to the White House to train all those dummies there . . . get them so they could read faster.*

Stefan received that Gavin Award for Disc Jockey of the Year in '71. Greg Shaw, in his fanzine *Bomp!*, described a "nationwide" Ponek broadcast he caught that summer.

GREG SHAW KSAN was on long distance with a DJ in Bishop, California, hearing about kids "cruising" town until three in the morning. Ponek played Jerry Lee Lewis records. That was followed by a call to a station in Fargo, North Dakota, to hear about the scene there. A little Chuck Berry, and we were listening to a DJ in South Carolina broadcasting from a studio atop a drive-in theater. Stefan asked what the top records were in Pekoe, Wisconsin, where cruising was called "shooting the loop and buzzing the gut." We were in Alexandria, Louisiana; Toledo, Ohio. KSAN listeners called Stefan, requesting stations (linking in by long distance was not cheap!). By "Highway 61 Revisited," I was pounding the table, swearing I'd never heard a better hour in all my years of radio listening. The guys at KSAN were drunk with laughter, flabbergasted how easy it was to make contact with 1961. It was a sort of spontaneous documentary. A magnificent thing. *Who Put the Bomp* salutes you, Stefan Ponek, for originality and true rock 'n roll consciousness in broadcasting!

SIDE TRIP

Milan Drops the Mic

BEN FONG-TORRES Milan Melvin was one of the most fascinating figures out of the '60s. A case could be made that he helped to shape the time of our lives.

DAVID CROSBY In a world of posers, Milan was the rare real thing. An adventurer and a strong friend.

BEN FONG-TORRES Light up, buckle up, and enjoy the flight.

In '68, facing the draft, Milan Melvin read over KSAN, a letter denouncing conscription and a government fostering "organized violence" in Vietnam and at home. He revealed his past ties to the FBI at UC Berkeley, where he spied on leftist students—until joining them. Metromedia ordered him to stop on-the-air political material. He said he couldn't yield to censorship and still function as a revolutionary.

JOAN BAEZ, sister of Mimi Farina Lean, lanky, self-contained, charming, and a natural gentleman—one of a dying breed even then.

Voco took Milan under his wing at Blue Thumb Records producing LPs. He was never inducted. KSAN Gnusman, Peter Laufer edited Milan Melvin's memoir, *Highlights of a Low Life*, and was his friend for more than thirty years.

MILAN MELVIN No joy remained in radio for me. I felt we had lost. Lost any chance to do anything significant. I wasn't interested in sales anymore because Metromedia started bringing in their own people. I wasn't in charge anymore, like at KMPX where we were personality-driven, playlist-free, honesty-in-advertising radio. When it came to the KSAN news department, I was wrong, but that wasn't my scene. I thought, if we'd created our own radio station, even the news department could have been better. But my heart wasn't in it—my heart was elsewhere, with Mimi Farina, whom I was marrying that fall.

PETER LAUFER Milan was a Zelig-like figure for the latter half of the twentieth century: he seemed to be everywhere and do everything—and do it first. From the postwar tedium of the paranoid '50s; through the sex, drugs, and rock 'n roll '60s; on to the world-trekking '70s, the self-reflective '80s, the capital-building '90s. In many ways, he lived the baby boomer fantasy life: rarely compromising, highly political, self-indulgent, seeking enlightenment and instant gratification simultaneously.

EDWARD BEAR After he died in 2001 at the age of fifty-nine, we took a life-sized headshot of Milan out to his favorite old San Francisco hangouts. It was Roland Jacopetti, my wife Lori, and I—we put the picture on the table, bought him drinks, and toasted him farewell. We took turns downing his drink. I wish my memory was still sharp, but it's not. Roland was the perfect person to share that night with. Roland is innately warm-hearted, very bright, and funny. He produced KSAN's Congress of Wonders comedy sketches, and lots of spots. We could use more men like Roland and Milan in these divided days.

Milan's memoir included this letter near the end.

Puerto Vallarta

Dear Family and Friends,

Please be informed that I have crossed over or as some say "gone paws up" or "assumed room temperature."

Not knowing, of course, what's on the other side, I promise you that if there is anything ever in eternity that I can do for you there, I'll get it done. But if the Tibetan Buddhists have it right, I'll be back around after forty-nine days for another go at learning the lessons I flunked this time. Look for the little boy in the cowboy and Indian pajamas with the pith helmet and safari jacket and know that Expedition Melvin rides again.

In closing, let me ask that you think of me as having a first-class seat on the nonstop bullet train to the greatest mystery and the grandest adventure of all.

YEE-HA!

YEE-HA!

And love,

MM

Bob Simmons: "I can name about 90% but damn, time has taken its toll. Jeff Nemerovski, David Bramnick, Richard Gossett, Sean Donahue, damn do not remember, Larry the Public Affairs guy, Dave McQueen, Tony Kilbert, Ben Fong-Torres, Phil Buchanan, Jane Oliver, Christi Joy Marcus, Danice Bordette, Helen Cleland, Scoop Nisker, Rick Sadle, Joyce Shank, Jerry Graham, Bonnie Simmons, Norman Davis, Doug Dunlop, Bob Simmons, Joe Lerer, don't know, Ed Ely, Don Ptoczack, Earn Morgan, Bob McClay, Vicky Cunningham, Donna Campbell, don't know, and Jeannie Chen, mid-'70s, but don't quote me . . ."

PHOTO BY STEPHAN RAHN

SIDE TRIP

Vermont, 1970

In the summer of '70, Tom Donahue and a gang of Jive 95ers blew in from out of the West, landing at Goddard College in Plainfield, Vermont for an "Alternative Media Conference," organized by revered radioman Larry Yurdin—Big Daddy once offered him a gig at KMPX. Featuring: Ram Dass (keynote), Wavy Gravy and his traveling Temple of Accumulated Error (in their Hog Farm commune bus), Art Spiegelman (counterculture cartoonist), Harvey Kurtzman (creator of subversive journal, *Mad Magazine*), and Paul Krassner (creator of the *Mad* for adults, *The Realist*). KSAN's San Francisco kooks turned on a lot of teenagers that weekend.

Alternative Media Conference in Vermont, 1970. Radio newbies in their twenties inspired by Donahue, Scoop talks, tripping, getting to know one another, the usual. Trish Robbins met McClay and other Jivers here, moved west, got a job! (L–R: Mike Goodwin, Wesley "Scoop" Nisker, and Larry Bensky).

PHOTO BY ROBERT ALTMAN/MICHAEL OCHS ARCHIVES/GETTY IMAGES

TRISH ROBBINS I was nineteen and on the air in Miami. When I heard about this conference—basically a call to the people—I had to go. That's where I met Bob McClay, Tom Donahue, Scoop Nisker, Larry Bensky, and Dave McQueen leading seminars for students on college stations or wanting to get into FM. I remember being too petrified to say anything, so the whole weekend I hung out with Stefan Ponek and the KSAN guys. I was just so stunned by the whole thing. To see brilliant people talking about changing the way people did broadcasting. It had been all AM. Now it was the KMPXs and KSANs. People who were doing progressive radio—"underground radio"—amazing! I remember a lot of people at the conference tripping. I absolutely was, I can't remember if I slept with anybody or not. And Bob McClay said, "Hey Trish, if you're ever in San Francisco, drop in!"

And after the conference, everybody went home and started their own little radio stations. There may have been one in your hometown. Now there are low-power, community and pirate stations sprinkled like KSAN's grandchildren all over the continent. (And podcasts going as far out as their narrowcaster's dreams, etc.) Vermont '70—some of it can be seen on YouTube—was an incubator for ideas that found their way onto the airwaves.

TRISH ROBBINS A year later, I moved myself across the country. And the first thing I did was drop on by KSAN. I don't think they expected to see me again! Bob McClay was on the air. He goes, "Hey Trish! Oh wow, we need a music librarian. Answer this question and you're hired." That was the way they did stuff there. (HR in 1971?) McClay said, "Who were the Mugwumps?" I said, "Really? That's all you're going to ask me?" I knew everything about music, which is how I got the gig in Florida when I was eighteen. "The Mamas and the Papas were first called the Mugwumps." He brought me in. Then they started using me as a weekend fill-in. McClay took me under his wing and taught me about San Francisco music. Bob was my mentor.

The Year of McClay! Bob McClay, Stefan Ponek, and unidentified per her request. 211 Sutter Street studio, mid-1970s.
COURTESY BOB SIMMONS

15

THE WONDERFUL McCLAY

Bob McClay was known for going to extremes to find the funny. "Using an eye-dropper in a cab after the Hooker's Ball, drive-time DJ Bob McClay accidentally squeezes three thousand micrograms of LSD in his mouth," said The *San Francisco Chronicle.* "He strips off his clothes, cowers under a desk until airtime, and then completes his show. Nobody notices." The same daily paper declared 1976, *The Year of McClay!* Tom Donahue said McClay was "pressed off center." He was also the first DJ to play Hendrix.

JOEL SELVIN In April 1967, Paul McCartney told the Jefferson Airplane about Jimi Hendrix, whom nobody knew in the States. Except for Bob McClay; he had the only Hendrix import in town.

BOB MCCLAY Shortly after KMPX got underway, a friend in England sent me an acetate pressing—or an acetate cutting—of a record that hadn't yet been released. It was by an American guitarist with two English backup guys. Collectively they were the Jimi Hendrix Experience. That afternoon we were the first radio station ever to play Jimi Hendrix in the world. The record hadn't even been released in England.

JOEL SELVIN At that time, April-May of 1967, you think the station had ten, twenty thousand listeners? They wouldn't even get rated! The record wasn't released in the U.S. until August. And there weren't any "pick hits" at KMPX. Every track was played: "Purple Haze," "Foxy Lady," "Fire," "Third Stone from the Sun." The station was just *slamming* the fucking thing. So Hendrix shows up in town in June, the weekend after the Monterey Pop Festival down the coas—he's the opening act of the Jefferson Airplane show at the Fillmore. Five days of shows. I think Gabor Szabo is above him on the bill. And I'll tell you, everybody that showed up there showed up to see Hendrix. He was a *made man* in San Francisco because of KMPX—because of this extraordinarily devoted, intensely tied-in audience. The culture was so tight at that point you could drop a dime in the underground radio station and it would just spread out through the whole whatever network there was. The listeners grew *exponentially* over the course of the next eighteen months.

1972 Promo

[Film noir-feel clack of shoes on cobblestones as a foghorn moans through the Golden Gate.]

MALE ANNOUNCER: Great Radio Mysteries! [reverb, howls, organ flourishes] Today, the strange disappearance of Bob McClay! Born the errant son of a dancer, under the boardwalk in Atlantic City! A soda jerk, truck driver, encyclopedia salesman . . . and then a famous disc jockey. Before he disappeared! No one has seen Bob McClay in the studio since that fateful day in 1972. Wednesday. Sometime between two and six. His voice continues to haunt the airwaves almost every afternoon on KSAN. How is it possible? Is the voice taped in some secret way? Not according to our bonded engineers. Today at 2 p.m., the Bob McClay show remains another. . . . Great Radio Mystery! [pianos' slam finish to Beatles' "A Day in the Life."]

Another typically atypical Bob McClay afternoon on the air . . .

MCCLAY [shuffles papers] I want everybody to get out your whips, your chains, the boots, and the spurs . . . here's a lady, every record she makes, it is extremely masochistic. That's Melanie and "Sweet Misery." Come here Melanie, we wanna rub a little salt in those wounds . . . Bob McClay, after three weeks in sick bay, feelin' fine. Do you wanna say hello to anybody?

AARON [Bob's son, four] Yeah, yeah.

MCCLAY Who?

AARON To Sean.

MCCLAY You wanna say hello to Sean?

AARON Yeah. And Eddie.

MCCLAY And Eddie, too? Well go ahead.

AARON Hi Eddie!

MCCLAY Who else?

AARON And Mommy.

MCCLAY [back-announces records] Yma Sumac, Grace Slick from *Manhole* and—what?

AARON Is that you?

MCCLAY That's me all right. Is that you? Who are you?

AARON Aaron.

MCLAY This is Bob McClay and Aaron. Are you gonna sing a little bit?

AARON May I talk to Sean?

MCCLAY Why don't you talk to the microphone?

AARON Hi Sean!

MCCLAY Say, "Hi microphone!"

AARON Hi Mike!

MCCLAY Microphone.

AARON I can't. I said hi to Sean. Hi Sean!

MCCLAY By the way, we also heard, Aaron—in case you're interested—Sons of Champlin, "El Condor Pasa" from Los Incas, and Simon and Garfunkel, "The Boxer." [reads spot] "Kaplan's new bib overalls come in Charlie Chaplin and UFO Painter styles with flared bottoms and—" what?

AARON Can I talk?

MCCLAY Well, I'm talking. Can we both talk at the same time?

AARON Yeah.

MCCLAY "1055 Market Street between Sixth and Seventh. They're open daily."

AARON Market Street?

MCCLAY You know where that is. Between Sixth and Seventh? Kaplan's? The place with all the tents?

AARON Yeah! Can I talk to that? [referring to his father's microphone]

MCCLAY No, I talk to *that* and you talk to *that.* Okay?

AARON [something difficult to figure out]

MCCLAY Say, "You'll never . . ."

AARON "You'll never take me alive."

MCCLAY "You'll never take me alive," what?

AARON "You'll never take me alive, copper."

MCCLAY [after spot] *Freebie and the Bean.* Rated R. Say, "Love the one you're with."

AARON Love the one two . . .

MCCLAY Gotta get a union card, kid. [after playing "Love the One You're With"] Stephen Stills. An example of situational ethics: Love. The one. You're with. From KSAN, the Jive 95 in San Francisco, I'm Bob McClay and Aaron, until about 5:45 when the news . . . will lay in your stomach. Richard Gossett will bring it all up at six.

https://clyp.it/nlwrvftj
Bob McClay and Aaron, guest in Daddy's lap, 1974.

BONNIE SIMMONS Bob definitely burned bright at all times.

BEN FONG-TORRES There were few people more masterful at a segue than Bob McClay. Bobby Dale, too, but McClay was a master of last-minute grabbing something and slapping it on the turntable. And making it work. I think there's an air check where he fell over his chair reaching for an album and knocked over the entire stand of cartridges that held all the commercials and jingles and IDs. You hear this cataclysm in the studio, and him awkwardly getting back up, righting his chair, and completing the segue.

VICKY CUNNINGHAM I saw Bob McClay do four or five things at once, managing to screw up all of them. Nobody cared. No one at KSAN, or in its audience, cared about a lot of things radio had long held sacred.

JOEL SELVIN McClay was playing the same records in 1979 he was playing in 1967.

BONNIE SIMMONS He was the absolute best long-track player in the history of radio. He knew every record that was over nine minutes long, because he would get on the phone with the woman who would later become his wife, and have these knock-down, drag-out fights—and they couldn't really fight if he had to keep segueing short records. So anytime you heard, John Mayall, "Thoughts About Roxanne," because that was her name . . .

JOEL SELVIN I remember when Bonnie put him on Saturday mornings. She wakes up, hears on her radio, "click, click, click." No one answers the phone, so she goes down there, and McClay is asleep at the board. Out. I remember once, there was a college reporter following him around, and in front me at a nightclub, he says to her, "You can write an article better than he can." I said, "Sure, Bob, that's easy, but I've never fallen asleep at my typewriter." But, McClay was such a real person on the radio.

BEN FONG-TORRES After leaving KSAN, McClay never worked for another station, and made a living selling antiques and estate items. He died in 1999 of complications from diabetes. He was sixty-nine.

BONNIE SIMMONS I will go to my grave with Bob McClay being one of my favorite people I knew on this planet. He had a twisted but also wonderful sense of humor. Born in New Jersey on the boardwalk, and it just showed. I believe his parents ran a booth there, something like that. He was a little older than most of us—he'd worked with Donahue at WIBG in Philadelphia before they both came west.

BEN FONG-TORRES McClay quintessentially came from Top 40, and like others, flourishing on the FM side.

BONNIE SIMMONS Fantastically smart and well read, but likely to get in trouble from time to time. He was also very kind, and I am lucky to have been his friend—he was one of the people I was always closest to at the station. One summer, Paul Wexler, who had been doing production, went back to the East Coast, and to make some money, he became a lobster fisherman. In the fall, he was coming back to work, and he called and asked if there was anything I wanted. And, I have fond memories of growing up on the East Coast and always getting a lobster when I would be driven to summer camp, going up the coast to Maine. So he brought back lobsters, packed in ice and everything. And he came into my office and puts these four live lobsters on my desk. They have the pins in their claws and they're just lying there. And McClay comes in after a particularly grueling shift on the air. I suspect he was "delightfully tired." It was dark, and he sees these things on my desk, and he says, "Wow! Nice shoes."

SIDE TRIP

Two Stones Spots, '68

Tom Donahue ["Street Fighting Man" plays] The Rolling Stones have a new LP, Beggar's Banquet, *it's on the London label. (Teenager in street: "And the cops caught up with me and they hit me in the legs, I started to fall, they hit me over the head, my head cracked open, I started bleeding and they shouted, 'Go back to the park where you belong—get out of here, you hippie!'") [Stones singing, ". . . think the time is right for palace revoluuuution . . . what can a poor boy do . . . but to sing for a rock 'n roll band."] The Rolling Stones* Beggar's Banquet, *on London Records, the whole thing in the Stones' new package with beautiful fold-out in the center, for just 2 dollars and 66 cents.*

[Unidentified voice] It's from White Front and it's from London, and it's evil . . . it's a dirty, dirty, evil, evil record. It's not good at all. I mean, it's good musically; it's just not nice . . . it's the Rolling Stones and they're singing about the devil, the salt of the earth and street fighting and dear doctors and parachute women and factory girls, and it's an evil album and you can buy all that filth and dirt for 2 dollars and 66 cents . . . 'cause they like to deal in dirt, and sell records . . . in evil Sunnyvale and dirty Pleasant Hill. White Front.

SIDE TRIP

Flash Mobs of the 1960s

1969: "Radio Tips Off Protestors," read the headline in the daily *San Francisco Examiner* newspaper. "The Berkeley street people and others staging demonstrations against the trial of the Chicago Seven are getting their instructions as to when and where to meet through the courtesy of a local radio station." KSAN would also announce where folks could find teach-ins or attend civil disobedience training for rallies. To learn about more cosmic events, listeners could hear Darryl Martini, "KSAN's Cosmic Muffin," phoning in from WBCN, Boston with daily astrology reports.

Wes "Scoop" Nisker: "I got the nickname when I was breaking stories sent to me by 'special sources' at the Chicago Conspiracy trials in 1969."
PHOTO BY ROBERT ALTMAN / MICHAEL OCHS ARCHIVES / GETTY IMAGES

16

NO GNUS IS GOOD GNUS, BUT SCOOP'S GNUS IS *THE LAST NEWS SHOW*

Wesley "Scoop" Nisker came out of Norfolk, Nebraska. He attended the University of Minnesota, and hung out with a blossom of Twin Cities hippies. Feeling San Francisco was the place to be, he loaded up the pipe and moved to Fog City. One hero was journalist I. F. Stone, who wrote that the journalist's task was to "take all the news of the world and make it sing like poetry." To this, Scoop Nisker added, "Music is news, news is music!"

STEFAN PONEK Wes Nisker just came in off the street one morning with his mandolin and said, "Hey, I've got a song about the news, and I've been hearing what you're doing and maybe I can help you do it." Scoop took over the news in '68 and really ran with it, to the proportions that he became famous for. "If you don't like the news, go out and make some of your own!" A classic. He was consumed by the desire to stop the war and ended up changing the way news was presented in America.

SCOOP NISKER As the counterculture's station, KSAN began to function as a communications center for the antiwar movement. And the main message was always the music. Rock songs were our liturgy, our anthems, the internationals for the youth of the world. The Youngbloods singing, "Everybody get together,

Scoop Nisker.

try to love one another right now." For some, the call to rebellion included the call to laughter and scorn. My own disaffection was fed by satirists like Ernie Kovacs, Sid Caesar, and Steve Allen. Since I never felt entirely at home in American society, I loved seeing it ridiculed. My first news with Stefan Ponek, we were doing riffs influenced by Lenny Bruce and Mort Sahl. It was tribal radio. After talking to people in the streets about an issue, I'd come back and mix their voices in with political speech on the subject, add the statements of a couple of cartoon characters, add sound affecting the scenario, and put it all together over a rock song or looping Indian raga. It would take about two hours to complete a five-minute piece. Politicians' words on tape revealed either the hidden truth or the essential nonsense of what was being said. In May 1970, mourning the Kent State protestors, I mixed Nixon's voice with students, soldiers, and the *Woodstock* album version of the Jefferson Airplane's "Volunteers of America." Metromedia wanted to censor me after hearing that one.

The true hippie agenda called for spiritual revolution, so I started interviewing Buddhist, Hindu, and Sufi teachers coming through town. With the growing countercultural interest in Asian traditions, they were offering Western hippies more new ways to pray and get high.

Read a passage in a Scoop Nisker book, you get high. *Try You Are Not Your Fault and Other Revelations*, or *The Essential Crazy Wisdom*; his ideas as he strives for a better world are, as the Swami from Miami might call them *sui generis*.

SIDE TRIP

John and Yoko and Scoop

In 1969 John Lennon and Yoko Ono spent their honeymoon in bed at the Amsterdam Hilton. This bed-in for peace ("and growing hair") spread worldwide, but a second one, in New York, was derailed by Nixon and his thugs denying the committed couple entry into the U.S. because of a pot conviction. Lennon responded, "It's because I'm a peacenik." However, Scoop Nisker, "pragmatic hippie and zen socialist," was able to reach the Lennons at their next stop, Montreal's Queen Elizabeth Hotel. These excerpts from their chat mention the People's Park rally in Berkeley, fascists, yippies, Gandhi, Abbie Hoffman's new book, kissing cops, and the Beatles' new record, Get Back, the one filmed fifty-two years later for an eight-hour documentary.

https://wesnisker.com/radio-archives.

MAN IN MONTREAL Hello, Scoop?

SCOOP Yes?

MAN I've got John Lennon for you in just a moment, darling.

SCOOP Okay.

JOHN LENNON Hi, Scoop!

SCOOP Hello, John! How are you doing up there in Canada?

JOHN Oh, fine, fine, fine. It's going great, y'know? We're broadcasting, like, every ten minutes.

SCOOP What kinds of things are you broadcasting?

JOHN Peace, baby, peace!

SCOOP Yeah, yeah, yeah! Are you in bed now?

JOHN Yes, yes, yes. There's a photographer photographerin' us, and me on the phone and Yoko next to me here bein' handed somethin'. And it's all goin' . . .

SCOOP Gee, I don't quite know what to ask you, man. Do you have anything to say to San Francisco?

JOHN Yeah! Peace to San Francisco. Y'know, violence begets violence, folks! If you smack him, he's gonna smack you back. The only way is through peace.

SCOOP Do you know about People's Park?

JOHN The People's Park, yeah.

SCOOP There's a big march tomorrow, and we wish you could be here.

JOHN Well, we send our spirit, we'll be there in spirit, y'know. And good luck to the march, and let's hope it just doesn't end up in another riot, 'cause I think marches are tending to just end up in riots. And what we're saying is there's many ways of protesting, or celebrating. And maybe bed-ins is one of them, or maybe it'll inspire people to have other ideas, y'know?

SCOOP Can we talk to Yoko?

JOHN Yes, she's here. [off phone] Yoko, would you like to talk to Scoop?

YOKO Hello? Yes, this is Yoko!

SCOOP Hi, how are ya, Yoko?

YOKO Fine, how are you?

SCOOP Marvelous. You're in bed.

YOKO Yes we are. [laughs]

SCOOP How do you like Canada?

YOKO Canada's beautiful! Very beautiful vibrations, and it's very young, you know. It's a young country with hope, y'know. Beautiful!

> *It's a song about stringin' up them beads,*
> *take a little walk down to People's Park*
> *Just a little place to crash*
> *Make love in the dark.*
> *Heard this song on my radio sitting all alone in my room.*
> *That's the first time I realized that I'd be leaving home pretty soon*
> *Up on Telegraph . . . Telegraph . . . Avenue.*
>
> —Phil Marsh song, "Telegraph Avenue"

SCOOP How do you propose we get our park back?

JOHN If Gandhi can get rid of the fascist British, you can get your park back, y'know. I mean, the people have been trying to get things done militantly for thousands of years, and it never works! Take France, Russia, Britain, Ireland. All the places that have revolution through violence—all they got was another establishment doin' exactly the same as the old one. What we gotta change is their heads! And San Francisco is one of the major centers for that. And it's a pity that "Make Love Not War" has become a trendy cliché, in that the people didn't believe it. And if they can't wait a year or two, if they think they're gonna get it by violence, they won't get it. It'll take just as long doing it nonviolently. That impatience, as Yoko was just saying here. You don't get a child and then stretch it to be an adult. You've gotta wait for it to grow. Peace is something like that. And change is like that. You smash the building down, you've got to build it up again.

[Scoop plays "Revolution #9" under their chat.]

SCOOP Beautiful. Beautiful. Have you read *Revolution for the Hell of It* by Abbie Hoffman?

JOHN No, I keep hearing about it, so I think I'll read it. He's a Yoopie, isn't he?

SCOOP Yeah. [laughter]

JOHN We think the hippies and the yippies, all us so-called hip people, are just playing the establishment game, saying, *We know where it's at, man. You just can't talk to those people, man.* And that's just as snobbish or whatever as the establishment. If we're the hip ones, we gotta extend a hand to those squares, use the hipness and do something hip! Let's kiss a cop for peace week! Promotin' peace is like promotin' anything, like soap, y'know? The thing is, you've gotta keep plugging it!

SCOOP What kind of feelings come from the new album?

JOHN Well, *Get Back* is from the album session, and "Get Back" is the most finished thing on it. The album turned out to be the rehearsal for the, for a show that never was, so we put the rehearsal out; after we finished the album, we filmed the whole making-the-album, then we were gonna do another album when we got halfway that album, and we decided to take a holiday, and this is my holiday.

SCOOP What about, "Get back, Loretta?"

JOHN What about it?

SCOOP Essentially you're saying we can't ghettoize ourselves.

JOHN I don't see the connection, really.

SCOOP Well, "Get back, Loretta," kind of obscure!

JOHN It's Paul with lyrics lately, so ask him what he's talking about. Are you playing "The Ballad of John and Yoko" there? ["Drove from Paris to the Amsterdam Hilton/Talking in our beds for a week/The newspapers said, 'Say what you doing in bed?'/I said, 'We're only trying to get us some peace.'/Christ, you know it ain't easy."]

SCOOP Yeah, we're playing it all the time. Some of the stations have banned it because of the "Christ" reference.

JOHN Yeah . . . why can't I sing about him?

SCOOP I don't know, John, that's . . .

JOHN I'm one of his biggest fans, man. They're just hypocrites, you know? The same hypocrites that Christ used to talk to. They don't know peace, man. It's the same game.

SCOOP Well, keep up the good work.

JOHN And you too, man. Spread the word like Buddha.

SCOOP Okay.

JOHN Okay, bye-bye!

SCOOP Peace!

JOHN Peace!

[Scoop plays "Ballad of John and Yoko."]

I asked Scoop if that interview was his most cherished memory of his years at KSAN.

SCOOP NISKER My interview with John and Yoko during their bed-in is at the top of the list. But I must say, meeting and working with Darryl Henriques is a never-to-be-forgotten part of my life. It was always inspiring, exciting, and, most of all, surprising. We met in Berkeley during one of his performances with the East Bay Sharks, an infamous street theater. Darryl brought to *The Last News Show* unbelievable characters: Jacques Kissmatoe, exploring the wild gefilte fish and other species; Charlie Chicken and the All Animal News Team, covering the treatment of species; Orlando Florida, a newsman who was on the scene but nowhere near the story; Rico Vaselino, so-hip preacher, desperate to "slip and slide" into heaven; the Reverend Clyde Fingerdip, minister for home repairs—listeners wrote in to heal a particular appliance; and of course, the Swami from Miami!

The Swami from Miami (on The Last News Show*)*
Om-shalom!
Welcome, welcome, children. You are welcome
to the here and there . . . and everywhere.
I am speaking to you this evening from high atop my meditation pillow,
somewhere in the suburbs of enlightenment.
Ahh, feels good! Just like Nirvana should!
For the clearest reception, please sit down.
Now, meditate as though your next life depended on it.
The incarnation you save may be your own.
To each according to their karma
From each according to their vibes.
Ah ja . . . Om-shalom! Om-shalom!

DARRYL HENRIQUES Everything I'm about to tell you is true: When Scoop returned from the Far East where he'd gone to become enlightened (and did!), he told me about a new religion, combining the inner peace and wisdom of Buddhism with Jewish know-how and chutzpah. Scoop, being the holy trickster, named me first patriarch of the *Buwish* faith! Can You Dig It?

SCOOP NISKER In the mid-'70s, there was a huge market in mysticism. Many Eastern gurus had come to the West to find *gurupies*. Swami offered "Cosmic Advice for Mundane Matters."

DARRYL HENRIQUES One of Swami's gurus was Swami Procrastinanda, who once said, "To act: that is easy because it fills one with the illusion of having done something! Not to act, that is difficult because it fills one with the reality of having done nothing." Swami's later teacher was Guru Lethargi, who once said, "Never mind."

SCOOP NISKER Darryl also played Joe Carcinogenni, the Purple Poisoner, who offered more "treats and eats from the wonderful world of poisons"—a character inspired by local consumer personality Joe Carcione, "the Green Grocer." Our Joe revealed the stories too toxic for other media to go near.

Wes "Scoop" Nisker, Paul "Rumpleforeskin" Krassner,
Darryl "Swami from Miami" Henriques at a Berkeley rally.
Darryl in the LA Weekly, *"We're doomed, pass the champagne."*
PHOTO BY FRED GREENE / GREENECREATIVE.COM

Darryl Henriques, "Swami from Miami" was known at clubs around the Bay Area as a stand-up philosopher. He could go for hours at Berkeley's famous Freight and Salvage, daring the audience to leave before he did. In 1990, his ecology primer, *50 Simple Things You Can Do to Pave the Earth*—ahead of its time—went out of print. Darryl can always be seen as Nanclus, the Romulan ambassador in *Star Trek VI: The Undiscovered Country*, and as a reporter for *Life* magazine in *The Right Stuff*. The philosophical message under his comedy? "We're doomed, pass the champagne," he told the *LA Weekly*.

http://www.jive95.com/mp3s/ads/jobs/econ.mp3
Scoop and Darryl did a commercial campaign for Job rolling papers. "No free papers," Scoop says, "but too much fun."

SIDE TRIP

Scoop on Randy Newman's New Album

In '72, to celebrate the new Randy Newman LP, staffers, incited by Thom O'Hair (see "SIDE TRIP, The Legendary O'Hair"), launched two thousand balsa-wood gliders from the rooftop of the historic Sherman Clay building as clocks struck noon in downtown San Francisco.

> *Boarding House spot*
> *Scoop: Berlin in the '30s had its Bertolt Brecht. Sunset Strip in the '70s has: Randy Newman. The Perverse Poet of the Apocalypse. Nothin' like him. In-bleeping-credible! Randy Newman has a new album out called* Sail Away. *And on Sunday, from 9 to 10 on KSAN, you can hear him live from the Boarding House.*

SIDE TRIP

Scoop's *Last News Show* Record

SCOOP NISKER When I got back from India—I made several trips in the '70s—KSAN offered me some time to do specials, so I was gonna try and enlighten the world, bring the beauty of Buddha dharma to everyone. But as the energy of the radio station would be bopping along, my piece would come on and just . . . *thonk.* So I faded away from radio work for a while. I did record an album for Bezerkely Records, produced by David Rubinson and based on my "Last News Show," but the company backed out; they realized what a nightmare it would be to get publishing rights to all the songs I used excerpts from. Only radio is free, fellow Jiveheads! (Well, before Sirius XM started charging money for it.) I got the master back from Bezerkely, took it down to a place in Ontario, way east of LA: the Rubber Dubber. Black market. Bootleggers. Got some dubs made, put a carton of them in my trunk, and drove back to San Francisco. Rubber Dubber was busted later that night, and everything disappeared. Except for one carton.

SIDE TRIP

PsyOps Is Listening

In 1966, Roger Steffens was teaching English and traveling the Midwest with his show, "Poetry for People Who Hate Poetry."

ROGER STEFFENS I voted for Goldwater in my first presidential election. After fifteen years of Catholic schools and miseducation. I was once American Legion New Jersey State Orator Champion! I remember the oration: "The Constitution: A Barrier against Tyranny." A lotta shit that turned out to be.

In '67, he was drafted, assigned to U.S. psychological operations (PSYOPS), and given an apartment in Saigon in which to write propaganda and win the proverbial "hearts and minds." (Eventually he became an aid worker in a South Vietnamese village—read his memoirs for more adventures.) In '68 and '69, Roger started hearing radio coming from America.

ROGER STEFFENS The Armed Forces Network was censored, totally controlled by the military, and made little or no mention of antiwar demonstrations going on back home. If you wanted to really hear what was going on, you listened to Scoop Nisker, who did these surrealistic collages on KSAN, telling the truth about what was really going down in the world. Scoop was thousands of miles away, and this was decades before there was a worldwide web streaming radio stations. I had a poet friend in San Francisco, Jerry Burns—he taped eight hours of KSAN and sent them every week. Every time I got a new reel, I put together excerpts and sent out ninety-minute cassettes to various battalions, to people who I knew would make their own copies for friends. So it expanded exponentially. Jerry shipped the reels from the Oakland Army Terminal, and they went out instantly to Saigon. I had eight hours of KSAN's Monday radio by Wednesday morning. Fresh as you could get! Those weekly tapes kept my head from exploding during my twenty-six months in Vietnam. I had these radio recordings from the States, so my place in Saigon became a refuge for disaffected GIs who came over for listening parties. Peace posters, candles. I brought black paint back from a leave in Tokyo, and my roommate, Jack Martin, a record cover illustrator, covered a wall with people floating through the cosmos—a space motif, and when you turned on the black light, the wall disappeared. It was like you were a hundred miles off the planet. I think KSAN was the absolute efflorescence of American radio, its highest moment. That station was the most important one in my life ever. (Along with WINS-era Alan Freed shows from '54 to '58. Greatest DJ ever.) Nothing topped those Scoop Nisker collage one-act masterpieces. Weird, satirical, profound, and righteously enraging—every day! Over the years, soldiers have gotten in touch over the internet, and they always talk about Scoop and those tapes. They said they listened in their hooches out in the boonies, with peace posters on the walls.

BONNIE SIMMONS One Thanksgiving, my hundred-year-old stove in Oakland broke. I called Apple Appliance. A guy actually picked up! I said, "I know it's Thanksgiving, but I have thirty people showing up in six hours." He came! He mentioned he knew who I was from my name and voice, and he went into a story about how, when he was serving in Vietnam, the KSAN tapes pulled them through. Good story, huh? Yeah, it was lovely.

SIDE TRIP

Sisters and Brothers

BONNIE SIMMONS Part of the reason why I believe we were so successful at KSAN is that we didn't have any idea we were doing anything important. Historical? We were just a bunch of lucky hippies who were being paid to do something that we would've done for free, forever! Sit on the radio and play records for our friends? Gee, that sounds like it'll really suck, doesn't it?

Bonnie Simmons started in the KSAN music library, became music and then program director, and had her own daily show.

BONNIE SIMMONS Now that I've been on the radio for fifty years—sigh—it's fun! What keeps you alive when you're doing this sort of thing? I change my mind fifteen seconds before the record ends at KPFA. I guess it really was and is improvisational. I had the pleasure of being right in the middle of it when I came there as quite a young person: my office was the record library, and there's sixty thousand record albums on shelves around me. The library is right in the middle of the station. One door led to the studios so jocks could run in and grab things when they needed them. Through the other door was the rest of the office administration.

NORMAN DAVIS The fact that creativity was encouraged—almost demanded—once you have that freedom, no limits, when you take the shackles off, an immense amount of energy comes with that. It's like a pump was turned on someplace.

BONNIE SIMMONS Tom had very few rules. Because we had no playlist, you stood behind whatever you played. If a listener called you and said, "God, that song sucks," you couldn't say, "Well, the program director made me." You took the rap for it. Tom's theory on choosing music was, "Only play the good stuff." There were no other barriers.

RAECHEL DONAHUE The rule was, it's not about you; it's about them. Just because you wanna hear eight Weavers tracks in a row doesn't mean they do.

NORMAN DAVIS I played Ken Nordine—everyone loved his storytelling—one track after the other, because listeners would tape it. His albums were not easy to find. One reason Tom told us not to talk over songs is people at home recording—the only way you could get that song then.

DUSTY STREET Tom was smart enough, from working in AM radio for a long time, to say: "They don't sit and listen 24-7 like you do. What you're burned out on they're not burned out on yet. So if you're burned out on it, play it for another two months, and then change."

BONNIE SIMMONS I have no problem playing big hit records. Because people like big hit records. And I like big hit records. I also know that if you present people with two hours of obscure music that doesn't have any threads of things they're familiar with, you're asking them to work too hard to listen. They're not getting grades. They're not in college; they haven't paid you for this lecture.

DUSTY STREET I used to be queen of changing the record in the last four seconds. One of the best all time was Reno Nevada. Reno once put on an LP at the wrong speed, stopped it, rewound it on the air, changed the speed, hit the mic and said, "And now the long version."

Reno X. Nevada (Dalton LeRoy Hursh) was married to Diane Vitalich, drummer with the Ace of Cups, a popular local band. Diane recalls Reno once slapped on an album, repaired to the men's room—outside the station in the 211 Sutter building—and locked himself out. Tracking an LP at 33 revolutions per minute gave a DJ time to climb a fire escape, kick through a window into Tom Donahue's office, and make it back into the studio for the flipside. Reno was the first DJ Donahue fired at KSAN.

DIANE VITALICH Reno had a good run later at KSML in Lake Tahoe. Known as the "Secret Mountain Laboratory," it was another KSAN—hippies like Chan were doing the news there.

The Ace of Cups was the scene's first female rock group, ubiquitous on the psychedelic posters announcing gigs at San Francisco ballrooms and clubs. Diane Vitalich, Denise Kaufman, Mary Gannon, Marla Hunt, and Mary Ellen Simpson recently recorded a new album. In the '60s, the Cups performed barefoot, often ending their sets with antiwar singalongs. In '67, they opened for Hendrix in the Golden Gate Park Panhandle after his breakthrough appearance at the Monterey Pop Festival.

MARY SIMPSON MERCY Jimi goes, "Can I borrow your amp?" "Oh! No problem!"

SIDE TRIP

Tom and Rae

In '69, Raechel Hamilton and Tom Donahue were married at the Jefferson Airplane house, large and black and standing just outside Golden Gate Park. Rae said she heard Enrico Caruso spent the night of the 1906 San Francisco earthquake there. Adding, "Where do these myths come from?"

RAECHEL DONAHUE I came down the staircase, nineteen, in a white satin, pleated, collarless minidress. My vow had to do with a *duprass*. From Vonnegut's *Cat's Cradle*, a duprass being a *karass* of only two people.

DUSTY STREET I saw all these little wood nymphs skipping about the mansion. Voco comes up and says, "Streeto, wanna do my show tonight? I'm a little fuckety-up'd." I see nymphs dropping acid into everything.

RAECHEL DONAHUE What happened was, we'd hired the Airplane's people to do the catering. Cut to forty years later: At a concert in Cleveland, I run into Brian Auger, and he says, "You know, I was at your wedding!" How he couldn't remember the words to "Season of the Witch" at their gig later. "Did you have the champagne Jell-O?" "I had *everything*."

DUSTY STREET After the party, driving to the radio station, my soon-to-be-ex-husband said, "Hey Dusty, how do you feel?" "I feel like I'm coming onto acid, man." "I wouldn't doubt it; there was acid in absolutely everything." So I get to do one of my first shows ever while high on acid. The first commercial read I did was about a KSAN contest to attend Woodstock: "How would you like to take a really far-out trip?" Here I was taking off for outer space somewhere. I mumbled something, reached over and turned the mic off, and didn't talk again for five and a half hours. I got good at playing the records that day. Putting them away was another thing; I understand it took them years to find albums I put away by color.

RAECHEL DONAHUE My dressmaker, mother, stepfather, seventy-five-year-old grandmother—everybody got dosed. My mother began snapping pictures; she even took one of Paul Kantner's dangling testicles mobile. My stepdad thought it was pot that had gotten him so high—he went back to Riverside and tried raising a crop. Nobody noticed when Tom and I left. They were all rolling around on the floor laughing. We're in a limo, going across the bridge to Sausalito; we hadn't eaten anything and decided to nibble on a piece of wedding cake. "Now we understand! And we've been living together for how long? Four years?" The honeymoon suite had no radio or TV. My friends Julie Driscoll and Barbara Briscoe brought over a Scrabble board, and we played until the sun came up.

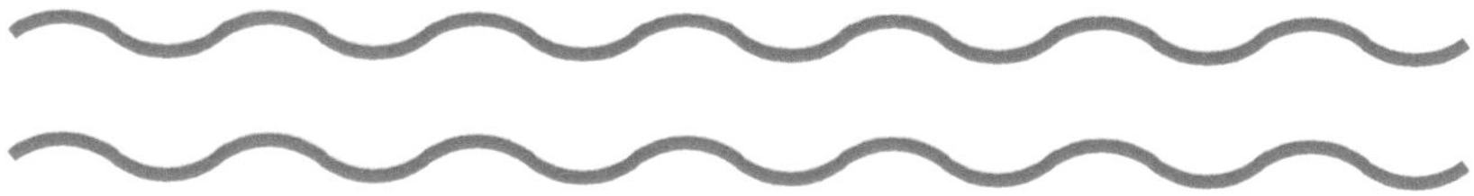

Jake Rohrer, gardener/musicologist, author of the memoir *A Banquet of Consequences: True Life Adventures of Sex (Not Too Much), Drugs (Plenty), Rock & Roll (of Course), and the Feds (Who Invited Them?)*, loved Tom Donahue

and sent Bruce Anderson of the *Anderson Valley Advertiser* ("America's Last Newspaper, Fanning the Flames of Discontent") this Big Daddy memory.

When I did cocaine with Donahue, it was a relatively new drug on the scene, and people sometimes just gave it to me as a symbol of their hipness and cool. For some uncool reason, I felt I should explain to Donahue how we would snort the cocaine rather than use a syringe—as though this might be his introduction to the drug. He smiled his huge, Cheshire cat smile and said, "My man, you are talking to the original Hoover." Whereupon he produced from his pocket a miniature upright vacuum cleaner cast in metal and used it for several lines of the offered blow. Donahue's cool seemed a visible aura, emanating all around him.

SIDE TRIP

Scoop Nisker and the Revolution of San Francisco Bay, November 1969

Just before the Altamont Music Festival, Indian activists took over Alcatraz Island—site of a former federal pen in the middle of San Francisco Bay—for nineteen months. KPFA ran daily reports from "Radio Free Alcatraz." KSAN had just one skirmish.

SCOOP NISKER Tony Pigg and I set off, on a journey to ferry food out to what the Miwok Indians called an "island of evil spirits." A listener helped us procure a boat—a mini-schooner (yeah, right)—which we filled to the gills with items, and headed across the bay. Boom! Out of nowhere, the coast guard rammed us. *Rammed.* Unreal. My clipper chum, Jiveman Tony Pigg, dubbed it the "First Naval Battle of the Revolution!" We really did believe that we were starting revolution: these Indians, once shackled in a nineteenth-century U.S. Army prison there, would win; we were going to stop the war and create a society of justice and peace and harmony. It was a hippie vision, but informed by some serious movements that had come before us. So, inspired by Adam Fortunate Eagle, we managed to cast some bread across the waters, throwing what we had overboard onto a dock—there were so many cops, we scuttled back to Fisherman's Wharf. Earlier that year, men landed on the moon.

17

KSAN AND ALTAMONT, 1969

Joel Selvin is the author of *Altamont: The Rolling Stones, the Hells Angels, and the Inside Story of Rock's Darkest Day*. I asked him to set the scene for what became another legendary airing.

JOHN SELVIN Altamont, in many regards, was a complete Rolling Stones miscalculation of the politics of the San Francisco rock scene. And they didn't understand undercurrents that were going through the counterculture at that time. It wasn't the Summer of Love anymore, man. We weren't happy hippies grooving at a free Stones concert in Golden Gate Park. There were signs of real conflict, there were signs of stress, there was factionalism. And you know how factionalism is always the death of any movement.

RAECHEL DONAHUE The problem with Altamont was when the Stones' manager, Sam Cutler—he's English—hired the Hells Angels to do security for five hundred dollars' worth of beer. He thought they were like the British Hells Angels, basically little guys on scooters with polished leather orange jackets drinking tea. He had no idea.

December 6, Dusty Street was in the studio, with Scoop Nisker and Stefan Ponek on the Altamont Speedway grounds, 30 miles east of San Francisco.

DUSTY STREET I'm on the air and I'm talking to Stef out there. "How's it going?" "Oh yeah, this is great. It's just like Woodstock. Everything is mellow." I go, "Oh, that's cool." We had the AP machine, just in case something developed. I went to rip out a newswire story, and it said this person was stabbed to death at Altamont. And I'm going, "Holy shit, what is this?" Stefan comes back on the air. "How's everything going?" "Oh, it's absolutely great!" I said, "Well, wasn't there an altercation?" He said, "Oh, well, there might have been." It wasn't until the next day that news broke of what happened. But in his defense, I understand it all happened very close to the stage and Stef was somewhere else.

SCOOP NISKER At about 11 a.m., as people began streaming into this dusty speedway scene, I was convinced it was gonna be a tragedy. I started telling people when I called in to the station, "If you haven't left yet, don't come out here." A bunch of us there actually tried to set up a different stage. Just to draw some of the crowd away to a folkie thing, elsewhere.

Ponek and Nisker had planned ahead for a Sunday concert special. The KSAN sales department got Tower Records to sponsor it—they imagined a rockin' good reminiscence. Santana! The Dead! The Airplane! The Stones! But combing through the *Sunday San Francisco Examiner*, Stefan realized the press completely missed what happened. Joel Selvin and Tom DeVries, reporters who covered Altamont, remember Stefan's take.

JOEL SELVIN KSAN's next-day broadcast was the first and most important corrective measure. The news media botched the coverage. One of the papers said, "300 Thousand Say It with Music." The sense was, *Oh, another great concert.* Then the whole city listened to KSAN's Altamont coverage.

TOM DEVRIES I went over to the station, and they took three straight hours of call-ins about the experience. It was terrific radio. And a gift for me; I'd been at the concert with a TV crew (pronouncing it, like everybody else, "Altamonte"), but the event was so large, it was only by tapping into all their different views on the air that I got a feel for it. KSAN, not the national media, explained what happened.

Excerpts from Sunday morning, December 8, 1969.

SCOOP NISKER Hello. We have a group of people here in the studio, and we're going to talk about what happened yesterday at the free Rolling Stones concert.

STEFAN PONEK A lot went on Saturday afternoon at Altamont. And there are probably three hundred thousand different opinions as to what exactly happened. We thought we had something before the concert, in proportion equal to that of Woodstock. The truth of the matter is, we don't really know what's going on.

SCOOP NISKER At Altamont, there was a miniature society set up of three hundred thousand and upwards people. It was supposedly a society of the new generation, the love generation, the brave new world, the children of the future. And, as far as I can say, I don't want to live in a society like the one I saw yesterday.

STEFAN PONEK I've gotta jump in here, because I was at Woodstock. And all the things you're saying went wrong . . . *they happened at Woodstock.* But it was a different thing. I can't explain the difference in feeling. Coming into this one, I felt the same way as I did coming into Woodstock. Coming into Woodstock, I was freaked, it was big, I was afraid. But it got together.

SCOOP NISKER What was the difference?

STEFAN PONEK That's what I'm trying to get to. Coming into this concert last night, I had that same good feeling I had at Woodstock when it all got together. But this one never came together. It never got together to the point of a universal kind of thing that sparked inside of everybody that said, "Hey, let's all get behind the spirit of this festival." The spirit of Woodstock was a getting together in the way that we're talking about it. The spirit of Altamont was, "To hell with you, brother!" You know? "I don't give a damn whether you've got a ride home or not. I don't give a damn whether you're on a bum trip or not. I'm on my trip, you're on yours." Okay, hello, you're on the air.

FEMALE CALLER Hi, I was right up front of the stage. I would like to report some specific things. I saw about five or six fights, a friend of ours was—I guess he took a picture of an Angel, and the Angel grabbed his camera and ripped out all the film. A friend of mine stepped on an Angel's hand, and the Angel threatened to kill him or something. And these things were going on—we were wondering why the Angels were like the guards on stage. It was very frightening. And I think whoever put them on stage as guards, like, it was a very irresponsible act, like we were all in terror of them, you know, like I was going to criticize them and everybody hushed me up because they were afraid they would be beaten. And just in the area that I was in, I saw so many fights. I saw a girl dragged across the stage by her hair. I saw a girl hit by a bottle. And then in general, there was no feeling toward people on bad acid trips. There was a girl beneath my feet who was getting kicked and walked on, and people wouldn't help her. And I had to try to help her up out of the crowd with another girl, and people around me said, "Oh, you should have left her alone because she would have worked out of her trip." You know? In general it was frightening. I think it was the Angels who were primarily responsible for the violence because out of the five fights I saw, like, an Angel was involved in every one of them.

Sonny Barger, head of the Oakland chapter of the Hells Angels, calls in.

STEFAN PONEK And here is Sonny Barger. Have I got it right, Sonny?

SONNY BARGER Yeah.

STEFAN PONEK Okay, what's up?

SONNY BARGER Well, you know, I can't tell you what happened. It was like four o'clock because we had an officers' meeting and we stayed behind—and we got there about four o'clock. And we were told by one of the clubs that if we showed up down there, sit on the stage and drink some beer and this and that, that the Stones' manager or somebody had bought us; and I don't know who any of these people are that are people running the Stones—or any of them people—because that's not my thing, knowing them people, you know? But we were told by members of the Angels that had talked to them, that we could drink some beer and sit on the stage and just keep people off of the stage. I'm bum kicked about the whole thing. I don't like what happened there—the whole show. But when we got there—we come in around four o'clock—we were told that we would park in front of the stage. The place was packed, man. But we come through, and the people there were outta sight, man. They just stood up, moved their sleeping bags and everything, and moved out of the way. They done everything really neat to let us through, the fourteen or fifteen of us officers to come in at four o'clock, or approximately there. Everybody got up really nice—some people offered us drinks on the way by—and we must have come in approximate contact with at least a thousand people. And out of them thousand people, we had trouble with one person. One broad jumped up and said something that pertained to a four-letter word to them Angels. And one of the Angels stopped his bike and he had his old lady on the back, and he said, "Are you going to let them talk about Angels like that?" And she jumped off the bike and smacked the other broad that said that—that was in the crowd—got back on the bike, and we proceeded down, no problem.

SCOOP NISKER Were you given any instructions as to how to keep order around the stage?

SONNY BARGER This is what we were told, we were supposed to sit on the edge of the stage and keep people off, and you know, a little bit back if we could, you know. And there's this cat running around on the stage, pretty frantic, sort of a burgundy-colored leather coat and long hair and long sideburns and talked with an English accent.

STEFAN PONEK That was Sam Cutler.

SONNY BARGER Ah, Sam Cutler. It could be. I was introduced to him, and I forgot it before he said. Anyways, this cat's sort of going a little bit, you know—he was hysterical, I would say. He don't know what to do, and there's a lot of people on the stage besides Angels, you know? And he's blown it, and he's saying to us, "Get these cats off the stage; the Stones won't come out!" I tell them, "Hey, they ain't coming out for a half hour anyways, they were back there tunin', man." I couldn't understand personally because I was there to sit on the stage and drink this beer that we were promised, you know, for sitting on the stage. I didn't go there to fight. I just went there to have a good time and sit on the stage. You know what, I'm in the way. So maybe somebody ain't gonna climb up on the stage.

KSAN staff member (unidentified woman) comes on mic.

KSAN Hey, Sonny, could I ask you a question?

SONNY BARGER Let me finish what . . .

KSAN Oh, I'm sorry.

SONNY BARGER Then you can ask me anything you want. Anyways, finally the Stones come out, and they start playin'. Everything's going, everybody's having a real good, good time. All of a sudden, somebody down in front—where this one bike that's parked right in front—is yellin', you know? So I myself jumped down there, and the wiring had shorted out somewhere, and the bike had caught fire, and I pulled the wires off of the bike, out of the battery, and the bike was in flames in a couple places, and we was trying to put it out, and the people were packed right up onto the stage, you know? And I kept telling them to back up a little bit so we can get this fire out. And nobody would back up. Now, I ain't saying anything about no Angel hitting anybody. I know some of them hit people, you know? But they moved them people back out of the way of the bike, and we got the fire put out on the bike, and in the process you know what? Some people got hit. And you know what? Some of them people—like maybe Friday nighters that got the front row, I don't know—they didn't want to give up that spot, even to put the bike out, to let us put the fire out, and they come back fightin', you know?

KSAN Yeah.

SONNY BARGER When they come back fightin'—they got thumped. And a lot of times there were six or seven Angels on one guy, and a lot of times there wasn't, in different areas. But then after that happened, we got the fire put out on the bike, everybody got back up on the stage with the Angels, and the people moved right back in again, and everything was cool. But outta all of them people in that front area, which maybe for twenty-five rows back—I don't know how anybody could even estimate at it—there was three or four people in there that come over to where the bikes were and kicked a couple of bikes over and broke a couple mirrors off of a couple of them and this and that. Well, I don't know if people think we pay fifty dollars for them things, or steal them, or pay a lot for them or what. But most people that's got a good Harley chopper got a few grand invested in it.

KSAN I can dig it.

SONNY BARGER Ain't nobody's going to kick my motorcycle! And they might think because they're in a crowd of three hundred thousand people, that they can do it and get away with it. But when you're standing there looking at something that's your life, and everything you got is invested in that thing, and you love that thing better than you love anything in the world, and you see a guy kick it—you know who he is.

KSAN Right.

SONNY BARGER And if you have to go through fifty people to get to him, you're gonna get him. And you know what? They got *got*. And after they got it, then some other people started yelling, and you know what, some of them people was loaded on some drugs that it's just too bad we wasn't loaded on, because they come every once in a while—one or two or three of them would come runnin' off the hill, yelling, "Ahhhhh!" you know, and jump on somebody, and it wasn't always even jumping on Angels; it was anybody that was in their way, anybody that was there and this and that. And when they jumped on an Angel, they got hurt. And it went on and on like that. But you know we moved them people to save that bike. And after that, they started trying to destroy our bikes, and we're not going to stand for it, and then that made it personal.

KSAN I really dig you; that's not a nice thing to do.

SONNY BARGER We tried talking to them, and Mick Jagger had the people sit down. Well, you know what, you grab on Mick Jagger and ask him who told him to tell the people to sit down. I told him to tell them to sit down, and if anybody was there in the front row can remember me telling them to sit down, but if you tell them to sit down and be cool, and the people in the back can see a little bit, and the show can go on and we can get it going. And he done it. And also, in the process of it, there was one girl, if you remember, that was quite a large girl that was going around topless and kept trying to climb up on the stage. And this Mick Jagger, he used us for dupes, man, you know? And as far as I'm concerned, we were the biggest suckers for that idiot that I can ever see. People were there lookin' for a good time, but you know what? Everywhere we go we're lookin' for a good time, but if somebody wants trouble with us, they're gonna get it. We don't wanna hurt them people, and you know what, they don't wanna be hurt. But there is some of them lousy people—you can call us lousy people just the same way back, I don't care. I've been called everything you can be called by experts. But some of them people out there ain't a bit better than some of the people think of the worst of us, man. And it's about time they realized it. And they can call in and call us all kind of lousy dogs, and we shouldn't be at these places and this and that, but you know what, when they started messin' over our bikes, they started it.

STEFAN PONEK Sonny, you got it right there, man. By lettin' people know where you're at, people should have known . . .

SONNY BARGER I am not no peace creep, by any sense of the word, but you know what, man? If a cat don't wanna fight with me, and don't wanna hassle me—then I want to be his friend. If he don't want to be my friend, then outta sight. Don't even talk to me. But if he don't wanna to be my friend, and he's gonna go get in my face, I'm gonna go hurt him, or he's gonna go hurt me. And you know what, it really doesn't matter if he hurts me, because I've been hurt before. And you know what, I've been hurt by experts. And over the years, I've learned how to get up and do it again.

STEFAN PONEK Okay, thanks a lot, man. I think you've done a lot to enlighten a lot of people as to just what was going on.

Calls come in from Sam Cutler, Stones manager; Jim Marshall, *Rolling Stone* photographer; and Emmett Grogan, an original Digger. Diggers were the freedom fighters in the Haight-Ashbury, providing free food, a free store—doing what they could—for the *thousands* of teenagers from all over the *world* who arrived for the Summer of Love in '67. Now, after two hours of phone conversations . . .

STEFAN PONEK We gotta leave it . . . I think it's—there's no conclusions to be drawn, except this has been kind of a weird experience. To give this much attention to a rock 'n roll show. And I was doing a heavy number on it—we were committed to doing this show before it came down. It's brought out a couple of good things from it, from just doing the show. One is, that it exploded and became an analysis of what the heck it is that made for the summer bummers, and maybe gave some idea—I think maybe some insight—of what a festival requires. Or what a big concert that involves a lot of people is about. And where people are at, and why the whole scene has gone so sour. I think it's not so much, this is my feeling, where the community is at, as it is where the people who put it together are at. And what they've got to work with. And a combination of factors is what made Woodstock such a huge success. And the reverse combination of factors is what made Altamont such a huge disaster. And I think it's kinda unanimous that it was a pretty big disaster.

The next day Sam Cutler of the Stones speaks to the press.

SAM CUTLER KSAN's whole take on Altamont was completely fucked. They got it all wrong before the concert, and even worse after the concert. It's just a fuckin' radio station. Meeting someone from a radio station is about as interesting as meeting the local postman. KSAN wasn't that fuckin' great.

https://www.youtube.com/watch?v=JUlyVSfhgaM
90 minutes of KSAN's Altamont special, December 8, 1969.
(KSAN also steals a scene in *Gimme Shelter*.)

SIDE TRIP

Pharm Chem's Cannabis Report and Other Benefits of Listenership

https://www.youtube.com/watch?v=PpLLv_zjuzg
"Psychedelic Relic," song for elders by Roy Zimmerman.

JOEL SELVIN There were shared values in the KSAN community, and that's the sorta basis of any community, right? Important values that represented different ways of thinking, serving different gods and, as a result, that tied us all more closely together.

Most radio stations involve listeners in fund-raising efforts. Jive concerts raised awareness of, and dough for, the United Farm Workers, the Abalone Alliance, and the hunger strikers at the Sonoma County Jail. The station urged its community to carpool to country markets for fresher, cheaper vegetables. In October '69, the schmooze-king *San Francisco Chronicle* columnist Herb Caen hunted-and-pecked: "Station KSAN raised $2,805.90 for the Biafran Airlift, but no scoffing. Most of its listeners are flower children, some of whom even donated their pot money." Bonnie Simmons remembers one particular holiday activity.

BONNIE SIMMONS Just imagine this happening in the world we have today. Every Thanksgiving, we would do the "Thanksgiving Turkey Trade." Hundreds of people would write in and say, "We have two extra places at our Thanksgiving table," and other people would write in and say, "We don't have anywhere to go for Thanksgiving." And we put together hundreds of groupings of listeners, some of which probably lasted beyond Thanksgiving. Nobody ever complained or said they had a difficult time of it. "We're a family of four, we live on Stanyan Street, we're having a vegetarian Thanksgiving, and we have room for four people, so if anybody is gonna be in that neighborhood and would like a Thanksgiving dinner and not have turkey, let us know." And we'd give out their phone number.

SCOOP NISKER How beautiful and so poignant to hear that story. Because it emphasizes what a moment in time this station existed in. Is there that kind of intimacy between a major media and its audience that you know of? That kind of participatory, *This is our station, this is our voice*? It just doesn't exist.

For most of its twelve years, the station presented the Pharm Chem Report.

MILAN MELVIN It was a most valuable community service, started at KMPX by Dr. Hip [see chapter 21].

SCOOP NISKER Pharm Chem was a commercial chemistry lab in Palo Alto near Stanford University. They put out a weekly review of the drugs in various neighborhoods.

DUSTY STREET We thought we should report who was putting garbage into what you were smoking or ingesting.

MILAN MELVIN It was a most valuable community service, started at KMPX by Dr. Hipp (see chapter 21 The Fantastic Krassner and Doc Hippocrates). Listeners would show up in the lobby with a baggie and a kind of pill inside, wanting to give a message not to take them. DJs would invite them into the booth to describe the pill and its effects. Bob McClay was one of the most helpful DJs with that. It really was the best we could do as a community outreach.

SCOOP NISKER f of bad acid, bad coke, heroin, or marijuana that was extra strong or had been sprayed with something toxic like paraquat. The Pharm Chem people never moralized. Sometimes they sounded like today's wine or pot connoisseurs with good buys and excellent vintages. "People should be curious about the Thai stick being sold in Berkeley in recent weeks. You may not be used to that much THC at one time." Other times it was, "In the Haight this week, we have a report of a bunch of methamphetamine with baking soda." And for a fee you could send Pharm Chem a small sample of your drugs along with a five-digit number, and a few days later call up for their chemical analysis.

BOB SIMMONS, producer Here's why we responded with the Pharm Chem Reports. Like all social networks, KSAN was a feedback loop. A loop with a certain psycho-demographic. We gave our peer group what they wanted; they rewarded us with their numbers, which we promptly sold to advertisers. We didn't have the solid dope on who they were individually, like iPhone or Facebook, but we had a pretty good idea. They used to come into the station regularly to rap. Or to drop off a listener's personal—another way of messaging with point-to-point communication. We were a mass medium, but unlike TV or AM radio (except for talk radio), we were on the phone constantly with our audience. Radio was the first social media, you know. Letters would come in. They loved the Pharm Chem Report.

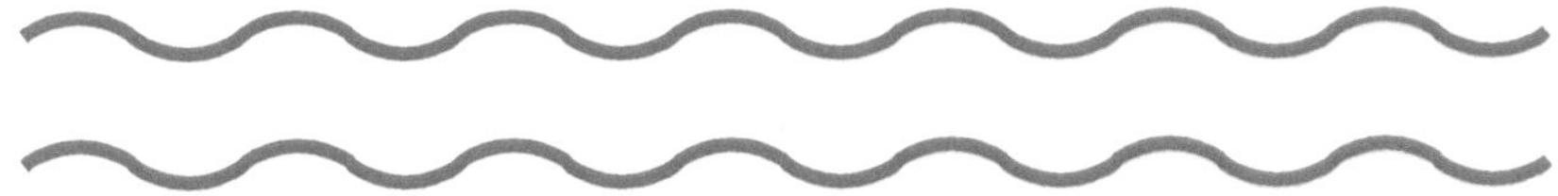

SIDE TRIP

The Radical

By December '69, Roland Young was one of KSAN's most popular DJs. Bay Area activists tuned in to hear his raps. The *Berkeley Tribe* called him a "KSAN Kommando" for refusing to read certain ads on the air. But "things are changing at KSAN," he told the *Tribe*. "We are being told to not be so hard on the commercials." During the United Farm Workers' boycott, about a Safeway spot, Roland said, "Management agreed to run free announcements for the grape strikers to offset the commercial, but they are trying to use us to break the strike by urging people to shop at Safeway. It's the same old story—using the workers to break the backs of other workers." Calling KSAN a "vulgarization of the original concept, a dream deferred," Young maintained the support of station general manager Willis Duff.

WILLIS DUFF I thought Mr. Young was an excellent disc jockey, with respect to his ability to communicate himself as a human being, as a humorist, his skill with music. Roland was a super bright guy. The sales manager asked me on numerous occasions to discharge Mr. Young, because he was more trouble than he was worth. I resisted.

Journalist Larry Bensky worked two stretches at the station: '69 to '71 and '77 to '79.

LARRY BENSKY After attending the '69 Vietnam Moratorium Day rally in Golden Gate Park, Roland came back and did his show that night. These were turbulent times; DJs talked about their own lives all the time.

Roland's December shift began at 10 p.m.

ROLAND YOUNG *Good evening, brothers and sisters. This is Roland Young, and I'm dedicating this show to David Hilliard—he got busted today—and to all political prisoners who . . . revolutionaries throughout the land . . . with a suggestion that a caller called in . . . people who stand in support of free speech. For less than one dollar you could send a fifteen-word telegram and have it billed to your telephone number. Send it to Richard Nixon saying, "I will kill Richard Nixon or anyone else who stands in the way of our freedom." As a gesture. "Seize the Time." [plays "Seize the Time" by Elaine Brown]*

LARRY BENSKY Well, Nixon was the president. It came to the attention immediately of authorities, who called Willis Duff, who fired him on the spot.

Listeners heard this recording throughout the next day:

"This is Willis Duff, vice president and general manager of KSAN. KSAN has terminated the employment of air personality Roland Young. This action was taken based on the judgment of management that Young acted in an improper manner during the broadcast of his program. The specific action that precipitated Mr. Young's dismissal was the reporting on the air, and the suggestion telephoned in to the station by an anonymous listener, that persons in the audience might send telegrams to President Nixon with essentially the same language that was used by Mr. David Hilliard, of the Black Panther Party, concerning a threat on the life of President Nixon. This resulted in an arrest of Mr. Hilliard. It was management's opinion that there was a clear possibility that the statement made by Mr.

Young could be construed as advocacy of sending such telegrams—an illegal act. Mr. Young has stated that he does not advocate the sending of such telegrams, nor would he do so himself. KSAN is extremely regretful that this event occurred and that there was a possibility of listeners construing any advocacy of an illegal act from one of our broadcasts."

http://www.jive95.com/stories.htm
Willis Duff announcing Roland Young's dismissal. This link also includes: Frank Zappa on drugs, Tom Donahue on earthquakes, Tim Leary on his campaign for governor, and other far-fetched ideas from that year.

This is an excerpt from a Jive 95 special, *What Was That? Or, Suddenly Lost Summer*, looking back at the '60s, featuring KSAN Gnus man Larry Lee speaking with Roland Young.

LARRY LEE You were one of the great stars of KSAN. KSAN fired you in 1969 because you were political.

ROLAND YOUNG Maybe they fired me because I was a great star. "We can't have any great stars in here; we just want some little bitty stars." [laughs] Everyone at KSAN was political. Everyone's doing something that's upholding the system or not upholding it. I was involved in a certain kind of conscious politics on radio at the time: doing interviews, playing music that I felt represented the full spectrum of conscious being. Which is originally, in our more naive days, what we thought a lot of radio stations were going to be. At the time we didn't understand that art and business worked hand in hand in a capitalist society.

LARRY LEE Anybody who gets out and performs or talks the way you did on the air gets their fans, and people who are not. Such as the owning corporation.

ROLAND YOUNG Some business came into play. And we didn't have any room in our program to incorporate that adequately at the time, you know? We were about something else. We said: Here's art. Here's business. If just by the very nature of it being high and groovy and right, the art will manifest itself. So the kind of music I was committed to wanting to present to people, and the kind of ideas that were happening, the kind of feelings and activity going on, I guess made me incompatible with what people who had the power to hire and fire had in mind for KSAN. And so I was removed from the air.

SIDE TRIP

Dave McQueen

SCOOP NISKER In 1971, I quit radio and went to Asia for a year to study Buddhism. I carried a Jelaluddin Rumi quote: "Start a huge, foolish project, like Noah. It makes absolutely no difference what people think of you."

DAVE MCQUEEN Scoop was under heavy attack at that time from the Berkeley Police Department, who accused him of *advertising* demonstrations. That put a lotta pressure on the station, and of course Scoop was spending twelve hours a day there, putting together broadcasts. And they were brilliant! But it just totally exhausted him. When he left, I became Gnus director. For its entire history, KSAN had sort of a fraught relationship with its news department. The company was vaguely scared. They didn't want problems; they didn't want police complaining. But we did what we did, and we proved to be quite popular—people listened to us. And that kept us going.

SCOOP NISKER Dave hired Larry Lee and Danice Bordette and two other folks. It was unimaginable that a radio station whose primary concern was rock 'n roll had a news staff of five people. And to have a half hour of news in the evening on a music station!

DAVE MCQUEEN If I wasn't familiar with the details of a story that came up, I would just ask to hear from people and would get expert advice from academics and professionals in every field. Before cyber communities, there was something called *a radio audience.* We had an amazing audience—it was astonishing. It wasn't just hippies hanging out and smoking dope.

Dave McQueen grew up in Port Arthur, Texas.

DAVE MCQUEEN In 1958, one of my teachers told me I had a good voice for radio, so I charged right down to the station to ask for a job! They laughed and laughed—I was fifteen—they thought that was really funny. But they let me fetch coffee, file records, and answer the phone. About a year later, I had my first weekend show; a station will always start you on a weekend. This was back when every region in the country had its own distinct music: you had doo-wop in the Philadelphia–New Jersey region, swamp rock from New Orleans to Houston. Today, whatever record is number one in San Francisco is number one in New York or anywhere else.

Did I know Janis, and Chet Helms? There were only about two dozen freaks in that whole part of the country, and we all knew each other. I took jobs where I could: Beaumont, Houston, New Orleans, Austin—did a lot of Top 40. But in 1967, I don't know why, I just decided I wanted to go to San Francisco and be a hippie. And if you grew up in Southeast Texas, you wanted someplace where things were happening. Of course, I couldn't find a job—everybody in radio wanted to work in San Francisco. I worked as a maintenance mechanic in a chemical factory in Richmond. A union organizer for the Teamsters. I went back to Houston and worked at KPFT, with Larry Lee—on the air for the Pacifica Foundation!

THORNE DREYER, author of *Making Waves: The Rag Radio Interviews* I worked with Dave McQueen at KPFT. He was a sweetheart.

DAVE MCQUEEN I came back to San Francisco, and shortly after I arrived, I got a call from Willis Duff, general manager at KSAN. He'd been looking for somebody to do news and said he noticed on my resume that I had been a helicopter traffic reporter—one of the first in the country. I guess he thought, *Hmm, seems to know what he's doing*, and I went to work for him. By then it was 1969. It was quite interesting, because it was Us against Them. One problem when I first got hired: Dusty Street and Bob McClay were determined I was not going to be there very long. They gave me a hard time because—there was no disguising it!—I sounded like a *standard radio announcer*. Kind of the opposite of what KSAN stood for in every way. I think they figured I'd just be giving the usual corporate spin. What I was saying was mostly just straightforward information about what was really happening in Vietnam. Of course I put my opinions right up front. I made no bones about that—there was nothing subtle about it. People realized that was real information.

ERIC MEYERS, music intern Dave was the consummate chilled presence delivering the news. Never saw him flustered. Some called him the Walter Cronkite of the counterculture.

PETER LAUFER McQueen's gift was in *talking* the news. Not reading it.

DAVE MCQUEEN Fifteen minutes at a whack. I'd rip up a bunch of wire copy and just have a stack of newspapers and stuff in front of me—and start riffing on it, at noon and 5:45.

THOM O'HAIR I came in as program director in 1971 and concluded that our morning audience was interested in news information, so I proposed that a member of the Gnus Department begin airing casts at 7 a.m. I was told by McQueen they started at noon. "That's the way Donahue had done it, and no asshole from Oregon is going to tell them different." Not wanting to order them to do it—that's not the way we did things—we talked and talked. I needed some fresh air, so I went walking along Montgomery Street—San Francisco's Wall Street—near the station. I hadn't banked on a revelation. I saw groups of people outside eating their lunches, and there they were: tuned to the noon news on KSAN! I saw some change stations, and I couldn't resist asking them why. They said they turned to the station primarily for the good news, and expressed the wish that the station aired good news in the morning, when they were getting ready for the work day. Bingo! The following day I got McQueen to let somebody else do his midday cast and took him to lunch. What he witnessed knocked him out—the same scenario.

DAVE MCQUEEN The morning is going to be the quarterback for your radio station. If you don't have a strong morning presence, you won't have a strong overall sales appeal to agencies.

THOM O'HAIR We worked it out, did some money shifting, and soon I had a good newscast twice an hour in the morning. The ratings and time spent listening went into double digits on "Drive" 95. It became a major reason listeners took the station seriously. The news front was from the left side of the street, and championed the capital "Every Man" in all of our listeners, no matter the gender—the person getting screwed by the system. History showed that the bottom-line story about Vietnam was not being told to Mr. and Mrs. America. To stop this unjust war, to bring home the troops—this became the motivation behind our newscast. Scoop, and the rest of us, were consumed by the desire to stop the war.

LARRY BENSKY We put everything we could on the air about Vietnam. We didn't have a budget to send anybody over there.

THOM O'HAIR Thursday was body count day—when the government released casualty figures for the prior weekend—so much bullshit. There is one thing that I want to put on the record here: we never, despite all accusations of the contrary, put the responsibility for the war on the shoulders of the servicemen. They were never referred to as baby killers; the spitting on them was a myth. The fault was laid at the feet of the political system, right where history has since placed it.

DAVE MCQUEEN Originally, Peter Laufer and Larry Bensky were there. Bensky, several times. One of my heroes in the business—I think Larry got fired more from one station than anybody in the history of radio. A tremendous mind. He's got it all in his head. His best work was done as the national correspondent for Pacifica Radio, particularly the Iran-Contra hearings in 1987—he broadcast live for the duration, May to August, and he narrated the whole thing, out of his head. Just a brilliant guy. A tremendous guy.

BOB SIMMONS Dave McQueen, secretly or not so secretly, despised Tom Donahue. I always admired McQueen for remaining silent over the years when people wanted to talk to him about KSAN. Not wishing to disturb the popular narrative. Good policy, I thought to myself.

DAVE MCQUEEN Mr. Coman—Donahue was a pseudonym—really didn't care for me at all. For the first year or year and a half that I was news director at KSAN, Donahue was in Southern California at KMET. Willis Duff ran KSAN. Only after Willis left and Tom was back as interim program manager did he and I have any real contact. We were not close. He was a powerful presence. Tom didn't think I had a sense of humor—he was probably correct. I was kind of oblivious. Eventually he fired me—he didn't say why—he just called me into his office one day and said, "Dave, I'm gonna let you go." I said okay, got up, and walked out of the building.

Mr. Coman had plenty of followers. I was not one of them. He was a greedy and dishonest person. One day, reviewing budgets with the business manager, he asked about a one-hundred-dollar-a-month garage item: a small van, traded out with a local dealer and used for news and promotion events. He sent Vicky Cunningham to collect the keys from me. Then he took it home for the exclusive use of the family. Such was typical of Mr. Coman.

Joanne Greene picked up McQueen's news operating procedure the first day she arrived.

JOANNE GREENE Dave's reputation as a brilliant, no-holds-barred journalist was stellar. In November of 1979, I arrived with some anxiety—having never anchored—and went directly to the newsroom. I saw an audio board, two typewriters, and piles of wire copy. I stopped someone, "Excuse me, I'm Joanne Rosenzweig, the new news person. Do you know where Dave McQueen is?" "Oh, Dave's probably asleep in the front office—that's generally where he is between nine and noon." I thought, *How am I supposed to prepare the newscast without any direction? Okay, I'll just read over the copy he pulled for morning drive and continue to rip updates from the AP and Reuters wire.* Rick (Rick Sadle, the production director; he introduced himself and I got the immediate sense he would become a friend and ally) said, "It's after eleven thirty. I think it's fine to go wake him." There was Dave, softly snoring away on the couch, long, *long* brown hair strewn across a throw pillow. He had a beard like R. Crumb's Mr. Natural, but not as white. I whispered, "Dave?" No response. "Dave." Nope. "David!" He opened an eye at me, stretched, reached to grab a hairbrush off an end table and, bending forward, poured all of those locks over his head and began brushing. I'd never seen a man do that. "Cleared the wires," I babbled. "Read over your morning casts, but I'm not sure how you want to handle the noon. It's 11:45, and I'm getting concerned that we need time to prep." Dave brushed away, stretched, yawned, stood up, and walked out of the office. We made it to his sanctuary, where he began cutting out lines of cocaine. I tried to give no indication of my shock. (I was pissed, frankly.) He handed me a rolled bill (*first turn goes to the lady?*) "No thank you. I'm really getting nervous about the newscast." *What a dork, he must be thinking. Why did we hire her?* He went through a pile of copy and looked up. "What else you got?" Somehow we divvied up piles—Dave fondling his beard, which he did when deep (or not) in thought—and I stumbled through my first KSAN Gnuscast.

McQueen signed his letters, "Philbert T. Desanex." Philbert was a newspaper reporter, and secret identity of Gilbert Shelton's underground comix hero, *Wonder Warthog*. A Marvel artist once drew a panel of Dave doing the news while a monster raged through the City (the illustration is on the Jive site). In August of '21, Dave died on his driveway in Berkeley. They said he was leaning over to get his newspaper. He always called them, "the daily fishwrap." I'd gotten an email a couple months earlier.

"I turn seventy-eight and am long retired and in rather decrepit condition. Reading books, taking lots of naps, eating the occasional doughnut and occasionally raging at shameless Repuglicans. I declined to take part in Jeff House's

Jive project because I don't like to travel down memory lane, or perhaps I was just cranky that day. I remember all the KSAN incidents clearly. Those were interesting times. Fun, too. I refuse to travel more than a few blocks, but if you find yourself in this neighborhood, it would be great to schmooze. DMcQ (aka Philbert T. Desanex)"

18

LARRY LEE, THE GAY LIFE, AND THE WATERGATE FOLLIES

Larry Lee, like many others in the Gnus Department, was editor of his high school and college newspapers. As a teenager in Texas in the late '50s, he was a copy boy at the *Fort Worth Star-Telegram.* In the '60s, he covered the civil rights movement in Alabama. Next, he co-founded KPFT, the Pacifica radio station in Houston, and then, he moved to the Bay Area to become program director at Pacifica KPFA in Berkeley. He was living at Dave McQueen's house when Dave brought him into KSAN. Jive 95er Bob Simmons worked with both men; he says they were all part of a "Texadus" to San Francisco.

BOB SIMMONS We all just wanted to be part of that whole tectonic shift underway in the culture. *Rip Off Press*, *Zap*, and other artist-owned underground "comix" came to the City. Lee and McQueen met in Houston at KPFT, the Pacifica station bombed twice by the KKK. Larry and I had become solid friends way back in Austin, 1964, where he ran *The Daily Texan*, and I was with *The Texas Ranger*, the campus humor magazine.

Larry Bensky met Larry Lee when both were in the Gnus department in the '70s.

LARRY BENSKY Larry was enormously bright, omnivorously interested in current affairs, and thoroughly versed in history and literature, politics and science. Not the kind of guy you run across often in electronic journalism. One phone call to Larry was worth about a dozen to other people.

DJ Terry McGovern did the morning shift during much of Larry's time at the station.

TERRY MCGOVERN I'd never met the likes of Larry Lee. He would come in in the morning—he had kind of a cast in one eye, one eye was a little wampus—and he'd sit down next to me at the console, fire up a cigarette, and I'd say, "Larry, what's goin' on?" He would talk for ten minutes without ever looking at his copy. Just held it in his hand like a prop. Like how Rachel Maddow—that same kinda brain—can talk endlessly and tell a story.

Journalist Randy Alfred, co-found of the *San Francisco Bay Area Times*, met Larry Lee in 1977.

RANDY ALFRED Just before the Pride parade in June 1977, a gay man was stabbed to death in San Francisco's Mission District. When the trial started, I called Larry Lee at KSAN and asked who was covering it for the station. He said, "Would you like to cover it for us?" That's how they did things there: the community reported with them. I started reporting for their four daily news shows. KSAN had a short-lived gay liberation show in 1973; then *The Gay Life*, co-produced by Larry Lee and Nancy Newhouse, Tuesdays at 10 p.m. KPFA had *Fruit Punch*, and its sister station in New York, WBAI, had a show. But it was KSAN with the first LGBT-oriented programming on commercial radio. KSAN broadcast the Gay Freedom Day parade and speeches live in 1978. That year the Briggs Initiative was on the California ballot prohibiting schools from hiring gays; forget about even talking about gays—a broad, sweeping, totalitarian proposition. But Larry Lee left KSAN for KPIX-TV, and *The Gay Life* ended. I called every month asking, "When will it start again?" In November we defeated the Briggs Initiative, and three weeks later Harvey Milk was assassinated. KSAN told me the show was starting up again, "And you're the producer!" I learned how to do radio and kept the show going from 1979 to 1985.

Larry Lee created a show in '73 called *The Watergate Follies*.

LARRY BENSKY He didn't call the series "The Watergate Con-spiracy" or "The End of Nixon," or some such ponderous designation. Larry would end our daily news stories with just enough of a chuckle to let the audience know that the follies of humanity mean, among other things, that we are all part of the joke.

BOB SIMMONS *The Watergate Follies* and *The Darkening Sky* were about the madness in '73–'74. Funny, great radio. Our first adventure into radio dramatizations! Larry Lee came over to my house the night of the "Saturday Night Massacre," in 1973, when Nixon fired special Watergate prosecutor Archibald Cox. That's when we planned it. The idea was to use the radio station as a call to arms to fight Nixon's lawlessness. We were helping to preserve the Union!

DAVE MCQUEEN The program ran every Monday night at nine, an hour-long, highly produced show, combining music and—I remember Allen Ginsberg coming in one night and improvising a *Watergate Follies* poem.

BOB SIMMONS Our sound effects producer was Rick Sadle—he made them really zing.

Production director through the '70s, Rick had a great studio, where it was a kick to go in and record characters and spots.

RICK SADLE Larry Lee wrote one scene with projectile vomiting, inspired by *The Exorcist*, in theaters then. I couldn't find an effects record that had anything close! We took turns tossing a big bowl of oatmeal slop onto a trash-can lid. There were trials. How hard? How much? How far a toss? Finally: just right and disgusting. KSAN was a transformative experience in several ways.

> ***OLD TIMEY ANNOUNCER*** *[over swing music] "By electrical transcription from San Francisco:* The Watergate Follies*! Brought to you by Leopold's nonprofit community record store, 2518 Durant, off Telegraph. Tonight, Episode 26: "Dick's Last Trip!" So dim the lights, strike a match, and suspend your belief . . . the* Watergate Follies *is on the air! [Bernard Herrmann's* Psycho *score] White House horror! Dramatizations of dark deeds. . . . A moonlit July night in suburban Maryland, in a torch-lit secret passage beneath Bethesda Naval Hospital . . . a group of men bearing a coffin-like crate make their way toward a hidden laboratory . . .*

OLD TIMEY ANNOUNCER 2 *I'm sorry to interrupt* The Darkening Sky, *but* True Espionage Adventures, *usually broadcast at this time . . . instead, we bring you a special address from the oval module, Skylab . . . the president of the United Snakes (shout-out, Firesign Theatre)!*

NIXON (DARRYL HENRIQUES) *My fellow Americans, I am speaking to you tonight from Skylab, where I along with Dr. K., General Haig, and my immediate family are in orbit. Haldeman, Ehrlichman, Bebe, and my dog, General Tamayo—we all send our warmest regards to those . . . who wish us well. But to those who wish us ill, we are fully prepared and well equipped to move up here, as long as necessary. We are in position with extremely sophisticated tracking and scanning devices, which can monitor enemy activities anywhere on the face of the globe. As General Tamayo remarked to me this morning, when you're this far out, that little red button looks a lot less frightening . . .*

SAMPLE CREDITS Watergate Follies *is written and narrated by Dave McQueen and Larry Lee, executive technical producer is Rick Sadie, based on an original idea by Gordon Liddy . . . and tonight featured: Donna Campbell as the landlady, Tom Donahue as Granny Bremer, Tony Kilbert was the FBI agent, Norman Davis was Daddy, and Bonnie Simmons as baby Ronda! Our thanks to KDNA St. Louis for tonight's Conspiracy Theory. [Bob Fass interviewed Mae Brussell and Paul Krassner on KDNA FM.]*

https://www.youtube.com/watch?v=3Tut2wsxuZA&t=12s
Watergate Follies excerpt. Reporter Orlando Florida (Darryl Henriques) finds Nixon digging life among the hippies in Golden Gate Park. 1974, 7 minutes.

In March 1990, Burr Snider, of the daily *San Francisco Examiner*, wrote, "A hot and brilliant light went out in the San Francisco sky," after Larry Lee died of AIDS at the age of forty-eight. "We won't soon see the likes of this many-faceted journalistic superstar, part of the most fearless and iconoclastic radio news show there ever was. It was at the wild and irreverent KSAN that Lee found his true métier, and a target worthy of his scathing hatred of political chicanery: the Nixon White House. 'Larry was equally suspicious of people on either side of an issue. But he was gallant and brave

and graceful all the way, and at the end he was still pissed off at the people who were wrecking this country,' said Danice Bordette, one of Lee's co-conspirators at KSAN."

I think of Larry Lee. What a guy!

SIDE TRIP

Acid, Grass, Banana Peels

Allen Ginsberg once suggested, "The president and our vast hordes of generals, executives, judges, and legislators of these States . . . go to nature, find a kindly teacher or Indian peyote chief or guru guide, and assay their consciousness with LSD."

Tom Donahue doing a PSA (public service announcement)

Wavy Gravy is part of the Hog Farm, as is Lou Todd, and the Hog Farm has been working locally for the marijuana initiative, and tomorrow registrars will be out to get you signed up so you can be in a position to vote for it: if you'd like to go to the Fell and Stanyan entrance of Golden Gate Park at 10 a.m. Or they will be at the Tea Garden at two . . . you might be able to catch them at the Tea Garden at two [off-mic, Raechel is adding information]. That's where they plan to be at two. The Hog Farm tends to get there. And I'm sure, man, they'll have peanut butter sandwiches someplace. Because when you're with the Hog Farm, you will never ever starve to death. That's tomorrow at the Fell and Stanyan entrance to Golden Gate Park.

ROBIN MENKEN I was being interviewed for the *Oracle*, the Haight-Ashbury newspaper, and I think I said something about, "Oh yeah, you know you can get high from smoking bananas, like in the Donovan song, 'Mellow Yellow.'" And that started the whole thing. *Time* magazine said you could toast the fibers of the peels or something.

KMPX commercial spot

CHAPTER 18

[Music of Indian drone, frogs on lily pads.] A peace garden hangs around our eyes and opens into poppies four-dimensionally waving leaves and fingerprint petals at our sudden glance anywhere . . . we push through . . . your cellophane dress snags in a tortoise parade under green pools . . . my hair collects peacocks who settle on its shaggy palm crown dreaming sleepy yellow under this branch . . . and then past the domes of lovers casting off cheeks and nostrils of iron mathematics . . . to penetrate the quiet body of cockatoos flapping electric circles . . . sparklers igniting at your lips . . . exotic postcards flash by! The loud-speakering sphinx postcard glues against your forehead in the rain everywhere . . . your hand around my waist . . . my face against your neck . . . heartbeats colliding . . . in this garden of music white fire speaks through our veins, while on wooden scaffolds in vacant lots of February paradise, Record City is having a sale, featuring all Jim Kweskin and Jug Band and Country Joe and the Fish sides on Vanguard Records, at 2340 Telegraph Avenue in Berkeley.

19

THE MEDICINE BALL CARAVAN, 1970

I've always been of the opinion that cameras film the truth. And liars make movies. The way I look at it, Raechel and I threw this party and invited a bunch of our friends along. There was beautiful scenery, fine dope, great music, and a lotta laughs.

—Tom Donahue

I met a lovely girl in her mid-20s, wearing a micro-mini culotte of pleated mesclun brown chiffon, and a matching see-through blouse . . . a Peruvian vest-coat lined with llama fur, vanilla satin pants, white patent leather boots: Raechel Donahue.

—John Grissim, author of *We Have Come for Your Daughters: What Went Down on the Medicine Ball Caravan*

Big Daddy was a big man with a bunch of big ideas. In 1970, he had a vision of leading a hippie caravan across America staging music festivals, "like a Woodstock on wheels." Donahue's dream—*Rolling Stone* called him "ringleader of this whole mess"—involved Warner Bros filming the trip, which would feature interesting characters like Milan Melvin and Chan Laughlin as Donahue's co-stars. What happened next can only be told by KSAN maven Jeff House, author of *Below the Moon: The Study of Literature Through Archetype*.

JEFF HOUSE The mythos of the journey is as old as Gilgamesh. The promise of the death of the mundane. Picture a band, traversing the land, pausing to play for the locals, from California to our nation's crapital. A medicine show offers tonics; it's the age of organic diets! Try our gentle mix of peaceful vibes. (Like those ridiculous Café Gratitudes.) Guaranteed: you will feel groovy! Taste-test a smoothie of blended, chemical concoctions. Feeling mellow? Riding out of the west, preaching hipster goodness to the young and unenlightened. There's hippies in them thar tipis! Only eighty pounds (when dry), and prophecies of the yearly Rainbow Gathering into the next millennium! Cut to: Warner Brothers.

MILAN MELVIN Donahue presents Warner acts on the road. Impromptu concerts from B. B. King, Jefferson Airplane, the Youngbloods, maybe Hot Tuna.

JEFF HOUSE John Grissim's hilarious account, *We Have Come for Your Daughters: What Went Down on the Medicine Ball Caravan*, according to *Rolling Stone*, "captured, without bias, all the scenes behind the making of one of the ten worst flicks in 1971."

JOHN GRISSIM I was twenty-eight. Technically pretty straight. Donahue's sixteen-track voice was hard to turn down.

JEFF HOUSE Tom was turned on by *Woodstock* the film, released in '70. Some of his pitch to Warner Brothers: "We have formed a caravan of love, discovery, and sharing that will retrace the steps of the pioneers from West to East and on to the Europe of our forefathers. We do not return to seek old philosophies or values but rather to bring a new lifestyle and new attitudes accompanied by the music that best of all expresses the new world in which we live—a new world in which Margaret Mead has said the older generations must think of themselves as immigrants. We come in a spirit of happiness and peace, with a party on wheels whose anthem is the music of the Grateful Dead, the band that more than any other represents the San Francisco roots of the Space Age Renaissance. The Hog Farm will leave behind a park we will create as a positive example of ecological action . . . the Earth People's Park."

Killing them softly with his charm and marijuana joints—the man's mountainous physique could absorb more and be affected less by whatever they were smoking.

MILAN MELVIN To French director François Reichenbach, Academy Award winner for *Love of Life*, about Arthur Rubinstein, it will be another triumph. To the French crew, it was an opportunity to come to the States in 1970 and consume mass quantities of psychedelics. We dosed them before leaving San Francisco. A few days out, François told the press, "The world has lost fifteen Frenchmen and gained fifteen freaks."

JEFF HOUSE Welcome to our world, says Milan Melvin, twenty-nine. Ex-dope man, record producer, craftsman, underground DJ, and Tom's consigliere. Right out of TV's *Wagon Train.* Wagonmaster on a Harley.

JOHN GRISSIM, in his book Milan conjures up a polished, businesslike rap that fairly oozes conviction. It seems to match his long-haired elegance, and he comes across as more of a personality than a freak, exuding a show-biz aura to which people can relate. He is fully aware and uses it to his advantage. I watched Milan cajole, charm, and con country realtors and civic leaders in five communities between Boulder and Bloomington, Indiana. It was like Milan and Donahue in the early days: cornering incredulous agents and accountants, trading riffs and ready answers with steamroller logic.

JEFF HOUSE And then they get them to buy time on KMPX!

MILAN MELVIN Donahue knew that painting on the lead bus, "We have come for your daughters," would create some "awareness" of our arrivals, if our appearance wouldn't, in mail trucks, buses, and hearses—a hundred and sixty freaks in thirty anythings that could roll.

JEFF HOUSE Who came along for the ride? KSAN asked listeners, "What can you bring to this parade?" Hundreds of letters arrived, from students, dropouts, street people, cooks, mechanics, anarchists, and other disenfranchised citizens of the United Snakes: housewives, secretaries, nurses, a doctor, a psychologist, an attorney, odd-jobber free spirits. John Grissim described it: "People who do batik and tie-dyeing, leather workers, weavers, seamstresses, wood carvers, dancers and poets, linguists, bookkeepers, a professor, and a young girl who can paint signs and cook a whole pig stuffed with rabbit, groundhog and squirrel."

Chan Laughlin—after this trip he'll transition into Travus T. Hipp—brought his three German shepherds. On this trip, unlike five years ago at the Red Dog [see chapter 2], Chan plays the walking boss, and camp master responsible for the orderly setup of sites, prepping tipis, etc.

MILAN MELVIN Chan spent all of his time fucking around with the shower tipi and sneaking into the refrigerator truck. I did nothing but answer questions about campsites and setups, money, laundry, diapers, routes, concerts, and busts. Mainly I remember working my ass off. Donahue spent his time hollering at Warner Brothers assholes from motel room telephones.

JEFF HOUSE Milan Melvin, Chan Laughlin, and Jack Towle, three-quarters of the KSAN sales department, had fancied a side trip to the Red Dog Saloon—the sheriff threatened to "deputize every able-bodied man in Washoe County and jail your leaders for disturbing the peace because these hippie types bring trouble no matter what you movie people say."

MILAN MELVIN After the first show, in Boulder, word rolled ahead: the druggies are on their way! When we reached Nebraska, every kind of uniform met us at the border—highway patrol, police, national guard, GIs, American Legion, guys from the postal service in Cub Scouts uniforms. Apparently we were not to take any of their daughters. They circled our wagons, and we were forced into a field. One fellow said: "You camp here tonight, and we'll escort you to the other side of the state in the morning." We'd never set foot in Nebraska. The irony of the thing was, the field was full of turkey weed, cultivated in Nebraska since World War II as hemp plants. Surrounded by the army, up to our necks in marijuana; unfortunately, when we tried to dry it and smoke it, there wasn't a high in the whole field. Just turkey weed.

JEFF HOUSE So, things were going well. The caravanserai had Warner Brothers freaking out. One exec asked Tom, "What if it attracts two hundred assholes that'll want to beat everybody up? Or SDS, Weathermen, the Black Panthers will want to take over the concerts?" Donahue said Warner was secretly hoping for a riot. Get it on film; that'll be the movie. "The Caravan people are completely incompetent," reads one internal memo as the budget goes to hell. "Donahue is exercising no leadership, and Milan Melvin has disappeared on his bike."

JOHN GRISSIM Placitas, north of Albuquerque, brought a beautiful vindication. A demonstration of the Melvin principle: given five minutes to cross the street, a hundred and fifty hippies will take three hours, but they will cross the street.

JEFF HOUSE A dozen of New Mexico's finest freaks drive over with a dump truck of peyote buttons. Grissim has a revelation: "It is hard to understand why straight America views hippies as the great unwashed. Longhairs, be they men or women, Hog Farmers or hitchhikers, can talk for hours about shampoos and cream rinses. The spaciest, most nonverbal freak will wax eloquent over avocado cream shampoo, rumored to be Beatle George's favorite." Speaking of Harrison, people have been taking his song, "Think for Yourself," the wrong way. Undergrounds on both coasts print the same smack. Must be the journalist/spies slipping on and off the caravan! They write how Tom is being used by corporate Hollywood, USA, ripping off youth culture, selling it at a huge profit, and returning zilch to the community. On the contrary, Big Daddy explains to the usually supportive alternative papers, "A corporation is shelling out big bucks for several dozen people *their readers'* ages to make a this-land-is-your-land by making music. If they want to make a movie out of that, may God hear their prayer."

JOHN GRISSIM The freaks made two thousand miles, through territory infested with the establishment, and reached an oasis of safety and sanity—a university.

JEFF HOUSE Antioch College in Ohio. Freaks versus Free Radicals (name of Antioch sports teams). The students want to bust up some cameras. Why? Because it's 1970. Nobody comes on their campus and makes money. *Off of them.* British musician John Peel gets into it with the Walking Boss. All your efforts are tainted, Peel tells him, by corporate America funds. Chan says, this film will change more heads than any speech making. "We're not making this to sell to freaks," Chan tells the college kids. "We want Kiwanis Club members—straight people—to see it and dig our lifestyle. That's why it has to be a good vibes movie, not about confrontation. You sit around here and complain because you haven't got the balls to go out in the world and do something worth filming; you're all whining in your little rooms. Not even living." When Peel fires back, "You're a Warner Brothers rip-off hippie!" Chan pulls out a knife. Peel runs, Chan chasing. Peel trips, and Chan is on him. A hippie from the Hog Farm commune jumps in. Chan apologizes; he was cool now. Someone says the whole thing had been guerrilla theater for the movie. By Ohio, the French despise the freaks. The freaks despise the French, for constantly filming the freaks skinny-dipping. The final act plays out at L'Enfant Plaza in DC. Eight thousand people (youth quake!) dance to Hot Tuna. The highlight of the show is a new quartet from Arizona, dressed like girls, called Alice Cooper. Now comes the European leg; Warner Brothers is kind enough to put Milan and his Harley on the same plane.

MILAN MELVIN Not bad for a kid from East Oakland flying overseas for the first time, right?

JEFF HOUSE When the caravan reaches Europe, future KSAN intern organizer Moe Armstrong is already there. He moved to England from a commune in New Mexico that he'd hitchhiked to after leaving a different commune in San Francisco.

MOE ARMSTRONG I had a British band called Daddy Longlegs; we were all expat Vietnam veterans. We had a minor hit called "High Again," a funky country paean to pot that got airplay at Radio Luxembourg. Banned by the BBC! Canterbury. But we opened for Pink Floyd at the Medicine Ball!

MILAN MELVIN The worst of the entire mess was Pink Floyd at Canterbury. We had seven cameras. Camera A was a track-mounted crane, doing avant-garde swoops in and out of Pink Floyd for three hours. But with no film in the camera. Of the hundreds of hours of film the French freaks shot, probably fifty were focusing in and out of a Coca-Cola cup on the grass next to a cigarette. You know, where the camera operator had seen God. Lots of sky.

MOE ARMSTRONG Our appearance didn't make it into the movie. I'm convinced playing "High Again" was the reason. Daddy Longlegs was too controversial for Warner Brothers!

JEFF HOUSE Nothing of that Pink Floyd concert made it into the movie.

MOE ARMSTRONG I would like to see what happened to our *Caravan* concert footage. The good news is Warner Brothers rereleased a Daddy Longlegs album in 2021!

JEFF HOUSE The edit was a disaster; the crew forgot to sync the tracks.

MILAN MELVIN The film editors in Paris had to hire Buzzy Donahue and me to figure out who was singing what.

JEFF HOUSE Warner Brothers begged for one young man's help—they recalled his editing on *Woodstock*. Twenty-eight-year-old Martin Scorsese said he'd do what he could. Too many performances—the Youngbloods in Boulder,

Van Morrison in Ohio, Cold Blood somewhere—were shot too poorly to make the cut.

MILAN MELVIN They missed the best of what went down.

JEFF HOUSE Like scenes with elders of the Winnebago tribe, of young people connecting around a campfire—they're nowhere in the movie. After the Canterbury show, folks split for San Francisco. Wavy Gravy and the Hog Farm bought a bus and met up with other pilgrims in Katmandu. Chan Laughlin headed to Asia to barter jewelry and trinkets he could sell somewhere else. He said when they did that in America, they were called traders. In Asia: smugglers. The Donahues stayed at Reichenbach's, trying to assemble ninety-two hours of out-of-focus footage. Milan Melvin rode on through Afghanistan.

In '71, *Medicine Ball Caravan: We've Come for Your Daughters* opened at the Plaza Theatre in New York. A bomb threat was phoned in from someone who declared the film a rip-off. In London, Rae gave birth to Jesse Lee Donahue—a name Tom said would look great on wanted posters. He figured he'd get around to seeing *MBC: WCFYD* eventually. Grissim asked him when, and Tom said, "When it's on a triple bill at the drive-in."

HOWARD HESSEMAN To this day you have to see it to disbelieve it.

BEN FONG-TORRES The Medicine Ball Caravan is how I got hired at KSAN: I was at *Rolling Stone* when Paul Boucher, KSAN program director, called to pass along an item for our "Random Notes" column: *Tom Donahue is taking a busload of friends cross-country and filming free concerts . . . all for a movie for Warner Brothers.* A couple of KSAN DJs would be making this trip, and Paul needed fill-in announcers. Might I be interested? Having been a radio junkie my entire life and a listener to KMPX and KSAN, I said, "Man, I am there!" It was baptism by air. I began with the most obvious of songs: Dylan's "Like a Rolling Stone." The hours passed swiftly, as did the following month. And as it turned out, several KSAN adventurers had wandered through Tibet and Morocco; they were in Paris or somewhere, with no plans for return within any measurable time frame. My temporary gig at KSAN lasted eight years. I'd get called in for fill-in work, or when someone was too stoned—I was known as a sober, straightforward journalist. One weekend, Steve Martin dropped in and did sight gags. On the radio. Yes! "It's great to be here," he said. Then running to a different part of the studio. "No, it's great to be . . . *here*, actually." So this is what happens when you say yes to a little temporary gig at the Jive 95.

BOB SIMMONS I filled in at the station then, too. When I told Tom that the caravan looked like "Altamont on Wheels," he said, "Don't say that again. It will catch on."

The arc of Donahue continued bending toward revolution. After *Broadcasting* magazine's Donald West noted a "bomb-thrower" taint to the name "underground radio," Donahue explained that it wasn't about violent revolution, but a social one. He never worried about sponsors being reluctant to lose their chains over FM radio. "The establishment has financed every revolution the world's ever had," he said. "And they'll finance this one, too." Especially now, "when more and more freaks are working in ad agencies."

SIDE TRIP

Moe

Moe Armstrong directed KSAN's internship program in the mid-'70s. Eric Meyers and Denise Dunne started long radio and TV careers as interns from San Francisco State.

DENISE DUNNE Moe!

ERIC MEYERS Moe! San Francisco State was the pipeline to KSAN. Dave Artale, Jill Fouch, Peter Rappalis, Denise—we all came from KSFS.

DENISE DUNNE I was on KSFS and told Moe I'd love to be at KSAN, and he said if you want to be an intern, you have to go back to school . . . ugh.

ERIC MEYERS I remember his heaven-on-earth rap, praising Cuban society after he came back from a radio conference in Havana. I loved it.

DENISE DUNNE Moe was just into everything at KSAN. Tons of energy.

ERIC MEYERS Another time I watched Moe talk a guy out of going out and jumping off the Golden Gate Bridge!

Moe Armstrong is the author of *Memories of a War Vet: A Hope for Many* and works with traumatized soldiers.

MOE ARMSTRONG After I got back in '66 and got out of the psychiatric hospital, I moved to the Haight and sold newspapers. KSAN and KMPX weren't around yet, and Neal Cassady lived upstairs from me and was always screaming about the speed. Annie Murphy was into acid, but she was never to touch his speed; nobody was to take his speed because speed was What. He. Loved. She could take all the acid she wanted, there was *always* acid—she could take as much as she wanted *of that*. Everybody has a Neal Cassady story, so I'll end mine there. Except two things he said to me: "Never shoot up." And, "You want to live high, get high—Vietnam, get some of this." Three things. "Stay high, keep moving, and give all of yourself away." You try talking to Neal Cassady—just like that, I was a full blown head, known as "San Francisco Moe." Became disenchanted by the antiwar movement. Tried Buddhism but was too jumpy for the meditation. The third path was rock 'n roll and taking drugs with your friends. John painted backdrops for the San Francisco Mime Troupe shows. He had just gotten out of the nuthouse. He was not ashamed for being crazy—he defined himself by how far out he was. We tripped and spent hours in conversation. We read the *Tibetan Book of the Dead* to each other and cried, watching flowers live. John and I went around San Francisco in garbage bags. I would wear sackcloth and become a saint! My hands were covered with blood; I would atone for killing Vietnamese. The way to make myself clean was to do good deeds: take in the hungry, clothe those in need, my home was a crash pad. I gave away my medal, clothes, my writing from the war. San Francisco Moe was my name in the ballrooms. Dancing, I was free. Nobody could take anything away from me. As long as I had no material wealth, I could live forever. In the winter, I wore boots with Vibram soles of vulcanized rubber, like I used to. The Marine Corps was never far away. I was able to live on the streets by what I learned in the Marine Corps.

DENISE DUNNE One night I'm watching TV, and Ted Koppel comes on and says, "Tonight's guest is the mighty Moe Armstrong," and I stopped dead in my tracks. Who else would call themselves "the Mighty"? Ted Koppel was talking about Moe's program for homeless vets, a safe place for them, because so many were dealing with PTSD. He's gone all over the country working with the VA and Plowshares programs. At KSAN, Moe was larger than life!

KSAN ran a contest where one lucky draft evader could win a free trip to Vancouver.

1971 staff on Mt. Tamalpais in Marin County north of San Francisco. Top to bottom, left to right: Stefan Ponek, Paul Boucher, (unknown), Dusty Street, Richard Gossett, Donna Campbell, can't remember lovely lady's name—she was receptionist before Hadwig Schneck, Bob Simmons, bearded salesman but I forget his name, Jay Oliver, Willis Duff, Dave McQueen, Ron ? (was sales guy, had a beautiful wife). Voco Kesh, Travus T. Hipp, Joan ? receptionist/sales, Whitney Harris, Trish Robbins, Winslow Thrill, (Richard Rollins) Pam Sanders, Mary Turner, Carl Truckload (Howard Kerr). Edward Bear, Goldie, Earl Pillow (Wesley Hind), Roland Jacopetti, Peter Laufer, Jeffrey Nemerovski, Bob McClay. Raechel and Tom Donahue were down in LA at the time. Other missing faces: Larry Lee, Larry Bensky, Tony Pigg, Roland Young, Jef Jaisun, Phil Charles, and a lot of weekenders.

PHOTO BY JOHN KARCICH / COURTESY OF KRISTEN KARCICH QUINT

SPILLAGE

The Oil Tanker Disaster in San Francisco Bay, 1971

Fresh Garbage
Look beneath your lid some morning
See those things you didn't quite consume
The world's a can for your fresh garbage.

Nature's Way
It's nature's way of telling you summer breeze
It's nature's way of telling you dying trees
It's nature's way of telling you something's wrong.

—Spirit, "Fresh Garbage," 1967,
and "Nature's Way," 1970

Save the Bay was organized in 1961 by Bay Area residents Esther Gulick, Sylvia McLaughlin, and Kay Kerr as an effort to raise ecological consciousness among their neighbors. Their movement grew, and resulted in community action on January 14, 1971. Dave McQueen and Peter Laufer were KSAN Gnus anchors that day.

DAVE MCQUEEN Late at night on January 14, two Chevron tankers, the *Arizona Standard* and the *Oregon Standard*, crashed into each other just off Alcatraz Island, spilling eight hundred thousand gallons of crude, soon washing all over San Francisco Bay and heading out of the Golden Gate onto Pacific coast beaches. It was a real mess.

PETER LAUFER I heard it on the car radio on the way into work. Driving in from Sausalito gave me time to figure out a game plan for what was a community-wide crisis. (I remember pulling my dilapidated Bug onto the sidewalk under a No Parking sign on Claude Lane and just leaving it.) I fell in easily with KSAN's allegiance to the community and it felt empowering in terms of engaging this immediate problem with an immediacy radio was ideally suited for.

DAVE MCQUEEN People were immediately looking for ways to help, not just read about it in the *Chronicle* and *Examiner*—tomorrow's news of the catastrophe would be too late to do anything about it in the here and now. Radio offered a continual stream of information.

PETER LAUFER It was so intense and nonstop. That we'd spend the first week of the spill sleeping on the studio floor was standard operating procedure.

BONNIE SIMMONS I remember we added phone lines by pulling phones out of peoples' offices and running the cords to put them on a desk together.

DAVE MCQUEEN We established a switchboard manned by listeners who spontaneously showed up and made KSAN kind of a clearing house for incoming data. Thanks to our incredible listeners, people learned the latest.

PETER LAUFER Witnesses went on the air, or we took down their information and talked it ourselves. McQueen went into the field, recording interviews from the shorelines. Dr. HipPocrates—Eugene Schoenfeld, our Sunday night sexual advice talk show host—reported on the size of the slick from one of the helicopters Standard Oil and the coast guard brought in.

BONNIE SIMMONS We had five hundred people show up at Stinson Beach the next day to wash the birds off. Thousands were cleaned. I remember we determined that Dawn dish soap was the best thing to get oil off the birds without hurting them. I still use Dawn dish soap to this day!

DUSTY STREET I was trying to work and there were birds being cleaned off in the middle of everything, these listeners had shown up with Dawn or whatever it was to help them. There were about thirty people in the studio and birds were being brought into the lobby.

DAVE MCQUEEN Paul Lambert was the listener who walked in and coordinated our response. He also turned us onto Ecology Action in Berkeley—they sent hundreds of spotters to parts of the coast that hadn't yet been examined for damage.

PAUL LAMBERT, listener I was a twenty-seven-year-old grad school dropout, and I heard KSAN say something about helping and called the number. It was the wrong number, so my friend José, a truck driver/junkie, said let's just go to 211 Sutter. It was the middle of the night; the DJ, Ed Bear, came to the door and invited us up. I told him KSAN was the community resource we trusted—they should be giving out the right phone number! He said, "Why don't you? "Me?" Jose took over logistics, I coordinated, and by morning we had three dozen volunteers. After three days without sleep, I collapsed at a meeting and went home.

JACK HINES, listener I heard KSAN sound the alarm: "Get to the beach! From the old Sutro Baths, south to the zoo, we need you!" Thousands of freaks were on the beach—I met a small army with rakes and pitchforks.

DAVE MCQUEEN North of the Golden Gate, fifty thousand folks, from the sands of Bolinas to Tiburon, spent days cleaning cormorants, pelicans, and gulls. We got a call: "We need baled hay to strew along the beach and soak up this oil." A farmer from the Central Valley called: "I've got a truckload of hay I can drive over there. Where are they?" It went on like that nonstop.

JACK HINES KSAN once had a "Speed Kills" campaign with the Haight-Ashbury Free Clinic that may have saved more lives, but I'll never forget how long and hard these freaks worked, because someone at their radio station figured out something to do when no one else had a clue. I've spent my life in commercial radio, and never have I seen a display of community service to match it. That's power, baby!

DAVE MCQUEEN That really established us; it was seen as a tremendous public service.

BONNIE SIMMONS A lot of what we did at KSAN was about service.

LARRY BENSKY I thought it was extremely opportunistic and hypocritical of KSAN to do that, because the spill was caused by, among others, Chevron—one of their sponsors. They were greenwashing their air by running the Chevron advertising. KSAN went completely overboard. Trying to help the birds, which we were all for, but that's what governments are for: cases of environmental emergencies. I remember at one point the station was picketed by people saying, "People are animals too!"

PETER LAUFER My radio comrade and longtime friend Larry Bensky makes salient points about greenwashing. But we Jive 95ers always were a productive compromise: licensed by the feds, owned by the mega-rich, and with our paychecks covered by corporate advertising. That reality does not discount the good we did, or the extended community we built during the oil spill.

SIDE TRIP

Basic Etiquette

STEFAN PONEK Drugs formed a brotherhood at underground stations. We were convinced that if the president got stoned, he'd call off the war. You could travel out onto the street buzzed and know who else was stoned. When your eyes met, bam! You both knew, and it was magic.

One DJ rolled joints on mic and invited listeners to meet him in the park after the show—"Hippie Hill" adjacent was a popular spot. And the station's basement was a warm place in the minds of many air staff. Gnus director Joanne Green and DJ Denise Dunne spent time on the classic, lumpy sofa down there that could seat three if they were sprawling.

JOANNE GREENE The basement at 345 Sansome was affectionately dubbed the Glaucoma Research Center. During business hours, staffers often went down to smoke. Other hours, and on weekends, marijuana was available and used anywhere. Sounding stoned on the air was never a problem for KSAN jocks. That was part of the appeal! Newscasters also used; somehow the work got done.

DENISE DUNNE My day would start at 8:30 a.m.: Arrive at the station, music director gives me a bag of pot—I go downstairs and roll the morning joints. While down there, the news crew—they'd been there since six—would be doing their mid-morning lines. Music director comes down, we smoke, go upstairs, and go to work. After doing some work, getting close to noon, we go across the street to the Financial Corner, get a couple of brewskies, come back, go down to the basement, then back up, do some work. The Beaver [DJ Beverley Wilshire] would come on two. By three, we'd go get her a beer run. She was on till around six. Then TK [Tony Kilbert], and he always had something good to smoke. By then the business staff had left, so everything was out in the open. You'd go through TK's show, or go to the clubs. Richard [Gossett] is on after TK, and while Richard was on, people would kind of drift in after the clubs—that's when the party would really start. Then we went into Sean [Donahue], who was on all night.

ROLAND JACOPETTI There was certainly a lot of dope smoked around KSAN. But it caused technical errors, and the deadlines were too tight to do that.

LARRY BENSKY Everybody was paranoid about the UPS drivers, who themselves, of course got high. The FedEx drivers, and the mailmen and maintenance workers who came in. All of them. We were in the basement of the Wells Fargo Bank building, where the vaults were. God knows what was in them—there was probably cocaine in some of those safe deposit boxes. But the bank had guards, who themselves, of course, got high.

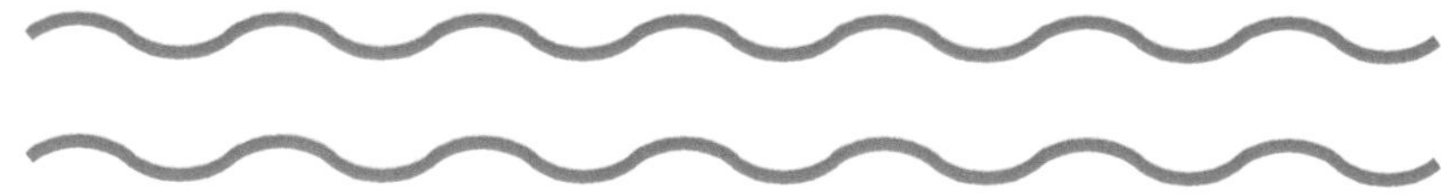

SIDE TRIP

Larry Bensky and the Jeans West Pantsing

"Executives get nervous about social ferment because of the reluctance to participate in a consumer economy by people who think they may be drafted, bludgeoned, or beat over their heads."

—Larry Bensky, *Berkeley Tribe*, 1970

Larry Bensky came to KSAN after a job at *Ramparts* magazine as managing editor, years at *The New York Times Book Review* and *Pacifica* radio. I asked about his involvement in an incident having to do with a KSAN sponsor.

LARRY BENSKY Actually, the ostensible reason I was fired was because I had an intern who went on the air, after he had done some investigating into city building inspectors. An inspector or somebody heard it and called the station, and Willis Duff went ballistic.

WILLIS DUFF, general manager Me "going ballistic" seems out of character with the me I remember. Certainly not over investigating municipal graft. I love that kind of news; it is vital to decent government. I remember when I fired Bensky. Bensky did something Metromedia couldn't handle.

LARRY BENSKY Duff had been put in by Metromedia because they wanted to sell the station. They eventually did.

WILLIS DUFF I was definitely *not* "put in . . . to sell the station." That's fiction. I was put in because Metromedia's station manager was too busy running KNEW AM to oversee the chaos of KSAN. Bensky was fired over the Jeans West incident.

Jeans West spot

A few years ago a certain street in London, England, was considered to be the fashion center for new mod clothes. Today the leader in men's and women's fashions has arrived in San Francisco to establish its fifteenth store in California, at 501 Pacific and Montgomery, Jackson Square. It's Jeans West. Jeans West guarantees they'll undersell everybody who says they're underselling everybody. In straight words: you can't beat the prices of Jeans West, because they're the lowest! Jeans West, the very clothes the heavy groups are wearing at their concerts. Jeans West—funny name for a guy selling clothes for young people and people with young ideas. The newest red, white, and blue Jeans West is opening at 501 Pacific. Drop by and get it on.

LARRY BENSKY KSAN was an open-source place where people from the community could come and get on the air and speak their piece. Not just in the news reporting, but on the deejaying side. You could go see Richard Gossett, go see Bob McClay, or Stefan Ponek, or Roland Young. In 1971, some sales clerks and stock boys from a chain called Jeans West came in to see us. Jeans West was lower-priced knockoffs of Levi's, an independently owned California company, whose groovy bellbottoms were a major fashion item among the *hipoisie* in San Francisco. I wore bell-bottom jeans! The four men said it was a serious situation: "We're being suspended if we refuse to take drug tests. Or refuse to sign papers saying we don't use drugs. Also, they want to know who on the staff uses marijuana—they're asking us to finger people!" This had nothing to do with their job description, so they weren't going to do it. And they got fired. I said, "Well, you should go on the air." So I put in: "Jeans West, reached in Los Angeles, had no comment on the story." I'd worked at the *New York Times*; I knew some news standards, you know? I knew that when you're reporting a story that's controversial, you reach out and get as many comments and opinions about it, including from those directly implicated. They left urgent, crazy messages for Willis, and when he came back, he saw them and asked me, "Did you run this story? I want to hear it." It had been on live, but everything is logged, and you have engineers who can pull it off the log, and you can listen to anything you want. This was just a three-minute story. Duff called me into his office the next day and said, "You're fired for putting unauthorized material on the air." I said, "My authorization is it's a news story, Willis. And nobody cursed, nobody broke any station rules, and no drugs were consumed on the spot. These kids were in trouble—they'd lost their jobs and they came to us as a way of getting justice. And exposing injustice." He didn't see it that way and fired me.

WILLIS DUFF Hmm. I never thought of Bensky as dishonest. Just a fervent idealist. I'm sure he isn't lying, but this sounds like some kind of self-protective, selective memory. Could be. My recall is predictably vague to the point of none.

LARRY BENSKY It became a cause célèbre. It was in the local underground press—at that point we had very active papers—and the Jeans West situation was reported with exact dates, places, and times. I heard that a memo was issued saying that anybody discussing the Jeans West story would also get fired. Just because I was fired doesn't mean that I wasn't rehired. Six years later the management had changed. In 1977, I was rehired, by Jerry Graham, and hosted *The Talkies*. Groovy Jerry. Nice guy, but he didn't dabble in the politics of anything.

KSAN, KMPX, KPFA—any kind of place that is disturbing the status quo—have to be supported from below. It's not the journalists; it's not the broadcaster that does this alone. There has to be grassroots sentiment for this in order for it to have an echo, to have an effect, in order for those who do it to have support. We had support in those years.

KSAN KOMIX presents fall schedule by Dan O'Neill, 1972.

SIDE TRIP

Dan and Chan and Travus

Cartoonist Dan O'Neill, a counterculture favorite, invented the syndicated strip, *Odd Bodkins*, the adventures of Hugh and Fred Bird—called a trippy *Peanuts*—worked with Joel Selvin at the *San Francisco Chronicle*. Joel has a Dan O'Neill story.

JOEL SELVIN O'Neill used to battle with Sunday editor Stanleigh Arnold over everything in *Odd Bodkins*. One day, Stanleigh came rushing out of his office waving a page proof, yelling, "He's spelled out *shit* in Morse code in the clouds!" Indeed he had. And Stanleigh had caught it because—sorry, Dan—Stanleigh was in the navy. Those two were in constant warfare, a blood sport on both ends. That is a great editor-writer relationship. Sneak attacks the order of the day.

In 1972, Dan O'Neill went to cover The Troubles in Northern Ireland with Chan Laughlin.

DAN O'NEILL I brought all kinds of tape back to KSAN after Bloody Sunday. One tape we did—me and Chandler—was with the Irish navy. The British authorities came in and took the master. Thirty years later, I found the tape and sent it back to Ireland, where it got into the tribunal where the British have to apologize to

"A man's not free who can't piss off his back porch." Chandler Laughlin became Travus T. Hipp and reported from Belfast and Wounded Knee with Dan O'Neill.
© DAN O'NEILL

Dan O'Neill's Hoksila stories about Wounded Knee, Episode 1.

Ireland for Bloody Sunday. Just after I get back from Belfast, I wake up to hear the FBI banging away at my apartment. There are two giants filling up the doorway. I see their necks are turning red, their collars too tight. Because I'm naked. Whatever question they ask, I say, "Search me." Finally, I lean into their space a little and say, "Your shoes are so shiny, I can see my dick reflected in there." They ran away. Years later, I want to get my FBI files to illustrate them. I call up, they tell me, "You have five files. We can't find the fifth one." I say, "Send copies of the rest." I get a letter saying, "You do not have any files." I'm sure it was because they didn't want a file out there that said they ran from my dick.

In 1973, they were in South Dakota gathering tape for a special about the Wounded Knee Occupation.

DAN O'NEILL Chandler and I were there forty-five of the seventy-one-day siege. We prepared a show called *It'll Be Treason If They Catch You*, sending back stories from Gordon, Nebraska, about half an hour from the reservation. Here's how that was done: You unscrew the mouthpiece of a public telephone, attach the little alligator clips, and play your tape. CBS and ABC were trading us whiskey and porterhouse steaks for the tapes we brought in. I drove there from San Francisco with four Vietnam vets in a '57 Chevy, took the car apart, and filled it with about three thousand pounds of freeze-dried food, battle dressings, and Winchester barrels. We had all these Indians disguised as reporters from KSAN. I'm busy taking pictures of them, rubbing bleach on the negatives to lighten them up, getting press passes from the highway patrol. We smuggled in Indians and guns through 1,500 miles of federal checkpoints. One day in Gordon, the FBI came up: "Do *not* go back to South Dakota. There's a list of four hundred to be killed. Seventeen are white guys. And you two are on the list." So that was it for us there.

At KSAN, I was Chandler's sidekick on a 5 a.m. weekend talk show, the *Rawhide Reality Review*. We had a good time—brawling with Hells Angels, that kind of thing. We were living in the same house; I was in the tower of this big old Victorian on Laguna, and he'd come up the fire escape and stick cocaine in my nose to wake me up.

I met Chandler at the press conference after getting fired by Stanleigh at the *Chronicle* for the third time. We shared a cigarette with [Mayor] George Moscone and some wino. We went up to a giant demonstration—Marshall Ky was in town, PM of South Vietnam—on Knob Hill, we see them all march around a corner, and a guy gets killed. A medic was screaming, "He's dead, he's dead!" So Chandler and I went down to the station right away. Chandler hooked me up once for an ad campaign. Once. An animated short called, "The City That Waits to Die." There's a skylight, and through it you see all the overdeveloped downtown San Francisco buildings fall together: one spelling K; another one S; the Transamerica shrinks down, as lights go on and off, to make an A; and two other buildings make an N. Then Donahue's deep voice . . . and crash! They played it on *Creature Features* when everybody's all coked up and paranoid in the middle of the night. Freaked everybody. Scared the shit out of them.

Dan O'Neill is completing *God Loves Me More Than You*, a memoir.

DAN O'NEILL It's not done yet—I'm still breathing. Only the good die young, and I'm pushing eighty. I was one of the first ones on Nixon's enemy list. You can Google it.

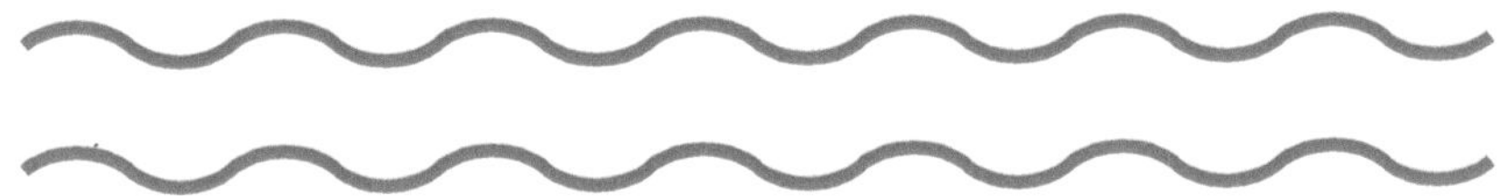

SIDE TRIP

The Poor People's Paul Harvey

Peace, love, and spare change don't work. There's no such thing as spare change, love ain't free, and peace is something you're going to have to fight for.

—Travis T. Hipp on the myth of the Haight-Ashbury

Before he changed his name during Donahue's Medicine Ball Caravan in '70, Travus T. Hipp was Chan Laughlin, student at the University of California during the Free Speech Movement in '64. He was co-proprietor at the Cabale Creamery, a Berkeley folk club that should do its own memoir. Travus once said, if a cat has nine lives, couldn't he get it all done in eight? After KSAN, his news and commentary were syndicated in Nevada and on California stations like KFAT, Gilroy and KPIG, Santa Cruz. Travus had a voice like he'd smoked gravel, and things came through it like, "Radio is the weapon I drew from the armory when we went into battle in the '60s."

Listeners could send KSAN a penny and self-addressed envelope to the station and Travus mailed out The Penny Ante Republican. *Around 2,000 received it weekly.*

TRAVUS T. HIPP I never expected to make a million dollars—KSAN was too far ahead of the trend to make a dollar on it. We were fucking lucky to have work.

Rick Gardner and Peter Laufer did stints with Hipp.

RICK GARDNER I learned the ropes of selling from Chan. He was a native San Franciscan; we rode around in his van for a few days, Chandler pointing out that *everyone* is on a scam.

PETER LAUFER This was in '70 or '71. I operated the board and eventually co-hosted *The Talk Show*, his Sunday morning call-in. We kept hearing these regularly timed clicks on the phone line, which we knew made the show difficult for the audience to listen to. Our engineer said, "Sounds to me like a malfunctioning tap." "According to the engineer here at KSAN," Travus told listeners, "this noise is a malfunctioning tap on the line. Now, whatever agency out there has tapped our phone lines, here's an idea for you: find a nice stereo or sit in your car, and just tune to our frequency: ninety-four point nine. You'll get a clear signal that you can record, dissect, study, and analyze all you want. But as long as your tap's on the line, it'll be hard for you, it'll be hard for us, and hard for our listeners. Thanks." Soon the noise stopped.

TRAVUS T. HIPP We were the relevant talk radio of that time. And like most good rock 'n roll, it disappeared from the airwaves.

PETER LAUFER Years after KSAN, we worked together at the *Gold Hill News* south of Virginia City. C. Atcheson Laughlin III and I remained close colleagues.

Travus died the day after his May 18, 2012, newscast, which he recorded at his home studio in Silver City, Nevada. The *South Tahoe Now* reporter: "He was 75 . . . as old as the Golden Gate Bridge. . . . Longtime associates credit Hipp with originating the word *hippy*." (Barry "the Fish" Melton, of Country Joe and the Fish fame, said Travus coined the phrase, "Question reality!") "He was buried next to his longtime companion Lynn Hughes," the obit concluded, "who went by the name Rose Hipp." Lynn Hughes from the Red Dog Saloon, who, in '68, fed radio hippie strikers with Chan from a Chevy van parked outside 50 Green Street in North Beach.

SEAN LAUGHLIN, son of Chan Whenever we called them hippies, they'd get this stern look and say, "We're not hippies; we're beatniks. And proud of it."

https://archive.org/details/tth_111007/01_nws_111007.mp3
Travus T. Hipp's Cabale news re "Ten Thousand Afghans Ago," and the busting of cannabis shops. October 2011, 4 minutes.

21

THE FANTASTIC KRASSNER AND DOC HIPPOCRATES

Comedian Dick Gregory once came on Paul Krassner's radio show to say he would stop eating solid foods until the end of the war in Vietnam. Krassner said that until the end of the war, he was going to eat all of Dick Gregory's meals. I'll always remember Paul Krassner's eighty-six birthday where he declared, "Eighty-six is the new eighty-five!" He died in 2019, but I saw him immortalized last year in a graphic comic history of the Underground Press Syndicate. The publisher of it was his friend. Paul had a million friends, and he mentored many of us, whom he called, "fellow Martians." And, in the fall of '71, he hosted one of the Jive 95's most memorable shows.

PAUL KRASSNER Sunday night, November 7, 1971. I had Ram Dass as a guest, and the topics discussed included the Attica prison riot, the ads in *Rolling Stone* magazine, and chimpanzee behavior. Five minutes before sign-off, into the studio walked Gene Schoenfeld, whose popular "Dr. HipPocrates" advice program was coming up next. With him was tonight's guest, Margo St. James—a mutual friend and my ex-lover—infamous convener of San Francisco's annual Hooker's Ball and founder of COYOTE, an acronym for Call Off Your Old Tired Ethics. COYOTE fought for sex workers' rights.

Margo was trying to, I couldn't help but notice, unzip my fly. She intended to give me head before the end of my show. As she began to perform fellatio, I said, "Margo, would you please say something, so that feminists who are tuned in will understand the context?" She looked up and said into the microphone, "I'm doing this of my own volition." I maintained my composure and finished by nine. "It's been a pleasure being with you," I told listeners. "This is KSAN in San Francisco, the station that blows your mind." We were both banished from the air.

Gordon Whiting, producer and radio connoisseur, offers some historical perspective.

GORDON WHITING The golden age of radio was predicated on the concept of theater of the mind, peaking, perhaps, with *War of the Worlds* in 1938. Audiences had no way of knowing for sure what was happening. The Krassner–St. James episode is part of that tradition—listeners had no way of knowing what was actually happening—but this was presented with an impish, rule-breaking '70s zeitgeist. Somehow I see Terry Southern in the KSAN control room, producing.

PETER LAUFER The story is an integral chapter in the history we alumni keep alive as station lore.

Krassner, in his defense, wrote to KSAN general manager Willis Duff, "What was happening existed totally in the imagination of the listener. . . . It was in no way a violation of FCC regulations, nor was it likely to really offend any listeners because it was being carried out in good humor rather than pandering lechery . . . and it was happening under the umbrella of a general permissive atmosphere at KSAN. . . . Oh well, please send me the fifty dollars that you promised."

But it was the next show that same night that threatened the station's license. After her brief head trip with Paul, Margo St. James went on Doc HipPocrates and introduced the terms, "snappy pussy," and "enlightened pussy power."

PETER LAUFER Eugene "Dr. HipPocrates" Schoenfeld was famous for addressing readers' health concerns in his weekly *Berkeley Barb* column with a directness that appealed to the counterculture. He approached his KSAN show with the same candor.

The Federal Communications reported receiving forty complaint letters. Willis Duff and Metromedia were called before the FCC in Washington. Herb Caen, "Mr. San Francisco," wrote it up in his *Chronicle* column.

HERB CAEN "The Brass at KSAN-FM have their fingers crossed after Dr. HipPocrates show. . . . Ms. Margo St. James, rising to a new low, out Lenny'ed the late Mr. Bruce to the point where there have been complaints to the FCC from outraged listeners."

Bonnie Simmons 11/10/71

Willis Duff

Paul Krassner Show 11/7

The shenanigans in the last 15 minutes of Paul Krassner's special program should not have been allowed on the air. Although I understand that the event was "staged" and did not occur,but the implications made by the sounds were too explicit. The program should have been taken off the air after one warning had been given to Krassner to cease. I am at a loss to understand how you let this continue until the end of the show.

(Under no circumstances is Paul Krassner or Margo Saint James to be allowed on KSAN again, since they clearly do not intend to abide by the most rudimentary standards of good broadcasting.)

Any future lapses in judgment of this dimension will be grounds for dismissal from your talk show production job.

WD mw

cc: Thom O'Hair

General Manager Willis Duff's memo regarding his disappointment in a Paul Krassner November 1971 show.
COURTESY WILLIS DUFF

One of the letters went to the Department of Justice in San Francisco, with a carbon copy (ask your grandparents) sent to KSAN. Some excerpts:

Gentlemen: I am not in the habit of writing complaint letters. . . .

Last night my wife and I had retired earlier than usual and decided to try FM radio for a change (and a change it was!). We happened onto KSAN-FM and tuned in to a talk show format run by a "Doctor Hip." The subject of the show was "Oral Sex." The guests on the program were proponents of this practice and spared no details nor restroom wall language in their conversation. I would be more graphic in my recounting of the program, but would probably be subject to arrest. Suffice it to say that every crude term in the book was on public airwaves. In seventeen years of marriage, there have been few times my wife and I have blushed at each other, but this was one of them. We could (and should) have turned off the station, but we just couldn't believe what we were hearing and wanted to find out what kind of station we were hearing it on . . . a radio station is hardly the place to . . .

I would suggest you procure a tape of Sunday evening from about 9:30 to 10:30 and get an idea of what goes on.

Warren A. Sugarman

Dr. Hip got some callers who went on to ask St. James about pussy power, about using psychedelic drugs during early pregnancy, what exercises did she recommend to keep from exhaustion during fellatio, etc. Margo offered complete answers.

Excerpts from Willis Duff's response to the complaint:

Dear Mr. Sugarman:

Generally the language used on Dr. Schoenfeld's program stays well within the bounds of medical terminology—a form of circumlocution that renders the most discomfiting subjects acceptable. In the program of November 7th, the variations from this practice with the use of the common vernacular are perhaps questionable from the point of view of taste, but not from the point of view of communication. (We know, for instance, that only a small percentage of most groups know what "cunnilingus" means.)

I personally apologize for embarrassing you and your wife.

PETER LAUFER This was captivating and riveting radio. It served the listeners with valid information that they sought, and it served the needs of KSAN—a commercial radio station seeking ratings—because this was the kind of information that lured listeners to stay tuned to the station. Duff had signed the letter, "Cordially," but he was unsuccessful at placating Sugarman.

Another Chronicle story said, "KSAN's broadcasting license looks about as valuable as used rolling papers until lawyers come up with an ingenious defense: Broadcast obscenity is judged against the standards of the peer audience. And does not San Francisco have, as Lenny Bruce once pointed out, the lowest morale in the nation?"

PETER LAUFER After a year of legal battling, Metromedia prevailed. KSAN's license was not jeopardized. I remember, in the same period as Margo's and Paul's escapade, the Supreme Court ruled that a T-shirt that read "Fuck the Draft" was protected speech. McQueen and I competed for who would get to read that story and hence say "fuck" on the radio for the first time—and legally. As I recall, I think he won—after all, he was Gnus director.

The complete transcript of the infamous Jive 95 show can be read in Peter Laufer's book, *Inside Talk Radio: America's Voice or Just Hot Air?*

EUGENE SCHOENFELD And I was the one who advised Margo to give Paul head!

WILLIS DUFF I love Gene. A total hoot. Genuine public benefactor. Wry and realistic. That giving-head-to-the-large-cocked-boyfriend piece starring *The Realist* nun was a history-making event. It would be SOP on a lot of today's podcasts. But then? Whoo-wee.

BOB MCLAY The Dr. Hip thing made everybody at the station paranoid as shit. I used to do "come" sets, but everybody had gotten touchy about playing certain records. It seems to me the only time we got in trouble was for the talk shows, never the music. The music people just ended up paying for it. Our selections fell under greater scrutiny.

When McClay spun "Sammy's Song" by David Bromberg, he found a memo in his mailbox: "That was a real lapse in judgment. That cut is definitely a no-play!"

THOM O'HAIR I remember once playing as many songs that were on the taboo list as we could! We read the Bill of Rights between records to make a point.

SIDE TRIP

Ram Dass

In the '70s, Ram Dass ("Servant of God") gave half-hour spiritual talks on Sunday mornings. His book, *Be Here Now*, changed the world, inspiring seekers to follow his path from acid to India. The beloved bodhisattva always maintained his sense of humor, and his teachings still air on Pacifica stations and on his website.

LARRY LEE, Gnus It's time again for the recorded talks of Baba Ram Dass, from Naropa Institute in Boulder, Colorado, as part of his course, "The Yogas in the Bhagavad Gita." For the complete catalog, please write Hanuman Foundation Tape Library, BOX 835, Santa Cruz, California, 95061. Now, here is Ram Dass.

RAM DASS There is a king and a wise man, and the wise man said . . . the wise man said . . . [to engineer] Can we turn down the volume in the earphones a little bit? Great, now I can't hear at all. Oh, I see, I control them. Okay, now it's cool. The wise man said to the king, "Sire, the wheat crop has been spoiled, and anybody who eats it is gonna go mad. But there's enough of last year's wheat for you and, of course, there'll be a little left over for me." And the king said, "Well, if all my subjects are gonna go mad, why would I want to stay sane? So, you and I will eat the poison too." (Probably the poison was ergot, I assume now, ha ha ha.) The king says, "But it would be nice if we could remember this moment when we decided to go mad." The wise man said, "Whatever for, sire?" The king said, "Well, there may come a time when it'll help you or me, or somebody or other. We'll put a mark on each other's forehead, so every time we meet, we'll know we're mad." And my predicament is that everywhere I go in the universe now, I look at people with a mark on their head. And I look in their eyes and I see, here we are, all mad. Stop at a red light in Des Moines, and look across, and there is a life. And there's a mark, and yeah here we are—far out—and drive away. So the mark of madness brings us together. Because those of you who are not sufficiently mad will have already tuned to some other thing. So I will assume we are already mad enough and now we can enjoy the madness, by asking questions and giving answers, as if that were all real.

Spot 1971

[Lightning strikes. Laughter ensues]

Bob: Bonnie, that was incredible, what can I ever do for you?

Bonnie: Well, if you'd like to do something for me, you could get your hair cut.

Bob: Are you crazy? It's just getting to be Leon Russell length.

Bonnie: You know my parents are coming from New York to visit. It's gonna be bad enough when they find out you dropped out of broadcasting school and I'm pregnant. But what will they say when they see your hair?

Bob: I don't care what they say. I'm not cutting it.

Bonnie: Look, Bob, you could go down to Mr. Broadway's at Broadway and Van Ness. They're supposed to do marvelous work on men's heads. How about a shorthaired wig? Mr. Broadway has a great selection of inexpensive wigs for people who want to change their image. They're supposed to look absolutely real!

Bob: No haircut. And no wig. That's final.

Bonnie: But Bob, what about the money my father promised to lay on us?

Bob: Mr. Broadway, huh? How do you think I'd look in a red wig?

Bonnie: Mmm . . . [laughter]

Tom Donahue: Mr. Broadway hairstylist. The other man in every woman's life. Broadway and Van Ness.

THE SAGE

Donahue's assistant, Vicky Cunningham, calls Bonnie Simmons "the hardest-working person I have ever met." Among the feats and pleasures she undertook, Bonnie hosted and co-produced many of the station's specials.

BONNIE SIMMONS I grew up in New York, Westchester County, and ran away from home to become a hippie. My brother gave me a copy of *Harry Belafonte at Carnegie Hall.* My brothers were a lot older than me and listened to New York radio stations that played a lot of R & B and rock 'n roll music, so that's what I cut my teeth on. I remember buying the single of Phil Phillips's "Sea of Love" very early on.

I started hanging around at KSAN when my ex-husband was doing fill-in stuff there. I got to know Dusty and her husband well—Luther Green, he ran the Straight on Haight. We all hung out, and I got to know almost everybody at the station. It seemed every few months they had a new music director. The person kept that job until they started selling our promo copies; the record companies would give us ten or twelve copies of every new album, which were supposed to go to all of the jocks. Little by little they would stop getting their promo albums! Then everybody voted to remove that person as music director. Tony Pigg interviewed me when I first applied for a job as record librarian. He told me that he couldn't give me the job because he had talked to his astrologer and was told that a Virgo would be the best person for that job. I'm a Sagittarius. All those great organization tendencies, I guess.

DUSTY STREET As a DJ, I was tired of not getting decent record service, so I kind of usurped the music director job away from Tony. I needed lots of records. That's when I hired Bonnie.

BONNIE SIMMONS I waited until Tony got thrown out as music director. Dusty became music director, she hired me, and I was in! I never had any aspiration to be in radio. I never had been the kind who called the disc jockey when I listened to the radio at night—it just didn't occur to me to make any kind of personal connection that way. I came to it for the music. One of my first jobs when I got to San Francisco was inventorying records in White Front stores. Every day I drove to a different White Front store in the Bay Area and would go through the racks and write down what had sold. And without even realizing it, I became this kind of computer brain—I knew all the serial numbers for these records. I helped Dusty get all kinds of arcane R & B records, because we both shared a love for those. Record librarian and public service director—I think those two jobs came together. If you seemed fairly competent, they also made you an engineer and producer for the talk shows on Sunday morning, so I would come to work at 5 a.m. and be the person that put on the Alan Watts tape. So, in a lot of ways, I owe it to Dusty Street.

DUSTY STREET We'd have great music meetings: sit around in Tom's office, somebody would have a six-pack, somebody else would roll a joint, and we played records for each other. Everybody was responsible for bringing in at least two records—one of the ways we got a cross-selection of music. If you talk to a disc jockey, they're very protective of their music collection. Not at KSAN. (But I never listened to anybody anyway; I'm a complete egotist. The only people I ever listened to were Voco and Bobby Dale. Everybody else bored the tears off me.)

BONNIE SIMMONS A few days into my library job, Willis Duff put out a memo: no one was allowed to bring their dogs to work any longer. Furthermore, no one was allowed to smoke dope anywhere in the building. The next morning, a large pile of dog poop appeared in front of his office with two roaches in it. I knew I had come to the right place of employment.

In a semi-related story, KSAN did lots of lost dog announcements; Big Daddy said, "Partly because Janis Joplin's dog seemed to get lost about once a week."

BEN FONG-TORRES In 1972, I got a call about a lost dog. The caller was Dianne Sweet, a devoted listener, and a fellow alumnus of San Francisco State, where I knew her as a homecoming queen candidate and she knew me as this geek editor of the campus newspaper, *The Gator*. We met after that call. By 1976 we were married. Just one story of a radio station's impact. There are thousands. KSAN, as my wife Dianne put it, was more than just hip in its music and presentation. It was a true bulletin board that allowed all its listeners to connect for any reason: a ride to Colorado; a rent party, waterbed for sale, lost dogs. This bulletin board was the community's Craigslist.

SIDE TRIP

Bonnie Simmons and Bill Graham

In '72, Bonnie shepherded a months-long project—just pulled together by airtime, of course—a seventy-two-hour tribute to Bill Graham. The rock 'n roll impresario was closing the Fillmore Auditorium, where he'd booked acts from all over the world who wanted to dig the San Francisco scene. Jive 95ers Milan Melvin, Ben Fong-Torres, Jeff Nemerovski, and musician Nick Gravenites join Bonnie and Joel Selvin, of course, as our guides to the event and the man.

BONNIE SIMMONS It was 24-7 in the studio. Milan Melvin, a wonderful guy, was tasked with producing.

MILAN MELVIN What happened was, after the Medicine Ball Caravan, I spent a year in Nepal. Two things became clear to me: One, I wanted to spend the rest of my existence in the Himalayas. And two, I had no money to do so. So I flew back to San Francisco, and with my tail tucked between my legs, I asked Donahue for work.

BONNIE SIMMONS *The Fillmore Special* would be one-hour segments honoring the seventy-two shows Graham put on. It took months. We found as much live music as we could—we went out to Bill's house in Mill Valley and asked if we could borrow a bunch of his shows. We knew Bill would tape them, though he didn't always tell the artist he was. And he had *all these reel-to-reels.*

Seven-inch reels, some moldy—rainy Northern California—and he said, "Sure, use them."

MILAN MELVIN We had hours of his recordings, and I brought in hours of interviews.

BONNIE SIMMONS We worked mixing all of that together. Each hour was a little "pack" we passed to everyone taking a shift: "Here's a bunch of this music that goes along with this hour, a couple of interviews of people talking about Bill." And we had Bill Graham. Basically, he tried to stay awake seventy-two hours and talk to us about the artists. The man didn't leave the station for three days. During long sets, he would take twenty-minute catnaps on a pasha pillow—one of those big waterbed pillows in the library.

BEN FONG-TORRES Bill Graham was a movie of a man.

JEFF NEMEROVSKI Wolfgang Grajonza was a Holocaust survivor who as a boy walked across Europe, and he didn't speak English when he arrived in America.

BEN FONG-TORRES His life of sixty years, which began in New York and came to an end in a helicopter crash in Sonoma County, was an endless reel of stories. In 1965, Bill Graham began staging concerts at the Fillmore in San Francisco.

JOEL SELVIN The rancorous side of his personality became a trademark. He'd flash a genial smile—after bellowing some poor character into submission over the phone—to let intimates know it was just another acting exercise.

JEFF NEMEROVSKI He told me going ballistic was an act. If people thought you were crazy, they'd back down.

MILAN MELVIN I always made the weekly call from KSAN to Graham my first call of the day because I knew he'd be sitting there at seven in the morning wearing his two watches—one for local time, one for New York—yelling into the phone, threatening some agent or manager that he wouldn't book their bands into the Fillmore ever again if the guy let his bands work at the Avalon or the Carousel. In the course of a morning's round of business, you could get loaded by Chet Helms at the Avalon or get a tongue-lashing from Bill Graham at the Fillmore.

JEFF NEMEROVSKI So, a volatile temper, but a remarkable man.

MILAN MELVIN We got into a fight at the Oakland Coliseum in 1969, rolling around on stage under the piano, with various members of our respective security details trying to break it up. The audience loved it!

BONNIE SIMMONS Michael Bloomfield—a very, very funny guy—did a piece for the special where he and Bill really got into it.

MILAN MELVIN The thing is, everyone I interviewed, it was adulation and worship. I asked Bobby Weir for something to balance his litany of praise, and all he said was, "Well, Bill's a real competitor. If he plays baseball, he'll push you out of the way if you're between him and the base." As I kept digging, I realized every damn musician depended on Graham for their livelihood. Finally, I cornered Honest Nicky the Greek. Nick Gravenites.

BONNIE SIMMONS Bill got into a fight with Nick Gravenites on the air—pretty good radio.

MILAN MELVIN Gravenites told me that Bill had told Janis and her band to stop smoking weed backstage. Janis was Janis, of course, and ignored him. After a set, she returned to the green room, and he was hiding in an armoire, waiting. When the scent of weed reached him, he burst out, grabbed her by the neck, and threw her down the stairs. Cut to the Fillmore weekend. I put on the Gravenites interview. Bill is sitting next to me, and all he can do is a slow burn. Janis had been dead just two years, and the loss was still fresh and painful to many of us. I ran into Gravenites a few years later and asked how it was going, and he said, "Terrible! Graham never hired me after that interview I did with you!"

A few dozen hours into his special, Bill has to go. He must go. He does not move. To set up what Bill and Bonnie talk about, this is Sammy Hagar: singer, songwriter, guitarist with bands like Montrose and Van Halen.

SAMMY HAGAR KSAN was all anyone listened to. It was the gospel. When I first got hip to it, I was like, this is the shit, man! This is like, wow, how cool is this? I just heard five songs in a row without a commercial! You could walk in if you were a local artist with an original song you'd written and recorded, and if it was decent, they'd just put it on the air.

Excerpts from the special:

BONNIE SIMMONS We talked about moving that Hammond B3 organ up sixty-four steps at the Fillmore. You've just played Montrose. Vanilla Fudge. This is *Bill Graham's Disc Jockey Show*! How did you happen to record Montrose doing "Town without Pity" along with "The Connection" when Sammy Hagar was still in the group?

BILL GRAHAM There must've been a full moon or something. It shows an artist's versatility.

BONNIE SIMMONS What's your next record here?

BILL GRAHAM One of the things about Elton John I've always liked is, before he got to the point where—everybody gets bored with seventy days supporting the product—before that, he really performed. He was not one of those to duplicate in concert the songs on the record. One of *the* great entertainers. . . . He never came close after that first album. That album to me, one of the dozen best of all the albums of this era. "Border Song," "Sixty Years On." The arrangements and the voice are exceptional. [Bonnie spins "Sixty Years On" from the 1970 LP, *Elton John.*]

BILL GRAHAM Bonnie, I have to go.

BONNIE SIMMONS We were going to do another day or two of this. Right now some people called up about the Kinks.

BILL GRAHAM Ray Davies. When they write the history of rock 'n roll, his name is gonna shine along with the others. A very inventive, creative wacko and . . .

BONNIE SIMMONS Why do you say "wacko"?

BILL GRAHAM Maybe it's the wrong word. A man who goes his own way and never wants to hurt anybody, but will take his own road, make his own paths, and will set a trend or fail to set a trend with what he's doing. He will not look for computerized solutions. He's a trendsetter. Maybe nobody follows him.

BONNIE SIMMONS [laughs] God save the Kinks!

BILL GRAHAM God save the Kinks is right. Without the Kinks, they'd all be pretty dull. The experimenters. The chemists of rock 'n roll.

BONNIE SIMMONS One of your favorite songs, is it not?

BILL GRAHAM Oh yes, my favorite band.

BONNIE SIMMONS Bill just mentioned that what he likes about this song is where they stop in the middle?

BILL GRAHAM And go again.

BONNIE SIMMONS It's the Grateful Dead and "Sugar Magnolia." K-S-A-N in San Francisco. Sean Donahue up next. [Bill, off-mic, says something that makes Bonnie laugh.]

SIDE TRIP

The Forgotten Waterbed Wars of '71

Jeff Nemerovski was known to roam everywhere in and out of the station, including leading a band of Jivers streaking—that means running around naked, in case you missed, luckily or not, the mid-'70s—after beating rival, KSFO, in the ratings. (Nemo also supplied the tequila and arranged the live audio taking listeners through a shocked KSFO.) He also played a role in the waterbed wars, producing spots with Scoop Nisker and Roland Jacopetti. Also during that campaign, Dr. HipPocrates got to test his personal brand for *Rolling Stone*.

JEFF NEMEROVSKI Roland looped Dylan's "Lay Lady Lay" into my Magic Mountain Waterbeds spot. Everybody got promotional waterbeds. The bag, that is; you still need a liner, a frame, a pad, or a heater. By the end of the war, for eighty dollars you could get two. The craze burned out in six months because the beds flooded apartments and weighed a thousand pounds.

EUGENE SCHOENFELD *Rolling Stone* magazine had Dr. HipPocrates test one for a story they called "The World's Biggest Muff Dive." The guy who ran the company wanted me to have sex on his *Schoenfeld*, with an "exotic lady from another planet." Passed.

Unduplicated
Exposure
KSAN FM/95

Roland Jacopetti: "During the waterbed wars that began in 1971—and ended in 1971—we were given one for the lobby. Willis Duff thought it would make a great prop. He's in tie and suspenders, goatee and bicorn hat, Napoleonic. Chan in keffiyeh. Naked woman from some print ad the photographer was scheduled to shoot later. After this was a series of shots of us naked and bouncing. Willis thought that was going too far and left. When he got back we were still at it. 'I've got people coming to the station!' 'We are the people!' *Undulator Waterbed Company, Neptune Waterbeds, White Tiger Waterbeds, Pasha Pillow Waterbeds, Embryon Waterbeds, Wet Dream, Joyapeutic, Environmental Valve Waterbeds, and Porpoise Mouth Waterbeds—all were sponsors that year. How was it possible?"*

COURTESY BOB SIMMONS

SCOOP NISKER Undulator Waterbeds, Neptune Waterbeds, White Tiger Waterbeds, Pasha Pillow Waterbeds, Embryon Waterbeds, Wet Dream, Joyapeutic, Environmental Valve, Magic Mountain, and Porpoise Mouth Waterbeds—all were sponsors. "If I can't have a waterbed, I ain't gonna be in your revolution!"

The station held a "Why I Want a Waterbed" contest—essays judged on "neatness, originality, and general lasciviousness." And, in Cameron Crowe's 2021 film, *Licorice Pizza*, a DJ based on Donahue's pal, Bob Mitchell, is pictured pitching waterbeds at KMPX's sister, KPPC in Pasadena. Some boomers may also recall Robert Heinlein's description of a waterbed in his 1961 novel, *Stranger in a Strange Land*. (A love generation favorite!)

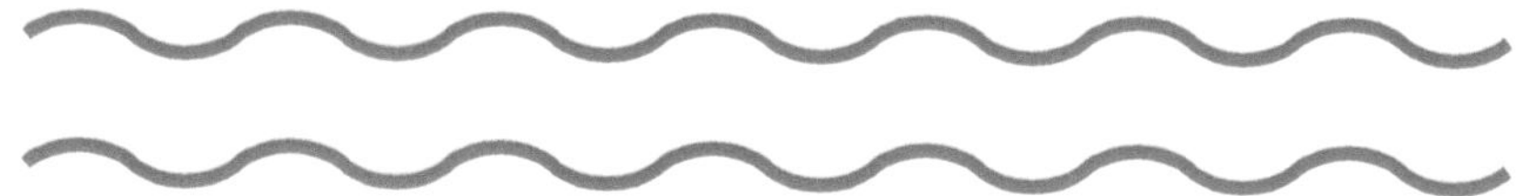

SIDE TRIP

Millhouse

Spot, 1971

Announcer: Emile de Antonio's Millhouse, *a white comedy in the tradition of the Marx Brothers, reminds us of how lucky we are we still have Nixon to kick around. [Nixon's voice] "I come before you as a candidate for the vice presidency, and as a man whose honesty and integrity has been questioned." The* New York Times *said,* "Millhouse *the film, not the man, is brilliant." The* San Francisco Chronicle *said, "We can only hope Nixon will not see* Millhouse, *for it is a real political bruiser." Direct from its premiere at the San Francisco Film Festival, now playing at the Presidio Theater, all seats are two dollars for this exclusive Bay Area engagement.*

http://www.jive95.com/mp3s/ads/ads2.mp3
Samples of PSAs and spots, the John Lennon movie *How I Won the War*, a "Hey Jude" revolt at Music Odyssey stores, contents of the new *Oui* magazine, waterbeds, bands like Pavlov's Dog—taken together worth a study, in *Adbusters* magazine. 58 minutes.

The arc of Donahue continued bending toward revolution. After *Broadcasting* magazine's Donald West noted a "bomb-thrower" taint to the name "underground radio," Donahue explained that it wasn't about violent revolution, but a social one. He never worried about sponsors being reluctant to lose their chains over FM radio. "The establishment has financed every revolution the world's ever had," he said. "And they'll finance this one, too." Especially now, "when more and more freaks are working in ad agencies."

SPOTS

Commercialization and Its Discontents

http://www.jive95.com/mp3s/ads/binaca.mp3
Two Binaca ads.

JOEL SELVIN The advertising agencies that first discovered underground radio, the first couple years—they couldn't believe it. Because the rates were nothing, you could saturate those things for bubkes. You could buy coolness and hipness, just by putting your stupid ad on underground radio, which had a really active listenership that was totally identifying with the product. It was the mid-'70s before FM radio really flexed their economic might—Ford and Toyota. Before then, there were all these independent guys. Remember, "Fall into the Gap!" The company used to be called the Generation Gap.

NORMAN DAVIS We were a most unusual kind of radio station, in that we were owned by a giant corporation, and yet we had a policy of not airing commercials we didn't approve of. I can't imagine a commercial station doing that today. Ain't possible. Metromedia had a national sales force out of New York and LA selling time to big sponsors and placing the spots on their seven stations. Revlon, Clairol, car companies. We wouldn't play the ones Metro sent us that insulted our audience.

STEFAN PONEK We liked the sales guys, but we made their job extremely difficult. We printed them business cards with psychedelic lettering on 3 x

5 stock, which didn't fit regular card files. And that was the whole idea. We worked hard to make these kinds of statements. For posters, we shunned the Peter Max flowers-in-the-hair, love image and held to a kind of purity of taste—underground radio featured underground artists—which frustrated the advertising community. But we'd also praise advertisers on the air.

Spot, 1970
Stefan Ponek: The situation with the new Beatle album Hey Jude *is a pretty interesting one. A few months ago, the manufacturer announced they were gonna release this thing at a list price of 6.98. Well that struck a lot of people outrageously. Especially Music Odyssey and a few other retailers. They made it clear to the manufacturer that they would not carry a 6.98 Beatles album. Well the album is now released, and Music Odyssey and the people from the other stores are pleased that after the months of pressure they brought to bear,* Hey Jude *is emerging with a 5.98 list price on it. And right now, Music Odyssey's featuring the new Beatle album at 2 dollars 99 cents, not only* Hey Jude, *but actually all one-record Beatle albums are being featured now through next Tuesday at just 2.99 apiece. This is a chance to pick up that Beatle album that you need to complete your collection. All but the* White Album, *at 2.99 each, at Music Odyssey, 3628 Geary near Arguello, open till at least 11 every night.*

BONNIE SIMMONS We found corporate ads insipid. Or hideous. Or mind chewing. We thought we knew the audience better. We would ask sponsors to let us make our own.

NORMAN DAVIS We did this for a while. But an awful thing happened to our spot for Binaca, the famous little breath spritz.

RAECHEL DONAHUE If you were a pot smoker, you had to have Binaca. Otherwise you would just reek.

NORMAN DAVIS Still do.

BONNIE SIMMONS Rick Sadle and our production team made these fantastic spots, with a jingle they pulled out of some English folk group's album.

RAECHEL DONAHUE "Fight air pollution with a little fresh in your breath!"

NORMAN DAVIS We didn't get permission in this case.

BONNIE SIMMONS Somehow we forgot to ask the client if we could run our own. And we ran them for four months. The most prestigious advertising award in the world are called the Clio awards, right?

RAECHEL DONAHUE The advertising world's Grammys.

BONNIE SIMMONS And we *won*. The Clios called Binaca and told them how great it was.

RAECHEL DONAHUE "You'll be presented with your award soon."

RICK SADLE The Binaca people and their ad agency were pretty excited—"Our spots turned out great!" Then they heard the spots. That's what brought us down.

RAECHEL DONAHUE "I don't think we have any paperwork on that."

RICK SADLE They demanded, on threat of lawsuit, that we run *their* Binacas.

BONNIE SIMMONS We end up with three times the Binaca spots.

RAECHEL DONAHUE We had to run their free Binaca spots forever.

RICK SADLE As a "make good," instead of us refunding their money.

RAECHEL DONAHUE But they still billed us on the hip ones. So go figure.

BONNIE SIMMONS And there was often a conflict, doing the kind of news we did. Many times the sales people brought us commercials that we vehemently opposed. I once went to the sales department and said, "You realize Gallo wine is just about to be in a strike situation, right? Our advice is, you might not want to take that buy." World War Three at KSAN. I remember thinking Metromedia's not gonna let us turn this down. McQueen said, "I'll take care of it." The morning of the commercial, there were four hundred UFW picketers in front of the station. They took the spots off.

DAVE MCQUEEN Once I did one that went, "Bank of America . . . just a stone's throw away." They didn't last as a sponsor, either.

DJ Richard Gossett: "Sitting in my little room on Fulton & Stanyan, I heard Traffic's 'Dear Mr. Fantasy' and stopped studying Forestry at SF State."
COURTESY BOB SIMMONS

24

THE PUNK

Johnnie Walker was a star at the BBC. He played records from the hull of a ship—Radio Caroline, the great North Sea pirate blasting the UK. But his dream was to work at the "most famous fucking station in the USA." Richard Gossett was one of the first DJs Johnnie met there when he came on board in '76.

JOHNNIE WALKER Richard Gossett was a tall, laconic DJ doing the 6 p.m. to 10 p.m. shift, playing the coolest collection of American and British FM music, which he presented in a wonderful, laid-back style. I loved to hang around KSAN watching Richard doing his show while he drank beer and smoked spliffs. Visitors popped by with coke, much as people bringing wine to a party, and Richard would gradually get more and more wasted, which was fine, really, as most of his audience was doing exactly the same. This was a far cry from my gig at Radio One. I loved it! I heard Mick Jagger once called KSAN "Radio One." It was said Clint Eastwood took a lot from Richard when developing his character for the film *Play Misty for Me*.

RICHARD GOSSETT Well, I don't know about that, but if you really wanna know about it: I was just a Bay Area kid, nineteen, and listening to Bob Dylan. Going to the College of San Mateo. Pretty soon I was coming up to the city a lot and going to the Blue Unicorn Coffeehouse, a poetry place. I grew up listening to Tony Pigg at KYA AM, and I got to meet him—he was dating Nikola, this English girl who was living in my house, a model at a Polk Street boutique called Orbit. Something like that. Tony invited me to come up to KYA. I was already a huge radio fan, listening to KOBY, KNEW, and so forth. I went up and was *mesmerized*. Tony had a great voice and a great temperament in the studio.

One day in '67, I was sitting in my little room on Fulton and Stanyan, and KMPX is playing Traffic, "Dear Mr. Fantasy," one of my favorite songs. And listening to that song . . . I don't know, suddenly I stopped taking forestry—I was studying forestry at San Francisco State University. (I got a D-minus in trigonometry, so that helped; I wasn't going to do any surveying.) The scene here was so huge at that point. There were just so many things to do, and music everywhere—but I was still going to school, mostly for the social aspect of it. I didn't need to be in school. I could've done something else probably—maybe be a farmer, because I love agriculture. But I didn't want to go to Vietnam, so I was studying. We were all going to school, the main reason being to stay out of the army.

When Tony Pigg and Tom Donahue went from KYA to KMPX, I used to sit on the floor and watch them do their shows. Watch and listen. I learned so much from those guys. When I started working at KNEW as a talk show producer, I would go into the back studio and practice my turntables and segues, use the microphone. I finally gave Tom a tape. "Tom, I want to be on the air." And he was just, "Kid, you need to get some experience." So after they all moved in '68 to KSAN, I went to their old station, KMPX. After a year of that, I got fired, but I had done really well, I guess, because when I went over to KSAN and asked Stefan Ponek for a job, he said, "Yeah, we've got the Sunday overnight show." I was scared, didn't talk much, because all I wanted to do was play music! I never really wanted to be an announcer—the kind of DJ who goes from any station to any station. I wanted to play music that would turn everyone on to the possibilities of a lot more going on.

TRISH ROBBINS Richard Gossett was gorgeous.

TERRY MCGOVERN I loved Richard Gossett. It was like listening to a guy drinking Heinekens in his living room.

DUSTY STREET

That's from the new Dave Mason album, Shouldn't Have Took More Than You Gave. *Anyway, I'm never gonna get tired of that album, man; it's just, really just so fine and mellow and pretty in your ears. That's called "Alone Together," it's on Blue Thumb, and the release date was today! So if you go out to your record stores tomorrow—or I think maybe Music Odyssey is open until midnight—you can run down, get your very own, and put it on your stereo system and just have yourself some fine music for the rest of your life. Or the life of the record. And knowing that record, you'll probably have to buy a couple of copies. This is KSAN Stereo 95 in San Francisco and Oakland. This is Dusty until two with music and things, just for you.*

In '69, Dusty Street, standing on a truck bed, introduced Country Joe McDonald and Sons of Champlain to fourteen hundred inmates at San Quentin.

DUSTY STREET It was on the prison football field. I jumped off the truck and danced under the rope line. I was twenty-two. I was wild. There were no fences in my life. "Hope the guys in cell block five are having a good day—there's a riot goin' on!" I said, "I understand you make a lot of jewelry. It'd be really cool to see some of your art!" I had to duck all the bracelets, necklaces, and rings they threw on the stage. Inmates made a poster, and they signed it, "Dusty, you're beautiful! Play more rock!"

John Grivas, a DJ in 1973, admired "Superchick."

JOHN GRIVAS That woman had soul; there was just something in the way she moved. Dusty was so hip. She knew everything about the musicians we played and had big-time artists just drop in and talk with her on the air. I thought of her as an older, wiser, big sister. She told me she grew up in North Beach and the Beats would do her homework for her.

Richard's show was on the air before or after Dusty's for years.

RICHARD GOSSETT Here's something I like to do when I'm with Dusty. Ready? "Mother Earth is pregnant for the third time for y'all have knocked her up!"

DUSTY STREET Parliament Funkadelic!

RICHARD GOSSETT Metromedia told us we couldn't play that. We had to cue past it, Street, remember? Somebody even took a knife and cut a little thing in it so we couldn't play it.

CHAPTER 24

When Dusty showed up for her shift, Richard might have a few friends with him in the studio.

RICHARD GOSSETT I got off at ten. And if I happened to be lucky to have a couple of ladies visiting, sitting and enjoying the show, Street, you were brutal! "Who are these sluts?" Four eighteen-year-olds, out the door in a flash. But that's okay. Actually, Street and I never did anything too goofy, except drop acid a couple times.

DUSTY STREET You dosed me, man!

RICHARD GOSSETT I gave her some acid as I was getting off the air, thinking, *cool*. I had to stay around for the rest of your shift and decide whoever was more . . .

DUSTY STREET Capable?

RICHARD GOSSETT Capable to be on the air. We kept playing music even though we couldn't talk. Big problem for disc jockeys.

Sitting Dog, Romilar, Novocaine, and Wavy Gravy

> *Lo and behold, I had what I simply could not deny being an experience of cosmic consciousness, the sense of complete fundamental unity, forever and ever with the whole universe. And not only that! But that what this thing was fundamentally—despite everything and every kind of appearance in ordinary life to the contrary—that the energy behind the world was ecstatic bliss and love.*
>
> —Alan Watts

Every year around Thanksgiving, Sitting Dog would come visit from his commune up in Oregon. With good cheer and amazing chocolate cookies, he left us wearing John Prine smiles into another year. "Enjoy a new orbit around the source of all life!" Sitting Dog would wish us, cosmically.

TERRY MCGOVERN Of all the stories from '67, my favorite was Scoop's, reporting from the Haight, which was no longer the "Haight-Ashbury"—this was 1977, and we were looking back for the special, *What Was That?* Our Scoop-on-the-street asking, "How did you get high back then?" This one fellow said he stole novocaine from his dentist. He was already a Romilar user—cough syrup—so he'd drink a bottle, inject his feet with the novocaine, and go out for a stroll.

THOM O'HAIR The low point was GL-70. GL-70 was the one with all the bad side effects of DMT combined with the bad side effects of DET. You wanted to put your face down a toilet bowl to cool off. We thought two grams isn't much, just two little pieces. We took a ride down to the Haight, and all of a sudden I was afraid to change my expression. It felt like if I moved, all these rocks would come tumbling down. Like I was Mount Rushmore. I was *stoned* stoned.

MILAN MELVIN Wavy Gravy used to do a five-minute set in Berkeley at the Cabale—which Chandler Laughlin ran—at midnight for five dollars and a joint, before and after. One of his numbers was called "Wavy Gravy's Time Number." About the little fellow, down on the corner one day to make a connection. Sees a weird guy in an overcoat, so he sidles up, says:

"Whaddya got?"

"I've got time."

"I've never tried time."

"Try this."

Hands him a little black capsule: "This is a second."

Did a whole handful. Great. But after a while he wanted more. So he went back.

The guy said, "I've got some minutes. But they cost."

Eventually, he wound up doing hours. And then days. And you can't just pop a day. You've got to break it open and pull it down over you. And eventually it occurred to him that, like anything else, he might be getting a little strung. So he went down to the corner again and said to the guy, "Man, you sure this stuff isn't habit forming?"

Guy looks at him.

"It's fine," he says. "I've been on time for years."

PSA Frank Zappa

This is Frank Zappa from the Mothers of Invention. I would like to suggest that you do not use speed. And here's why: it is gonna mess up your heart, mess up your liver, your kidneys, rot your mind. In general, this drug will make you just like your mother and father.

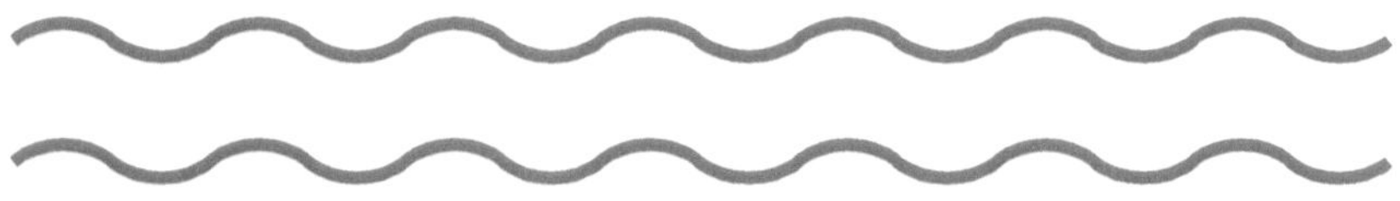

SIDE TRIP

The One and Only Terry McGovern

Good morning friends,
Here's your friendly announcer . . .
Love's in need of love today.
Don't delay, send yours in right away.

—Stevie Wonder, "Love's in Need of Love Today"

Terry McGovern was your morning fiend from '74 to '78.

VICKY CUNNINGHAM One morning he announced that you could get a decoder kit from KSAN and figure out our secret messages sent to listeners. I wanted to kill him. I had to find an artist to come up with a decoder so Terry could send the messages, after we'd gotten hundreds of requests for decoders that did not exist!

TERRY MCGOVERN As most things are, how I got there was a series of events: I was friends with Dusty Street; we would close a bar here and there. She got so deluded, she ended up thinking I would be a great addition to KSAN. I said, I love that station; we listen every Saturday night I'm partying. (Every radio in the fucking town was wired to KSAN.) She prevails on Donahue, Big Tom, three hundred and God knows how many pounds of fun. And he calls. "I'll tell you what, grab your wife [Molly] and come see me. I'm in Acapulco."

Terry McGovern, Beth Elliot, and Fee Waybill play outside the station at 345 Sansome, mid-1970s.
PHOTO BY RICHARDMCCAFFREY.NET

I thought, *This sounds like my crowd.* We get down there and discover he has two hotels rented out, in case he can't get to the other? Molly was just a little skinny thing; I didn't weigh more than 150 myself. And Tom, this enormous man, we all get into the hot tub. Salinger has a line in *Franny and Zooey*, "like the *Queen Mary* had just sailed out of Walden Pond." That was my picture of it. Don't splash around too much—he could crush us! And those gigantic paws with turquoise rings. He says, I want you to do the morning show. I say, I need this much money. He says, well, that's more than I pay. Not that much. I started doing the morning show.

VICKY CUNNINGHAM Terry McGovern was a ball of fire on the air. He stood the whole time, moving fast—his mind was really fast.

DAVE MCQUEEN It was nonstop with Terry. It never stopped being funny.

TERRY MCGOVERN One reason I wanted to be on KSAN was I knew I would toss it to Dave McQueen for the news! We worked together every morning. We weren't friends. Grudging respect—that was the most you could hope for from Dave. God almighty, what a voice! One of my favorite stories has to do with the Gnus Department. There's no closed doors at KSAN—I couldn't have been there more than a few days—and Peter Laufer comes flying in. He takes the needle off the turntable and says, "Gimme the mic! This just in from Cleveland! A woman from Shaker Heights was detained for killing her pet poodle by putting him in the microwave, thinking she could dry him that way. We'll have more in four hours!" I'm still standing there. "That's Peter Laufer. You only get him here."

PETER LAUFER I was twenty.

TERRY MCGOVERN I loved Python and played "Spam" a lot—every morning. Tom called me on it. "I think you're overdoing Monty Python." I said, "You do the rock 'n roll. I'll do the freaking comedy." I thought, *I must be out of my mind to say that.* He said, "All right, then," and hung up. Sometimes I thought he thought I was kind of a cute little bauble he'd acquired. KSAN was the experience of a lifetime: Raechel Donahue carrying a huge plate of mozzarella marinara into a staff meeting. General manager Willis Duff coming out to party in his three-piece suit.

WILLIS DUFF I never—well, damn near—wore three-piece suits. None of our memories are what they used to be.

TERRY MCGOVERN Before I got there in '74, I used to listen during stolen moments where I worked, at KSFO. Like when they had the strike in '68. A strike at KMPX? The most fantastic thing I'd ever heard in my life come out of the radio: a station on strike. What? Then I find KSAN. I had joined the circus! I kept my shit together, so never did the drugs. Certainly not on the air. We always had good dope: Jamaican. Thai stuff. Record promoters, bless their pointy heads. One day, we were notified another bomb had been planted by another wacko group just this side or the other of the Weatherman. (Depending on the weather, ladies and gentlemen.) They sent a note: "We're writing to you the people's station, because at 9:05 this morning we're going to blow up the Bank of America on Kearny Street." So McQueen and Thom O'Hair read the thing and split. Left the building. Not that they didn't want to save lives, but they had scored a bunch of Thai stick and had had it hermetically sealed in a B of A safe deposit box. Their stash. "And it must not be destroyed." Or discovered.

McQueen & McGovern one morning in 1977.
PHOTO BY RICHARDMCCAFFREY.NET

BONNIE SIMMONS I never heard that Thai stick story before.

TERRY MCGOVERN Oh shit, it's a Rashomon central. You couldn't get three people to agree on a story at KSAN.

BONNIE SIMMONS We're like any other group of people. It's always Rashomon. When is it ever not Rashomon?

TERRY MCGOVERN Who knows if that's true? McQueen would just smile and nod his head. Could have been a Wells Fargo.

SIDE TRIP

Terry & Harry & Fred

FRED GREENE, Producer In 1978, after Terry McGovern left his morning show to do movies and TV in LA, we were auditioning a variety of DJs, including Peter Scott, Ben Fong-Torres—I vaguely remember, Johnny Walker —for the 6 to 10 shift. And I got to work with all these great people for a day or two. I remember, after Peter Scott's tryout, he ended up in the hospital; I saw him several months later and he went, "You! You!" And I went, "I didn't do anything!" Then Harry Shearer did two mornings that were incredibly fun and entertaining.

TERRY MCGOVERN Harry also filled in for me sometimes. We were good pals. I used to call his phone just for his outgoing message. I remember we wrote a piece at the Comedy Store called "Two Guys Stereo Asylum." We were the Comedy Store Players (Martin Short joined our group). Harry found a sweater that was big enough for both of us to put on, so when the lights came up there were these two heads coming out of one shirt. "Two Guys Stereo Asylum!" screaming back and forth at the audience.

FRED GREENE For his audition, Harry brought in all this produced stuff—I was running it on reel-to-reel—similar to the character sketches he did later for "Le Show" on KCRW in Santa Monica and then KCSN in Northridge. Great stuff. With about fifteen minutes left in the show, general manager Jerry Graham walks in and says, "You're hired. You got the job." Jerry begged him to take the job. And Harry's like, "That's okay, thanks very much. . . ." Jerry said, "You don't understand. We want you to be our morning man here at KSAN." And I'm dying, man, I wanna work with you! I grew up listening to him with the Credibility Gap on KPPC down in Los Angeles, so I knew who he was and I loved him. I was completely floored that he hadn't accepted. Jerry kept making offers. Getting nowhere. When the record was over, Jerry had to walk out of the studio and we saw him through the glass, head down, totally rejected. I asked Harry, "Well, why not?" And that was when he taught me an important lesson. He said, "I love radio too much to do it every day."

SIDE TRIP

Live Jive! The Record Plant in Sausalito

https://archive.org/details/audio?and%5B%5D=KSAN&sin
The Record Plant in Sausalito, north of the Golden Gate in Marin County, recorded dozens of shows for KSAN.

The Record Plant, north of the Golden Gate, in Sausalito recorded dozens of KSAN shows.

BONNIE SIMMONS The quality of the Record Plant broadcasts was unsurpassed: twenty-four-track with a half-inch master. A small audience in the studio. KSAN, as it turns out, pioneered live broadcasts of rock 'n roll performances.

CRAIG CHAQUICO, guitarist, Jefferson Starship Our band Steel Wind did a live show that KSAN broadcast from there. State of the art! The band had a place in the Tenderloin when we drove in from Sacramento. We all lived together in one apartment. Boy, those were the days!

BONNIE SIMMONS Before the Record Plant, wherever we could, we set someone up to play. I would come to work, and Dan Hicks & His Hot Licks were already in the record library.

RICHARD GOSSETT We had José Feliciano in the library.

BONNIE SIMMONS Commander Cody set up in the library. Musicians would look to KSAN when they'd come to town. And, having worked with bands, I know this well: you're kind of disoriented on the road. You don't really have any constants in any given city. We became this sort of hub for musicians. We'd see artists and record company people coming to KSAN as though coming to the altar. I remember when Sun Ra set himself up in the library. He went and stationed the group in different cubicles around the entire office, because he thought it'd be fun to see how that sounded.

Station ID
If I had my choice I would never leave my house or car
Leaving my radio behind is going a bit too far
And the station that I listen to is the one that you do too
It's San-Fran-cis-co, K-S-A-N
Folk jazz blues and rock 'n roll, K-S-A-N!

—Dan Hicks & His Hot Licks

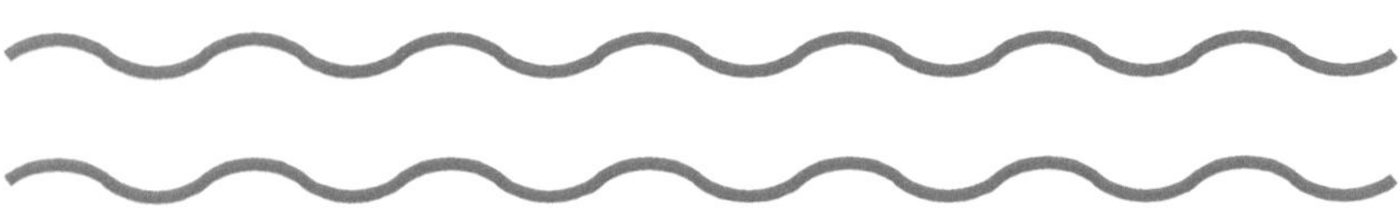

SIDE TRIP

The First Dead Interview

https://archive.org/search?query=phil+lesh+kmpx

Jerry Garcia and Phil Lesh were the first guests Donahue interviewed on KMPX. Given space-time limitations (find the complete chat via the QR), consider this an eavesdrop on San Franciscan radios on a spring night in '67—with the Dead going to New York City for the first time.

TOM DONAHUE [record fades] Okay, that's by the Swan Silvertones. Some of the first music I got with was gospel music. As a matter of fact, the first record I ever made was with a gospel group in Charlestown, West Virginia. That's a super bad record, man. [laughter]

PHIL LESH Like our first record.

JERRY GARCIA Oh, he knows all about our first record.

TOM DONAHUE Yeah, I was trying to get clearance on playing some of the early stuff on the air, but we'll get around to that some other night . . . you'll be up here. The immediate reaction with most groups, "Look man, I'd like to play your early stuff," and it's, "Whew, don't do that."

JERRY GARCIA Some of it's really interesting.

TOM DONAHUE Yeah, some of its interesting, because you can see the differences. I was talking about writing album notes last night, and I said that I finally figured out a way to do it—sign a different name, so years later my name isn't on there, 'cause I know how ridiculous it's gonna look [laughter]. I notice you didn't have any liner notes on your album.

JERRY GARCIA No, none of us can read very well.

PHIL LESH None of us can write, either.

JERRY GARCIA Yeah, right.

TOM DONAHUE What would you wanna say on liner notes?

PHIL LESH The only person who could have conceivably written ours would've been Kesey. And by the time the album came out, it just didn't seem right to even approach him on that.

JERRY GARCIA After all, it is a record; it's not a magazine [laughter].

PHIL LESH However, if anyone wants to peel back the label, there's hieroglyphics engraved in the wax.

TOM DONAHUE Beautiful. People will be tearing LPs apart all over the city [laughter].

SIDE TRIP

Congress of Wonders/Firesign Theatre/ Duck's Breath Mystery Theater/ the Credibility Gap

In '68, the Congress of Wonders was the "first three-man disc jockey team ever, 6 to 10 a.m. on splendiferous KSAN." The troupe, Wesley Hind ("Earl Pillow"), Howard Kerr ("Karl Truckload") and Richard Rollins ("Winslow Thrill") produced, with Roland Jacopetti, sketches and public service announcements.

Father: Son, you've got to get a haircut!

Billy: Aww, dad . . .

Mother: Billy, Billy!

Father: I can't understand what's gotten into you.

Billy: Aw, Dad . . .

Mother: Billy, Billy!

Father: You've been hanging around with those musicians.

Mother: Billy, Billy!

Billy: But Dad, we're forming a rock band!

Father: Psychedelic brain rot!

Billy: Oh, Dad, you're so uptight, you'll never understand. Never, never!

Father: You know what I think? I think you're on the stuff! If I thought you were on the stuff, I'd turn you in for your own good!

Mother: Robert, Robert! Don't be an idiot. It's true you are uptight.

Billy: Mother, mother!

Father: Uptight? I'm not uptight! I'm never uptight!

Billy: Dad, dad!

Mother: Just because you don't agree with what Billy is doing, you don't have to turn him into a criminal!

Announcer: If you know what were legalized, it would save a lot of people a lot of pain.

PHIL PROCTOR, the Firesign Theatre After the release of our second LP, *How Can You Be in Two Places at Once When You're Not Anywhere at All*, we started performing at KMPX's sister station, KPCC: *The Firesign Theatre's Radio Hour Hour*, for a live audience in a Presbyterian church basement in Pasadena. Radio is the most marvelous of media. Our comedy album material was disseminated and inseminated by the FM radio revolution. Underground radio blossomed at the same time as the recording industry started to grow. FM allowed Firesign to change the expectations of comedy for listeners—some freaky broadcasting major on a college station could play an entire side, which allowed listeners to steep themselves in the soundscapes we created. A listener would go, "What's that?!" buy it, and play it for their friends. That's a different culture. That's not exactly the iPod culture.

Station ID

PETER BERGMAN Hi! This is Gary the Seeker, and we're here in the Golden Gate City with the Firesign Theatre! Listening o'course to—

DAVID OSSMAN K-S-A-N FM! The Jive 95! 95 point nothing on your San Francisco dial!

PHIL AUSTIN Uh, no, Ray. While you were talking that went up again to, uh, one thousand and 95. [different voice] Well, I guess this proves once again I was right! I'm Dr. "Happy" Harry Cox and, ya know? Everything you know . . . is wrong!

PETER, DAVID, PHIL So long, Seekers!

GARY The longer the better!

PHIL PROCTOR I was working out of town during that. But satire is really what fueled us, us fools in those days.

In '78, Duck's Breath Mystery Theatre (Jim Turner, Leon Martell, Merle Kessler, Dan Coffey, and Bill Allard) created a serial for KSAN, produced by Rick Sadle, called *Rodo the Monster from Outer Space.* Duck's Breath also recorded a local hit, the "Herb Caen Blues."

https://steampoweredradio.com/ksan%20audioclips.html
Some funny IDs: from the Persuasions to Peter Tosh, Mel Brooks to Martin Mull (does a Neil Young zinger). The Jive site has others, including Bob Marley and Carol Doda.

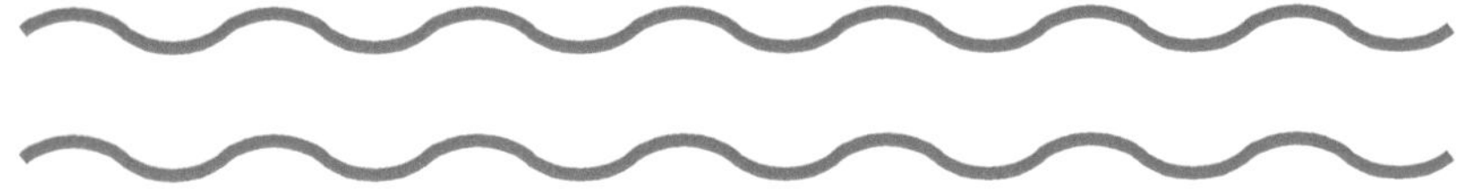

SIDE TRIP

John Lennon Dies in a Movie

Tom Donahue Ramparts *magazine spot 1967*

"A Beatle is [echo effect] DEAD*! ["A Day in the Life" plays] John Lennon dies right there on the cover of* Ramparts *magazine in a scene from his new motion picture,* How I Won the War! *Lest we forget,* Ramparts *has produced large posters of this bloody scene in full color. And they are only available as a gift to you with each subscription to* Ramparts. *The posters will not be sold. To get yours, just send a special introductory price of two dollars eighty-seven cents for a six-month subscription, to Beatle, care of KMPX,*

50 Green Street, San Francisco. And send it soon. They can't last long. And then look for your copy of Ramparts *with the full story on John Lennon's newest and most controversial film . . . the one where he dies! That's two dollars eighty-seven cents to Beatle, care of KMPX, 50 Green Street, San Francisco. To get* Ramparts *for six months and John Lennon forever!*

LENNON AND DONAHUE

The *Walls and Bridges* Interview

https://www.youtube.com/watch?v=rESDzsROwSM
Excerpt of Donahue with Lennon. 1974, 27 minutes.

In 1974, John and Yoko visited the Donahue home on Telegraph Hill.

RAECHEL DONAHUE The thing I remember most was, she was the most hated wife in America. But we really got along with them. They were staying down the street from us. All of a sudden in the middle of the night you'd hear, "Waaa!" They were doing their primal scream therapy at the time.

Lennon had just completed *Walls and Bridges* and brought it to play for Tom, a friend since the Beatles performed their last American concert, in '66 at Candlestick Park (see chapter 1). Lennon is more gleeful now. He knows he can be playful with possibly the hippest mate he met in '66. They discuss *Rubber Soul*, *Revolver*, ELO, writing a hundred songs, TM, escaping a mad guru, and falling in love with Dylan.

TOM DONAHUE That song ["I'm the Greatest"] has a lot to say about you too, right?

CHAPTER 25

JOHN LENNON Yeah, I started this song and kept wanting to . . . Oh, hello, Tom! How are you?

TOM DONAHUE Hello, how are you.

JOHN LENNON [In his "I hope we passed the audition" funny voice] *Long time, how are you, great!* Yeah! I had the bit about "I'm the greatest" around. And the little piano lick. For quite a bit. And I always thought, I can't sing that, I can't sing that, they're all gonna say, "It's him singing he's the greatest." [Tom laughs] And I kept trying; I'll change it, I'll change it. And I could never change it! *Oh. Ringo!* So I finished it off. I sort of, I wrote it for him. But it's really me, him, all of it, Tom.

TOM DONAHUE You've been real busy of late, right, working on what, two albums?

JOHN LENNON Yeah, I was in the middle of a Phil Spector album. It was '73, actually. And then Phil was ill, or had a car accident, and I waited, y'know. And he didn't get—[that voice again] *he didn't get better, like.* So I decided to go in and start me own album. Three days before I went in—I booked the time—suddenly he sent me the tapes. So from doing nothing for months on end, I'm just hanging out, suddenly I had all this work. Which I liked. So I went in to do me own album [that voice] *which I brought with me of course!*

TOM DONAHUE Only thing to do with Phil Spector is wait.

JOHN LENNON Yeah, he still thinks we're working on the *last* album. [they laugh]

TOM DONAHUE He has a different concept of time than the rest of us.

JOHN LENNON So I finished one, while we were waitin', and I'll go back and deal with Phil's tapes, see what we did!

TOM DONAHUE Right. And you've done the Nilsson album, recently.

JOHN LENNON Oh yeah! I forgot about that! Yeah. Yeah. *Pussy Cats. Pussy Cats.* Did that while I was waitin' for Phil. And I just sorta got turned on to not being a singer, being behind the board, so I thought, *I might as well do me own,* now. So I went straight from Harry's into my own—used basically the same musicians, too.

TOM DONAHUE Doesn't sound you've been loafing very much.

JOHN LENNON No, it's all or nothin' with me.

TOM DONAHUE Right. Okay, let's just start through the new album. With side one, cut one. That's where they put the song they like the most, or do ya? How do you figure it out?

JOHN LENNON It depends, ya know. I try and start it off with that. Except for when I did *Imagine.* I supposed *that* was the album, really. I usually try and put something that brings you in, but not too much. Just sort of medium. And that's what this is. It's called, "Going Down on Love." [Tom plays "Going Down on Love."]

TOM DONAHUE Okay, we're listening to John Lennon's new LP. And that was, "Going Down on Love." And you just go down on the microphone there, John.

JOHN LENNON Okay, that was "Going Down on Love," with Arthur Jenkins on his beautiful conga! He's the percussionist on the album. And the song really speaks for itself. I can't describe it. And, "we'd like to play another cut here now. Which is an instrumental. Which ended up on the B side of the single," he says, like he's on AM! Ha ha! It's called, "Beef Jerky," and I get off on this 'cause I don't have to hear me voice all the time. [Tom plays "Beef Jerky."]

TOM DONAHUE There we are, we're back.

JOHN LENNON There we are!

TOM DONAHUE You were gonna rap a bit, while I . . .

JOHN LENNON Okay, so let's think about it. That was an instrumental, that I just had the lick, and the thing is, I couldn't. I never played the lick on the guitar. Couldn't sing it and play it at the same time, so I never got any lyrics for it, so it ended up as instrumental. And I'm rather glad of it, really—what's that?

TOM DONAHUE "#1 Dream"?

JOHN LENNON "#9 Dream," yeah, that's fine. So this next one's called, "#9 Dream." For no reason at al'.

TOM DONAHUE You've numbered things a lot over the years?

JOHN LENNON Yeah, number 9 seems to crop up in me life. Even the cover of the album, I used a picture that I drew when I was a kid of twelve. It's a football picture, and the big, the main guy's got number 9 on the back, so, *that's my number*.

TOM DONAHUE Well, your birthday's October the 9th.

JOHN LENNON We had "Revolution Number 9," number nine, number nine . . . so, let's go.

[plays "Number 9 Dream"]

TOM DONAHUE This is Tom Donahue. I'm gonna do it till midnight tonight. John Lennon is our guest, and we're playing cuts from his new LP and it's uh . . .

JOHN LENNON It's all right!

TOM DONAHUE *Walls and Bridges*?

JOHN LENNON That's right, that's right.

TOM DONAHUE I'm always curious to know why people call an album what they call it.

JOHN LENNON Oh. Yeah. Well, normally I try not to think about the title until the end.

TOM DONAHUE Yeah.

JOHN LENNON And as usual, I didn't have a title. And I think I heard it on a public service announcement. You know, one of those "Brotherhood" or—late night, y'know? When they make you miserable in between the movies? [they laugh] I just heard somebody flash something about walls and bridges. And it stayed with me, and I almost called "#9," "Walls and Bridges." But it didn't make sense; it was one of those I liked the title, and I kept trying to fit it into somethin'.

TOM DONAHUE I figure it's never legitimate to ask a songwriter what a song means, but a title's a little different.

JOHN LENNON Yeah, a title's, I liked the thing, y' know. "Walls *and* Bridges." Like walls you bump into or that close you in, and bridges you go across or somethin' like that. And it was just puttin' it somewhere. Putting. It. Some. Where.

TOM DONAHUE There ya go.

JOHN LENNON Right.

TOM DONAHUE Puttin' it to 'em!

JOHN LENNON So I finally put it on the album. Nothing else came; I'll stick with the title until something better comes. And as the album finished, it seemed to be, without any thought, what it was about.

TOM DONAHUE Huh.

JOHN LENNON *Some kinda communication problems, ya know.* [they laugh] So, it fit in.

[Off mic: "Remember what we set up."] Oh! From the album. Oh. [whispers talk up of track] "What You Got."

TOM DONAHUE You were prompted on that. I forget a lot, you know?

JOHN LENNON Yeah, well I wasn't sure. I *wanna* play "Angel Baby."

CHAPTER 25

TOM DONAHUE We're gonna get to "Angel Baby."

JOHN LENNON Yeah. ["What You Got" plays]

JOHN LENNON [comes out of it singing] "Whatcha got, whatcha got . . ."

TOM DONAHUE I like that a lot. "What You Got."

JOHN LENNON Thank you. I like it, too.

TOM DONAHUE I guess you gotta like it all. I mean, you do more than is on the album.

JOHN LENNON Usually I have—on this album is eleven, which is odd—I usually have ten. Meaning, not for any reason other than, if you go over eighteen, nineteen, twenty minutes, it gets a bit *low*. So I just left one off this time. But usually I only have, exactly what I'm doing.

TOM DONAHUE Uh huh. We were talking about old records you liked. And "Angel Baby" was one of the first ones that came to mind.

JOHN LENNON That's one of me all-time favorites.

TOM DONAHUE I was trying to think what year "Angel Baby" would be.

JOHN LENNON I have no idea. I'm getting too old to remember. '62? I don't know; it sounds earlier than that. It's a pity we haven't got the B side, because the B side is one of the classic all-time funny records. It's not even the girl singin'. It's obviously somebody else singin'. They must've had five minutes to cut the B side—and the drummer's on beat all through it. Sax solo comes in too soon, so there's a big hole. The guitarist comes in, it's the funniest record. But "Angel Baby" is a beauty.

TOM DONAHUE It's one of the great bad records' there's a special category of records.

JOHN LENNON The B side of "Angel Baby" is one of the all-time great bad records. ["Give Me Love."]

TOM DONAHUE I think "Angel Baby" is, too.

JOHN LENNON Oh no! Aww, I couldn't. Don't say anything bad!

TOM DONAHUE I'm not saying in the sense of bad, I mean *bad.*

JOHN LENNON *Bad*, you mean *bad* bad.

TOM DONAHUE Bad bad, right.

JOHN LENNON *Baaad* bad. Yeah, that's it.

TOM DONAHUE And sometimes bad, too.

JOHN LENNON Sometimes bad. Here's a song about, "I love you so much." [plays "Angel Baby" by Rosie and the Originals.]

TOM DONAHUE That's "Angel Baby."

JOHN LENNON Ah, are we . . .

TOM DONAHUE Yeah, we're back. I wanna turn you on to one that . . .

JOHN LENNON Yeah?

TOM DONAHUE I think is in much the same *space*, as freaks say. It's by a fella named Ron Holden; it's called "I Love You So."

JOHN LENNON I'm writin' down a list of all the oldies here, y'know?

TOM DONAHUE Okay, let's get back to work. With ELO.

CHAPTER 25

JOHN LENNON I think they once said they were taking off where the Beatles left off with "Walrus," and I think this is a good result of it. ["Strange Magic" by Electric Light Orchestra]

TOM DONAHUE As somebody here was saying, that's another one that was, uh, stolen from the Beatles in a sense. Or borrowed, how's that?

JOHN LENNON No, I wouldn't call it stealin'. There's little movements here, y'know? That you can, almost pick which songs. But you can do that with Beatle music, too, if you know where our influences came from. And, what was it? On the "Showdown" one. We won't name where the pieces came from, because somebody might pick it up and sue 'em, y'know? [Tom laughs] There's two records there, but it's beautifully done, and it's improved. Well, it's uh . . .

TOM DONAHUE "Grapevine."

JOHN LENNON "Grapevine" and, uh, "Thunder," what is it, "Lightning Strikes Again." Lou Christie. But you could never place it. You know, if you wrote it out, it would look nothin' the same, if you wrote music.

TOM DONAHUE This is Tom Donahue, and you're at Jive 95, and John Lennon is our guest tonight, and we've been . . . well, we started off playing things from his new LP, and then took a turn somewhere down the road, got into some favorite records of his. We'll get back to that, but I thought it might be nice, since he is in town, to go back to *Walls and Bridges*.

JOHN LENNON That would be nice. We almost forgot about it, didn't we? We've got a pile of records here I been orderin' up. Uh, yeah, we're gonna play track two, side two, called "Surprise Surprise," and, yeah. Believe it or not, when I first started writin' this, it sounded like, "Little darlin', do do do do," but listen and you'll hear it's *nowhere* near it. Just 'cause I must mention there, that was Elton John singing harmony on that record. And we almost lost him on the mix. But it's there. [Tom laughs] On earphones, you really get it.

TOM DONAHUE How about the album Spector came in and worked on?

JOHN LENNON Is that the Beatles one?

TOM DONAHUE Right. Was there ever any thought about putting out the original version before he sweetened it?

JOHN LENNON Until you mentioned it, I'd even forgot there might even be one! I don't think we ever mixed it, ourselves.

TOM DONAHUE Uh huh.

JOHN LENNON Because by then, we hated it so much. Some of the tracks are pretty rough. Because we weren't cookin' at all. And nobody could face playing it, or mixin' it and going in; nobody wanted to do it, nobody had an interest in it. And . . .

TOM DONAHUE I suppose you, from time to time, listen to things you did with the Beatles.

JOHN LENNON Oh, I like listening to it!

TOM DONAHUE I mean, are there things that have gotten better to you over the years, you look back on and think, *Oh that was dynamite!*

JOHN LENNON Some have gotten better, inasmuch as I thought, I didn't like them at the time, y'know? Because I wanted it to be somethin' else. You know, you often go in with a sound in mind and come out with some, y'know, you go in and [deep voice] *you wanna be B. B. King* or whatever, and you come out, and you're not. And for years that hangs with you, you're trying to . . . and then I hear it and think, *Oh! That's okay. It wasn't as bad as I thought.* And, where were we?

TOM DONAHUE Uh, well, we're back on an album called *Walls and Bridges.*

JOHN LENNON No, we're in San Francisco!

TOM DONAHUE Right.

JOHN LENNON Hi! Yee!

TOM DONAHUE Did you do the drawings?

JOHN LENNON No, this is the first cover of an album that I didn't do meself. I like doing them. I mean, I like even pasting them together. But I was really too cookin' on the album to even think about it. So I let the guy at Capitol do it, Roy Kahara, and he turned out a nice job. Actually, it was originally gonna be the cover for [deep voice] *the Spector album*. Which we keep going back to.

TOM DONAHUE But you will be going back to it.

JOHN LENNON When I leave here, I'll go back to it. Back to New York. And so we used it for this instead. And it works the same.

TOM DONAHUE So we're back to side two.

JOHN LENNON Uh huh.

TOM DONAHUE No, I'm sorry, side one.

JOHN LENNON Side one. This is uh . . .

TOM DONAHUE "Bless You."

JOHN LENNON "Bless You." You can dance very slowly to it. ["Bless You" plays]

Well! I enjoyed dancing with you, Tom.

TOM DONAHUE Delightful. We could be on *Come Dancing*, if they just brought it back.

JOHN LENNON Yeah, we could trade it with you for Lawrence Welk.

TOM DONAHUE I always thought we could go together incredibly well! *Come Dancing* is a BBC show. And it's a program that is devoted to various clubs around England that do ballroom dancing, and they dance competitively on this TV show.

JOHN LENNON "Mary's wearing four thousand sequins, hand sewn to the back of her neck."

TOM DONAHUE "By Roy!"

JOHN LENNON Yes! Right, right!

TOM DONAHUE "He's a mechanic during the daytime, and this is the last night they'll be dancing together because Mary's engaged and her fiancé doesn't dance." [laughter] And the great military dances, I used to love them, when a whole lotta people are teams of . . .

JOHN LENNON Ah, they do the sort of, like, formation dancing they call it. Oh yeah, that's the big trip. With ten people all doing the tango. The men like doin' them Spanish ones, y'know? Where they can put their hands up and hold their guts in.

TOM DONAHUE I always thought that and Monty Python, they're the two funniest programs.

JOHN LENNON They're bringin' that show over here! On cable, of what do you call it here, public what is it?

TOM DONAHUE Public TV.

JOHN LENNON Public TV. National Educational you call it, yeah. That's coming shortly.

TOM DONAHUE I hope you're around to see it, man.

JOHN LENNON Yeah, I might even introduce it. They asked me to.

TOM DONAHUE How're things going about staying in the country?

JOHN LENNON Well, you know, every now and then they give me thirty days to get out, which is . . . and then we appeal it. And taxi drivers say, "Oh, you're still here?" [they laugh] So it goes on like that.

TOM DONAHUE Okay, let's get to the album you do with Harry Nilsson. [plays "Don't Forget Me"]

JOHN LENNON Yeah! Well, this is the first take we did. And it was in Record Plant West. And it was the first night. And you can tell!

TOM DONAHUE Let me ask you this though, first. How did you happen to get with Harry on it? I know you've known him for a long time.

JOHN LENNON Off and on. I wasn't hanging around with him much. Ringo was a lot. I met him years ago through Derek [Taylor].

TOM DONAHUE Derek produced the album.

JOHN LENNON So I really didn't get to know him till this album.

TOM DONAHUE I think that's one of the cuts that people really enjoy hearing lots of.

JOHN LENNON Yeah, I like it because it's sort of . . . mad.

TOM DONAHUE Oh yeah, totally.

JOHN LENNON It's really mad, yeah. A lot of edits in it. Which I still hear. "Spot the edit, folks! And you win an invisible T-shirt!"

TOM DONAHUE And he did some—I have in mind the ending of "Many Rivers to Cross."

JOHN LENNON That was . . . second night.

TOM DONAHUE Right.

JOHN LENNON Second or third.

TOM DONAHUE Sounds like he listened to your albums.

JOHN LENNON No . . . well, no doubt he's heard them. But he was singin' it, pretty much as he sang it. But he was holdin' back. So I just said, y'know, 'cause really, it was him brought the song to me. And I loved it. And I just kept asking him for more on it.

TOM DONAHUE Yeah.

JOHN LENNON And it turned out like it did. And I liked it. I knew there was gonna be, "Oh, it sounds like he's doing John." But there's a certain point when you get . . . high, right? By the singing of it, anyway, where you're gonna go to the same place! There was nowhere else for him to go but there.

TOM DONAHUE I think he has a tremendous voice.

JOHN LENNON Yeah, I love it.

TOM DONAHUE I'm trying to think of the song that Richard Perry did with him.

JOHN LENNON Oh, "Without You."

TOM DONAHUE "Without You."

JOHN LENNON Yeah.

TOM DONAHUE You know, just great.

JOHN LENNON Just lovely. I love it. I just heard they cut the piano and the vocal first and then laid everything else on it after! Amazing. I've never done that.

TOM DONAHUE Here's the Dylan song that you wanted to play.

JOHN LENNON Oh yeah. "Corinna, Corinna." This is one of the early Dylan records I got turned on to. And I like this one, and he didn't write it or nothin'. But when I met him he was saying . . . y'know, we were swapping . . . shit and that. I said I like "Corinna, Corrina"; you know, it's a nice backing. And he looked at me, like surprised, y'know? "Backing?" I said yeah, the backing is great! So let's hear it. [plays "Corinna, Corinna"]

TOM DONAHUE Bob Dylan's "Corinna." And you said you heard that in Paris the first time?

JOHN LENNON Yeah, I think that was the first time I'd ever heard him at all. I think Paul got the record from a French DJ. We were doin' a radio thing there, and the guy had the record in the studio and Paul said, "Oh, I keep hearing about this guy." Or he'd heard it. And we took it back to the hotel and [daintily] *fell in love, like.*

TOM DONAHUE Just to jump off here for a minute before we get on to some commercials and some other things. Do you have any desire to appear live again? I mean, does that turn you on, would you like to try again?

JOHN LENNON I get the buzz to do it now and then. But I always get . . . like I project and see it all. I tend to do that about everything, y'know, even going downstairs, or puttin' me trousers on.

TOM DONAHUE That's good.

JOHN LENNON Hmm. Right. So sometimes ya feel ya already done it. And then you think about, the percent of good shows one has, out of, say, you're lucky to get three out of ten where you really hit the moments that you're looking for.

TOM DONAHUE This is Tom Donahue, and John Lennon's our guest tonight, we've been playing cuts from his new LP, and we'll be gettin' back to that. And right now, we're just playing some records he likes, and we're up to the Wailers.

JOHN LENNON Yeah. I've forgotten who turned me on to the Wailers. I think it was Gary Kellgren from Record Plant West. He played it to me at a party, and it [funny voice] *blew me head off, like.* It's very good. Eric got "I Shot the Sheriff" from the album. That's one of the tracks. This is the track I like best: "Get Up."

[Tom plays "Get Up" by the Wailers, then into Lennon's "Whatever Gets You through the Night."

TOM DONAHUE We really knocked that around . . .

JOHN LENNON It might work anyway. It could.

TOM DONAHUE I played the song at the right speed.

JOHN LENNON Ah, yeah, this afternoon you played it. Well, the guy playing saxophone, Bobby Keys, he heard it on the radio. And he said, "Oh, that's a nice sax solo." And at the end of it, he realized it was him playin' it. Amazing, isn't it?

TOM DONAHUE What's the most expensive album the Beatles ever made?

JOHN LENNON *Sgt. Pepper*. Because it took nine months. It wasn't nine months in the studio, but we'd work and then stop a bit. Work it out. Rest. Work. Of course, the record company was screamin'. They screamed at the price of the cover. Et cetera, et cetera. And now it's probably [funny voice] *pinned all over the walls!*

TOM DONAHUE How many tracks was that?

JOHN LENNON I don't remember.

TOM DONAHUE I think it's four-track, yeah.

JOHN LENNON Oh, I see what you mean, that kinda thing. [laughs] I thought you meant how many tracks on the album. I don't remember it bein' four, now that you tell us we worked on four, so we must have. I remember we were always waiting for somethin'. And I thought, by now I keep thinking it must have been sixteen-track, but I think you're right. But it was four or eight *is the answer to that one*! [laughter]

TOM DONAHUE With Nilsson you worked on a sixteen, right?

JOHN LENNON Oh, sure! Yeah. It's been sixteen for a long time.

TOM DONAHUE Doc Pomus.

JOHN LENNON Oh, Doc Pomus. Oh, there's a nice story about that!

TOM DONAHUE You can do more than sixteen now.

JOHN LENNON Oh, I know that. Yeah. I couldn't . . . I've never gone over sixteen. I mean, I've used tracks, y'know, mixed down and mixed together, to get more available.

[off-mic: clop clop clop like chops of razor blade]

JOHN LENNON But that twenty-four business. And thirty-eight. Couldn't deal with it. Back to music, y'know. Somebody told me a story about this song. Which is that Doc Pomus, who lives in a wheelchair. I only met him once. *I was thrilled.* And he wrote this for his beautiful wife. "Save the Last Dance for Me." And it's Harry singin' it. [plays "Save the Last Dance for Me"]

TOM DONAHUE Ahhh . . . a couple of incredible records. The John Lennon–produced Harry Nilsson version of "Save the Last Dance for Me," and the Drifters doing the original. And the album you were working on with Phil is oldies, isn't it?

JOHN LENNON Yeah. Ah, it's all oldies . . . what did we do, what did we do? Oh, I don't wanna say what we did, because people're coverin'. Ha ha.

TOM DONAHUE Yeah.

JOHN LENNON And it's '73 we started. And if it ever comes out. Ah ha!

TOM DONAHUE Ya see, you're safer with an oldies album; you don't have to feel rushed.

JOHN LENNON That's true, that's true.

TOM DONAHUE It isn't gonna lose that thing of being of the moment. This is Tom Donahue, and we're talking to John Lennon. And I thought it was about time we got back to what he used to do and played some Beatles things.

JOHN LENNON Yeah, I'm still doing the same, only I know a bit more about it, I guess. Wanna use something from *The White Album*?

TOM DONAHUE Yeah, let's . . .

JOHN LENNON The Chocolate Box?

TOM DONAHUE Go for a bit of that . . . [they play "I'm So Tired."]

JOHN LENNON Written in the hills of the Himalayas!

TOM DONAHUE Ah.

JOHN LENNON Mmm. That's one thing transcendental meditation does for you is make you so tired. You fall asleep.

TOM DONAHUE I know the Beatle experts—and the world's full of 'em—point to *Revolver* as the big turning point. I think a lot of people that aren't rock 'n roll critics today, that may be the first thing they ever heard.

JOHN LENNON Well, ah, like everythin', people go in trends, and the trend now is to think that was the change. And the trend before was to think *Rubber Soul* was the change. And then the other trend was, *Sgt. Pepper*, right? But the whole thing was a gradual change.

TOM DONAHUE You weren't conscious of being spun around or anything?

JOHN LENNON No, but we were conscious that the, some *formula* or somethin' was, it was moving ahead. That was for sure. But we were on the road, ya know? Not physically. I mean, on the road in the studio. *And the weather was clear!* I think the songs suggested—going from, "Out of the Blue," from the *Mind Games* album, to "Sexy Sadie," or vice-versa—the chords are similar. Be interesting to hear. Be pinchin' meself! [plays "Out of the Blue" into "Sexy Sadie."]

JOHN LENNON That set us on a trip, talking, right?

TOM DONAHUE It's easy to drift away doing this.

JOHN LENNON Yeah! Especially, when I was there, ya know?

TOM DONAHUE Hmm.

JOHN LENNON Hmm. Amazing!

TOM DONAHUE Do you find specific memories coming back . . .

JOHN LENNON Yeah! Oh yeah, yeah! I remember singing them. And writing them. That was written in India, too. Just as we were leaving. Waiting for our bags to be packed. And the taxi that *never seemed to come, we thought* . . . they're deliberately keeping the taxi back so we can't escape from . . . this madman's camp! We had the mad Greek with us, who was paranoid as hell. Kept saying, "It's black magic! It's black magic! They're gonna keep you here forever!" So that was what I was doing while all that was goin' on.

TOM DONAHUE But you got away.

JOHN LENNON I must have got away, 'cause I'm here.

TOM DONAHUE Yeah, you're here . . . and, uh . . . what'd you say a little while ago? You like the way that—what meditation has done to your voice?

JOHN LENNON Well, whether it was meditation or, I mean, we were really away from everythin'. It was like a sort of recluse holiday camp. Right at the foots of the Himalayas. It was like being up a mountain, only they call it the foothills. Hanging over the Ganges. With baboons stealing your breakfast. And everybody flowing around in robes and . . . sitting in their rooms, for hours and hours meditating. It was quite a trip! I was in the room for five days meditating once. That was quite a trip, I wrote hundreds of songs! I couldn't sleep, and I was hallucinating like crazy! Having dreams where you could smell! No, I'd do a few hours, and then you'd trip off, y'know. Or half, or whatever you're supposed to be doing, y'know, three- or four-hour stretches. And you'd *really* trip out! And it was just like, a way of gettin' there. How do you go? Amazing trips! It was never the bit where, when you got back to, y'know, cookin' and livin' daily in the, *in the Western world like*. Getting up for breakfast and going to work or making records or back to so-called reality. You just can't fit it in it. Well . . .

TOM DONAHUE Well, John, thank you very much for coming up. It's been a pleasure.

JOHN LENNON It was a pleasure, Tom. I really enjoyed it. We really got down to the, uh . . . [that voice] *long trip down to the old dirt road.* Which is the last track we're gonna play.

TOM DONAHUE And you got a gig here anytime you want it.

JOHN LENNON Thank you. I'll be back. I enjoyed it.

TOM DONAHUE We'll be expecting you . . . believe me.

SIDE TRIP

More Tales of Broadcast Glory

You are a holy man on the FM radio.

—Joni Mitchell, "Rainy Night House"

EDWARD BEAR I was doing the all-night show at KSAN in the early 1970s. Every night I flew into the show on the sound of a jet taking off, leading into my theme, from the movie *A Patch of Blue.* One day in 1971, I got a message that I'd be getting an advance test pressing of a new Joni Mitchell album. New music from a major artist I love? Always a happy occasion for me. I like nothing better than to sit and listen, without interruption, to a new album while I read the lyrics to each song. And in my world, it doesn't get any better than when it's a Joni Mitchell album! Except, sometimes it does. The next night I got a call that she was going to bring up the new record and do an interview. Joni showed up late, alone, handing me *Blue.* It was thrilling to meet her, and we settled in quickly on the air. She talked about going on tour to promote her new album. I asked if she would introduce some of the songs, and she did, telling the audience stories behind writing the tunes. Four gorgeous tracks later, Joni said that she was tired and it was time for her to leave. We thanked each other, and she was gone. Joni was such a presence that I immediately started to miss her. I told listeners I was going to let a few more Joni tunes track, and I went running out of the studio, into the elevator, down four floors, and out onto Sutter Street looking for her. There was a limo parked half a block away, so I ran toward it calling out,

"Joni!" The limo window slid down, and there she sat in the back, gazing out at me. "Joni," I said. "I just wanted to kiss you good-bye." She smiled and put her face out the window. I leaned toward her, and we kissed. Sweet! Delicious! Joni! Mitchell! We looked at each other, smiled again, her window rolled back up, and the limo rolled out onto Montgomery Street. She was gone. Again. I floated back to work and, while in a daze, the rest of my night felt magical. This is a memory that has warmed me for a lifetime. The fiftieth anniversary of *Blue* was celebrated in 2021. It has come to be regarded as one of the best albums of all time. I agree.

Bear's first intern in '68 was a promising young student at the San Francisco Art Institute.

EDWARD BEAR She was bright and helpful and a perfect assistant. After working with me for a time (paid in promo records and concert tickets), she went on to work for *Rolling Stone.*

ANNIE LEIBOVITZ, author of *Annie Leibovitz at Work* He had the 2 a.m. to 6 a.m. slot. I would make tea and pull records for him. He did great mixes. He would segue into Aretha Franklin or Etta James from Martin Luther King's "I Have a Dream" speech. Because there was no advertising in the late time slot, his mixes could go on forever.

EDWARD BEAR Not exactly forever, but the mixes were no longer confined to ten- or twelve-minute runs. Those were wonderful days.

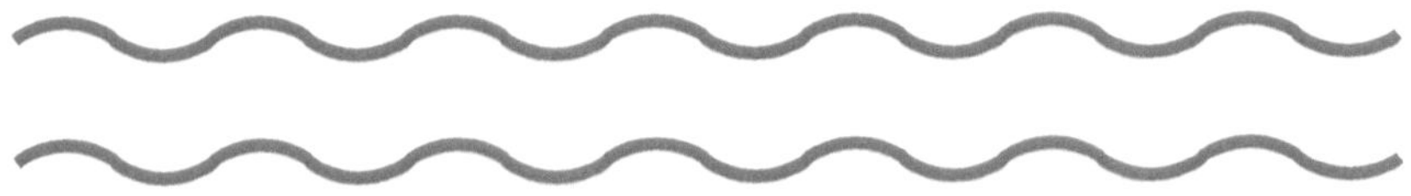

SIDE TRIP

Memo from Tom

"We've had some complaints from sponsors," Donahue began a memo in June '74, "about remarks made by the disc jockeys in connection with the commercials." While back-announcing, some air staff was bad-mouthing spots. "We have also received four complaints from listeners that spots are being turned down, not because they want to hear the commercials, but that they're tired of having to walk over to their radio to see if there's something wrong. It is inconsistent to want more money and want to screw the sponsor at the same time." He called it childish, a drag, and a bore, "and I would rather not be dragged or bored. Just don't talk about the God damn commercials." Plus a postscript: "The record thief who has stolen over a hundred LPs out of the library in the last two months is that jerk using the razor blade sitting at the end of the console."

Tom Donahue plays SLA communique for local reporters, 1974. Patty Hearst on it: "I would never choose to live the rest of my life surrounded by pigs like the Hearsts . . . fascist pig media . . . corporate state, et al . . . . Venceremos."
COURTESY BOB SIMMONS

26

SYMBIONESE LIBERATION ARMY COMMUNIQUÉS, 1974

In the spring of '74, *CBS Evening News* anchor Walter Cronkite reported: "There's been a big kidnapping on the West Coast. The victim was Patricia Hearst, daughter of newspaper executive Randolph Hearst, and granddaughter of the legendary William Randolph Hearst." Dave McQueen has a role in this story; Terry McGovern and Raechel Donahue portray it with merriment.

TERRY MCGOVERN Let me paint the picture. It's 1974. Patty Hearst has not been found. ICM has not dropped her yet. Terrible show business joke. Anyway, it's very tense. KSAN is getting all the SLA communiqués because they *want it should come through our microphones first*. The TV networks are coming to us because we're getting tapes. Patty's captors, the Symbionese Liberation Army, thought of us as "the people's station." Because we were being rebellious—or sounded that way—KSAN was their station, and they could send us their secret messages? Communiqués! This was a very dangerous group of people.

VICKY CUNNINGHAM The FBI set people up in an office across Sutter Street so they could watch our front door! The Symbionese Liberation Army [SLA] just liked KSAN. The news department had its own slant on everything: I remember, whenever Patty Hearst talked, Larry Lee ran tape of birds chirping.

DAVE MCQUEEN One of the craziest times in the history of broadcasting. It was surreal, because we were used to dealing with politics being stated in a rational manner. These people were completely crazy. COINTELPRO, the Counterintelligence Program that Hoover ran for many years at the FBI, infiltrating radical groups with subversive operatives; I'm still convinced the "Symbionese Liberation Army" came out of that in some way. Whoever thinks such a thing could happen? Their first two tapes went to KPFA in Berkeley. The next one came to KSAN.

RAECHEL DONAHUE Federal agents wanted to meet us at our house, and it's a shame this get-together never took place. It had forced me into domesticity mode: there were pot seeds all over, so I had to vacuum for the FBI.

DAVE MCQUEEN It really complicated our lives. I lived in Berkeley on Delaware Street. And it turned out that the Harrises, two of the prime movers in the SLA, lived a block away. Around the corner lived another one of them. I'd rented another house I owned to a former cell mate of Theo Wheeler, one of the original SLA founders. The FBI took a look at all of that—me, in the middle of this SLA ring—suddenly there were Fords up and down the street with guys in blue suits and brown shoes watching me. Constant surveillance. I've never been so safe in my life!

RAECHEL DONAHUE Hadwig Stadleman was our receptionist, this German woman with legs from here to there and back again. I was in charge of hiring. The boys said, "Could you get us a woman with legs from here to there and back again?" So I did. She once dated Ferlinghetti. Also good with a vaulting horse.

TERRY MCGOVERN An Olympic-class athlete!

RAECHEL DONAHUE Yes, she was.

TERRY MCGOVERN From Switzerland. Still is!

RAECHEL DONAHUE The woman on the phone said, "Can we speak to Tom Donahue please? This is the SLA." Hadwig said, "Vell, he's busy." "No, you don't understand; this is the Symbionese Liberation Army."

TERRY MCGOVERN They're the hottest thing in the news.

RAECHEL DONAHUE "We have a tape." Hadwig says, "Sorry, leave a message." "We're not gonna leave a message!" *And we're gonna kill you, right?*

TERRY MCGOVERN Hadwig says, "Ve don't play any new artists."

RAECHEL DONAHUE "It's a tape for KSAN news!" "Vell, okay, vere are you?" "I'm calling you from a phone booth—I can't tell you where I am!" "So tell me, vere you going to leave the tapes?"

TERRY MCGOVERN Sutter and Powell, close to where the station is.

RAECHEL DONAHUE Powell?

TERRY MCGOVERN Sutter and Union, something like that.

RAECHEL DONAHUE Kearney! They say, "You gotta get over here!"

DUSTY STREET There's a tape in the phone booth between Sutter and Montgomery, and before the SLA hung up, we hear, "I MUST GO NOW! GET OUT OF MY VAY!" Hadwig vaults over the desk, leaps down nine flights, goes whirling down the street, throwing people aside, leaping over small children. Heaven forbid, some poor person was trying to make a phone call—she'd grab them by the scruff of the neck and pull them out, phone dangling. "I am on an important mission! You make that call later, ya?"

DAVE MCQUEEN Hadwig got there as the woman was inside the booth, taping the envelope to the bottom of the thing. Apparently they struggled over the tape, and our intrepid news source ran back with it. Kind of amusing when you think of it. Also, a little bit scary too.

RAECHEL DONAHUE Hadwig got to the phone booth *before* the girl with the tape. She's dutifully waiting, looks across the street and the girl is wearing—in San Francisco—she's bundled up like a little snow bunny with the hat with the hood and the sunglasses.

TERRY MCGOVERN A scarf over her head like Mary Magdalene.

RAECHEL DONAHUE An envelope wrapped around a cassette in her hand. Hadwig runs across, "Are you the voman I am supposed to meet here?"

TERRY MCGOVERN "Are you Moonbeam?" This is to a Symbionese Liberation Army fugitive wanted in nineteen countries.

RAECHEL DONAHUE "You weren't supposed to meet me here!" Moonbeam bolts.

TERRY MCGOVERN Hadwig runs back to the station . . . and we put it on. Certainly put us on the map, the SLA.

DAVE MCQUEEN The SLA had picked *us*. We were the safe haven; we didn't have our fingers in anybody's pie.

Kenny Wardell was on the air Saturday night, April 3.

KENNY WARDELL I was doing Tom and Raechel's shift, and I kept seeing the studio hotline flashing. It wouldn't go away, so I picked it up, and a person was saying, "We just dropped off a tape through your mail slot." It was another cassette tape. So, I threw on a long record and took it to the production studio to give it a listen. Patty was coming out as Tania! Oh my fucking God! I called Tom. He said he'd be right down—he'd wanted to stay home and party that night—and I shouldn't let anyone into the station until he got there. Once he heard what we had, Tom knew what a publicity bonanza this was going to be. It didn't take long for the TV crews to get there.

VICKY CUNNINGHAM I'm sitting alone at home on a Saturday night, I'm wacked out of my gourd, right? Raechel calls and says, you better get in right now. I said no, no, no; it's Saturday night, I'm home, I'm relaxing, I'm stoned. She says, if you know what's good for you, you'll get in here right now. All these news people were there! I wrote up a little news release: how the SLA had delivered another message. Tom remained ensconced in his office, waiting for his great moment of glory to come out.

KENNY WARDELL Tom wanted to play the tape on the air before calling the cops.

BONNIE SIMMONS The reporters sat on the floor and daisy-chained their recorders together so they could all get a recording of the tape.

VICKY CUNNINGHAM The news people were really interested in the SLA tape, so they all got that and left. Tom comes out to have his great moment, and everybody's gone.

KENNY WARDELL Before calling the news, Tom had me dub the cassette onto reel. It would make a better visual for television to show a reel-to-reel tape spinning in the studio. "And put the cassette away." I suspect he wanted to keep the master.

DAVID MCQUEEN I suspect not to keep the master, but to keep everything at one step removed. Which is much the safest thing to do when you're dealing with as unstable an outfit as the Federal Bureau of Investigation. They could do great damage to you. He wanted to keep them at a remove. That would be my interpretation. I don't think anybody blamed us, because we had no idea what the hell was going on. These people were quite nutty. You had no idea what they were capable of doing—they kidnapped Patty Hearst. She was someone who was accessible to them, was a name that was, first, recognizable, and they could get mileage out of her. Which of course they did.

BONNIE SIMMONS I remember Donahue was sensitive in calling Randy Hearst to tell him that we had gotten another tape before all the police activity around it would happen. You know; they were both fathers. I always thought it was so right that Tom did that.

With the FBI surveillance, anyone who left 211 Sutter—the FBI would follow. Salesman Doug Dunlop wore three-piece suits and had shorter hair because he was in the national guard. So McQueen sent him out with any information.

TOM DEVRIES, TV reporter Person for person, KSAN was the most literate broadcast news operation ever. The newsroom crew of my period—McQueen, Larry Lee, Danice, Scoop, sometimes Laufer—jumped in as actually formally educated and smart. What they were interested in, and the intellect they brought to bear wasn't common. One evening I came by just as they got a bomb threat by phone. Cops were standing there, kind of unsure what to do. Somebody guessed the bomb was probably disguised as a record album; funny, because there were about a hundred thousand of them. As McQueen, Larry Lee, and I left to go eat supper, the DJ there asked sadly if we knew what kind of music bombers might like.

For historical context, check out *Revolution's End: The Patty Hearst Kidnapping, Mind Control, and the Secret History of Donald Defreeze and the SLA* by Brad Schreiber (he also did comedy sketches at the station in '79).

Dusty Street, Terry McGovern, unknown, Tom Donahue, Raechel Donahue, Norman Davis, Bob Simmons, unknown, Bonnie Simmons, Bob McClay, Richard Gossett, Sean Donahue, and many missing, 1974.
PHOTO BY JIM BALDOCCHI

Scoop Nisker, Bonnie Simmons, Terry McGovern, and Richard Gossett in KSAN booth at "Radio Day By The Bay" sponsored by the California Historical Radio Society (CHRS). Early 21st century photo taken by Kenny Wardell.
PHOTO BY KENNY WARDELL

27

BIG DADDY, 1975

TIM DAUGHERTY, English teacher, LA High In '68, I went to one of the radio station strike benefits at the Aquarius. I had just bought Moby Grape's second LP, *Wow*, a two-record set. I got to see Big Brother, Smokestack Lightning, Steppenwolf, Tiny Tim. Robert F. Kennedy was supposed to drop by. Tom Donahue was the *godhead.*

Bob McClay was in the studio playing phonograph records the morning of April 28, 1975.

BOB MCLAY [Blood, Sweat & Tears, "Variations on a Theme by Eric Satie," ends.] This is KSAN in San Francisco. And I'm Bob McClay and we have a very sad announcement to make. And that is that Tom Donahue, our vice president–general manager and disc jockey here for many years at KSAN, died this morning of a sudden heart attack. He was forty-six years old. Tom Donahue was known as the father of progressive radio, bringing free-form broadcasting to KMPX in 1967, and a year later we moved over to KSAN. Tom was a broadcast veteran of twenty-five years. He began his radio career at WIP in Charleston, Virginia, in 1948, moved to WIBG in Philadelphia, 1950—which is where I met him some years later. And then as music director and air personality, he helped to keep WIBG in the number-one position for ten years. He joined KYA in San Francisco in 1961 and, together with Bob Mitchell between 1961 and '65, reshaped San Francisco radio. In 1964 and 1965, Tom Donahue was the city's top-rated disc jockey. Following a strike in 1968, Tom Donahue moved with the entire staff from KMPX to KSAN, which under his direction has become

San Francisco's number-one station. His imaginative programming drew new attention to radio in the Bay Area.

We're repeating that our vice president–general manager and friend, Tom Donahue, died this morning of a sudden heart attack. He was forty-six years old. Tom Donahue will be missed. [Plays Rolling Stones, "Sympathy for the Devil."]

BONNIE SIMMONS Raechel didn't come to work that morning. She was supposed to be on at ten, and I went a little goofy looking for her. We would all be late sometimes, but nobody just failed to show up. Finally got ahold by telephone after ten, and she told me that Tom had died, and my brain didn't accept it. "What? What did you say?" I always felt bad about that; I couldn't absorb it. McClay was on for Rae, and I went into the booth and told him. After, he played "Sympathy for the Devil." Might not have been the most tasteful choice, and he was sorry about it later. That whole day is kind of blurred to me.

VICKY CUNNINGHAM Bonnie and I were planning to go into Tom's office that morning to get all the pills. We found a poem he'd written for Raechel.

BONNIE SIMMONS I kept hoping it was an elaborate Donahue ruse, some kind of insurance scam—he was so good at things like that.

VICKY CUNNINGHAM I would say he committed suicide. We were mad. He'd lost weight. Bonnie and I would come in the office, and he'd be shaking a few more pills out, then pass out—and Metromedia called to wake him up.

ERIC CHRISTENSEN That whole night of cocaine and backgammon; I remember it being in Marin, but Kenny Wardell thinks it happened on Octavia Street.

KENNY WARDELL I was living in an apartment on Sacramento, right around the corner from Tom's house, which I believe was on Washington. From what I remember, Buzzy Donahue had stopped by Tom's place and found him deceased. She called me and I ran right over. When I got there, a medical vehicle had just put Tom inside. This was one of the saddest days of my life. I hugged Buzzy and tried to console her, but we were both horrified at what had happened. Tom was a good friend, and we did a lot of fun stuff. Perhaps my favorite memory was when Tom and I took a plane full of KSAN-ers and friends to Hawaii for a week. The night we got there, we saw Elvis Presley perform his

"Aloha from Hawaii" concert, and the night we left to come home to San Francisco, we saw the Rolling Stones.

BOB SIMMONS He was in there playing backgammon for thirty-six hours straight, and his old heart just couldn't take it anymore. I think I said, when he died, "Tom believed in the three-day work week. Tom called his body and said he wasn't coming in today." I was saddened but not shocked.

BUZZY DONAHUE This is not what happened. I did not find Tom; he was with Raechel at her apartment with some other people. He had not been playing backgammon for thirty-six hours. But they had stayed up late that night from what I understand.

NICK GRAVENITES How he died: he was having a party with all the heavyweights of Marin County, the theater people and the music people, and they're playing for big money. You don't play backgammon for big money, you play it for pennies. Tom won over two hundred thousand dollars and a piece of the radio station. A few hours later he has a heart attack, and he's lying in bed dying, and he turns to Raechel and he says, "Bitch, I'm going to paradise and I'm not taking you."

BEN FONG-TORRES Rachael called an ambulance. He was dead on arrival at Mount Zion Hospital. His doctor said, "He's had extra heartbeats for years." At the end, he'd reduced his weight to 310 pounds. A simple burial took place at Mount Tamalpais Cemetery in San Rafael. He was buried in a simple pine casket. . . . His actual wish, he said, was to be cremated and have his ashes mixed with a pound of the finest dope and have his friends smoke it.

DUSTY STREET When my mother died, the first person I called was Tom Donahue, because I was so devastated. It was like my entire childhood, my entire basis of what made me me, was gone. And the one person I turned to was now also gone. But I had a lot of drugs and alcohol, so I dealt with it just fine.

BONNIE SIMMONS The audience was in a grieving period with us. It rocked the station. But there were no freak-outs, and everybody kept going.

On May 3, four hundred people at the Orphanage on Montgomery Street in North Beach, saw Tower of Power, Van Morrison, The Tubes, and Peter Yarrow perform (Tom broke Peter, Paul & Mary's "Lemon Tree" in

1962). The *Chronicle's* music reporter John Wasserman wrote it was, "suffused with the warm . . . Irishman's wake . . . everyone got appropriately wrecked." Wasserman concluded, "I will miss his influence . . . famous and respected."

BONNIE SIMMONS His wake was lovely. Quite a gathering of the "tribes," and a bit chaotic, as we put it together—this giant wake party—while we were all pretty much in shock. For some odd reason I remember James Caan came from LA, and not all that much more. As Tom had requested, at the funeral I did "wear a dress, drink a beer, and smoke a joint." I was only twenty-six when Tom died. He was so much like all of us that he was almost ageless. He was in quite a lot of pain from different back problems, but he never bitched about that. That wasn't his way.

BUZZY DONAHUE I adored him. He was extremely funny; he was very generous and charming. He loved women and he loved giving the underdog a chance. When I look at the people he brought in—he had this way of managing that just let people blossom. That's a really unique talent. And of course I loved that voice. He had one of the best voices I'd ever heard. He loved musicians and was extremely supportive of them—if he liked their record, he had to play it more than once. I picked that up from him without even knowing. This was pre-Pandora and Spotify. And that was one of the reasons he told the jocks not to talk over the songs—he knew there were people at home recording it, and it was the only way they could get the song.

RAECHEL DONAHUE Tom was one of the smartest men I'd ever met. He was a voracious reader, like I was. He changed the energy in any room he entered. He was a visionary, who built a creative vortex that drew everyone in: employees and listeners, deal makers and idea generators, socialites, and hoi polloi alike. I would say Tom was the Rock of Gibraltar, balanced on the head of a pin.

JOEL SELVIN The last conversation I had with Ralph Gleason at the *Chronicle* was about an article I'd written about Tom. And this was like the ultimate Ralph Gleason benediction—about Tom, he said, "Yep, he was a good cat."

San Francisco Chronicle, Sat., May 3, 1975
Donahue: A True Visionary of Rock
By Joel Selvin

Few disc jockeys have ever affected the actual development of radio, but Tom Donahue was no mere disc jockey. In a field where a person with just one good idea can look like an intellectual giant, Tom Donahue, who died Monday of a heart attack at age 46, was a true visionary. The whole country noticed San Francisco radio when Donahue created what quickly came to be called "underground radio" on KMPX-FM here in 1967, opening the FM airwaves to rock for the first time.

His mark is stamped throughout the history of rock music in San Francisco. He spent five years as one of the city's most popular AM radio rock broadcasters on KYA, produced giant rock concerts here before Bill Graham even moved to San Francisco, and owned the record company that spawned San Francisco's first home-grown hit rock records.

Donahue became general manager of KSAN-FM in October 1972, a position he held until his death. He came to KSAN in May, 1968, with almost his entire KMPX staff, following a bitter strike at the original station. With Donahue at the helm, KSAN has remained virtually unchallenged as the top progressive rock station in town.

At the zenith of KMPX's influence, Donahue broadcast nightly both in San Francisco and Los Angeles on KMPX's Pasadena sister station, KPPC-FM, using tape recorded shows to overcome the geographic problem. Later, he served as programming consultant for KMET-FM in Los Angeles, which memorialized Donahue there throughout the day following his death. At KSAN, commercial announcements were canceled for 24 hours; a KSAN memorial program is scheduled for 6 o'clock to midnight tonight, Donahue's regular time slot.

Tom "Big Daddy" Donahue came to San Francisco in 1961 from Philadelphia. With his partner, the late Bob Mitchell, he presented a series of early rock concerts at the Cow Palace, including shows by the Rolling Stones and the Beatles. The pair also produced the 1966 Candlestick Park performance by the

CHAPTER 27

Dan O'Neill remembers his old friend, Tom Donahue.
© DAN O'NEILL

Beatles; the final public performance by the quartet, and opened the country's first psychedelic nightclub, Mother's on Broadway, where the Lovin' Spoonful played for peanuts.

He ran Autumn Records, which recorded San Francisco's first hit rock group, the Beau Brummels. "A whore told me about them," Donahue liked to recall, "and I always listen to whores." Bobby Freeman earned a million-seller on Autumn with "C'mon and Swim" in 1964. Rock star Sly Stone worked as a producer for Autumn, and the Jefferson Airplane's Grace Slick made her first records (with the Great Society) for Donahue.

"The disc jockeys have become robots," he wrote for Rolling Stone in 1967, lambasting AM radio in an article titled "AM Radio Is Dead and Its Rotting Corpse Is Stinking Up the Airwaves." They are "performing their inanities at the direction of programmers who have succeeded in totally squeezing the human element out of their sound, and reducing it to a series of blips and bleeps and happy, oh yes, always happy, sounding cretins who are poured from bottles every three hours. They have succeeded in making everyone on the station staff sound the same—asinine. This is the much coveted 'station sound,'" he said.

His voice rolled from his throat like thick oil pouring from the can. His musical selections never betrayed his age and experience; he was always up-to-the-minute hip. His work earned him awards from Billboard, San Francisco State and the Bill Gavin Radio Conference, among others, over the years. "He always laughed and threw them away," his secretary, Vicki Cunningham, said.

Donahue is survived by his wife, Raechel, who has become one of KSAN's most popular (and best) disc jockeys herself, and five children: Catherine (Buzzy), 25, Tom Jr., 23, Sean, 20, Deirdre, 16, and Jesse, 4.

BEN FONG-TORRES After his death, it was reported that Tom Donahue and Francis Ford Coppola were talking about taking over another station and doing free form without corporate constraints.

BOB SIMMONS People don't realize, we were in the process of bailing out of KSAN. The FFC had offered to buy back the old KMPX and give it to Tom. And Bonnie and I, and Jeff Nemerovski—we were all going to go with him. I quit my job (at Arista Records working for Clive Davis) and waited. It wasn't that there was anything wrong with KSAN. This looked like it was going to be a grand new opportunity: We could have a piece of ownership—we would not just be hired help—and then Tom. . . . We thought we could tempt Coppola into still doing it, but no; he wanted Tom running it. He wanted that type of guy at the helm. In a way, maybe it was a good thing, because if the deal hadn't gone through, Tom owed a lot of money to a lot of people.

BEN FONG-TORRES He was making deals to the end.

TOM SMOTHERS He never turned the corner. He never got that financial edge, to be really comfortable.

JOEL SELVIN The last time I saw Tom, it was about a week before he died, there was some bay cruise or something. And we were up in the captain's cabin and were snorting a lotta blow. And Tom was getting real nostalgic, and he said something about, [does Tom's voice] "Ten years ago we'd all be on LSD." I didn't have any great nostalgia for ten years ago, but I made note of that, right? Tom's so hip. And he's looking for the next thing already. I could see he was getting tired of that. And then, of course, a week later he's snortin' his way out of this world. So, I guess that was the plan. I don't think Tom was getting rusty. He had those plans, he was ready to jump into the next big thing. He brought Metro to their knees! And as long as he had his guys selling off the top of the card, and full booking, he just told them to fuck themselves. And they said, "Okay, Tom. Thank you." Tom could do anything he wanted to do with that station. There was no corporate control on him at all. None.

VICKY CUNNINGHAM Metromedia was mad he was always giving people raises. He told them, "These people will demand a living wage." Another thing I loved was when Tom had the company car, the gold Mercedes, painted—covered in a mural of the sunrise.

https://www.youtube.com/watch?v=Cchja88Rn5w
Donahue and Van Morrison, between sets at the Orphanage, 1974. Twelve intimate minutes about cats they dig. Tom says something that Van will write into his song "Wavelength," released in '78. (We played it on KSAN. A lot.)

SIDE TRIP

One More Tom

Donahue was inducted into the Rock and Roll Hall of Fame in 1996 as a nonperformer, one of only three disc jockeys to receive that honor.

BONNIE SIMMONS Tom's great skill was not only in finding the most unlikely people to hire. Even when he would tell me we were going to hire someone, or *suggest* to me on his nicer days, I would cringe. I would make every argument against it. He'd say, "No, no. Just try it. I have a hunch about this." And damn if he wasn't right almost all the time. The guy couldn't lose. But also, Tom had the miraculous ability to get people to work like dogs on a particular project and think that we were having a good time. That's a great manager. An extraordinary manager would be one like Tom, who would not be there for any of the hard work. He could be at the racetrack, he might be out at Enrico's, he might be playing backgammon, he might be at home taking a nap. But it was all right, because Tom did his job by inspiring all of us to do ours. And the idea of Tom coming into an office and being there from nine to six every day was preposterous. It just wasn't gonna happen. Tom would stay away when things were unpleasant. I remember one miserable day when Tom had disappeared. And then he popped up with a box full of antique buttons. I stood there yelling at him, and he kept sorting through the buttons, labeling them, because he was going to give them to the staff as gifts. I kept on yelling, and he kept on showing me buttons. "Who do you think this one is right for?" The point was those buttons were actually more important in the long run than all those problems. He'd stare at you with those big eyes and say, "Nothing matters." Hippie bullshit or not, it worked.

"What Was That, Or, Suddenly Lost Summer," a 12-hour special on 1967 KMPX roots. Poster by Alton Kelley, 1976. Bob Simmons: "We convinced Alton that our week-long documentary needed him. A whole final layer of black outlining was left out of the composite and made the lettering look kind of blurry. He was furious, but just shook his head, not wishing to weep publicly. I felt badly for him, he did the poster for $150, ridiculously low. Sometimes I think the poster was better than the show."

POSTER BY ALTON KELLY

WHAT WAS THAT?

Ten Years After

https://clyp.it/g1hehm41
WWT episode, Dave McQueen on the Haight, 20 minutes.

https://archive.org/details/01-track-01_202104
From KSAN special *What Was That? Or, Suddenly Lost Summer.* Concert tapes by Bob Cohen, from Winterland, Fillmore, and Avalon ballrooms, with Santana, Zappa and the Mothers of Invention, the Byrds, Mother Earth, Moby Grape. Produced by Paul Wexley and Mark Salditch. Additional production: Haight/Ashbury Research Project. Norman Davis said, "Moby Grape was one of those bands who were really good when they were good. But when they were bad, they were terrible." 67 minutes.

A year after Donahue's death, the staff produced something their Big Daddy'd inspired: *What Was That? Or, Suddenly Lost Summer.*

BOB SIMMONS Tom Donahue had suggested we do a history of the "Summer of Love." After Tom died, the idea gathered steam. Several of us were having dinner at Victoria Station when the topic came up again. An audio history of the rise and fall of the Haight-Ashbury—it would be a tribute to both Tom and his business partner since 1963, and fellow KYA DJ, Bobby Mitchell.

BONNIE SIMMONS In 1968, Bobby Mitchell had leukemia, and while he was on his deathbed, Donahue's story always was that, with all of his friends and family gathered around close to the end, Bobby Mitchell suddenly sat up in bed and said, "What was *that*?"

BOB SIMMONS Mitchell said, "What was that?" and promptly died. That's the story. I'm just repeating the mythology. It's true, history is made by historians, not events. It might have been Beverley Wilshire who suggested the title. Here are some facts: I produced the Texas special that Tom put me up to, twenty-four hours featuring all Texas music. I had the idea that Texas's huge contribution to music needed to be recognized—Waylon, Willie, Jerry Jeff, Guy Clark, Doug Sahm, the Jazz Crusaders, Ornette Coleman, the Huey Meaux archives—and it was a successful program, meaning it almost paid for itself, and it got okay ratings for such an esoteric event. Now could we try to capture the spirit of the decade in San Francisco and perhaps the country?

BONNIE SIMMONS It was all hands on deck for what was a pretty damn ambitious project. Bob did a bunch of really good interviews. I did a lot of interviews. It was just crazy.

BOB SIMMONS Ralph Gleason, Jerry Garcia, Alan Cohen, the Thelin brothers, the poster guys Alton Kelley and Wes Wilson; I wrote Ken Kesey in Pleasant Hill, Oregon, to contribute, and two reel-to-reels arrived at the station, a few minutes of which added flavor. [See Supplementary Reading.] Luther Greene produced a wonderful segment on the Straight Theater, with funny audio from Hillel Resner and Brent Dangerfield; audio of Neal Cassidy rapping with the Grateful Dead as sidemen; live recordings "from the psychedelic ballrooms of yesteryear"; and there was a Janis number recorded by Bobby Cohen, a version of "Ball and Chain" that would *chill your bones.*

BONNIE SIMMONS We just bit off a little bit more than anyone could have been able to chew. Thirty-six hours. We always made them a little too long.

BOB SIMMONS We had a closet bursting with audio, tons of garbage, and jewels hidden in it. It was tough. We tried to do in two months something that we should have had a team of a dozen on for a year, like Ken Burns does. Few of us knew much about how to produce an audio documentary; we didn't have a National Public Radio as a kind of teacher for audio producers.

BONNIE SIMMONS I was doing my regular job on the air and was program director. Corte Madera was just too far away; we ended up sleeping in the office.

BOB SIMMONS Bonnie and I convinced the great underground artist, Alton Kelley, that *What Was That?* needed his work alone. He became super pissed off at Cal Litho for their printing job; they left off the last color separation. Kelley just shook his head at the mistake, not wishing to weep publicly. He did the poster for $150. Ridiculously low. When the show ran, I was told no store in San Francisco had any quarter-inch tape left because there were so many tapers doing home recordings. Joel Selvin hung around a bit when we were cutting tape. So he knew the background. He wrote a column about it in the *Chron* "Pink Section" after it ran. It was pretty accurate. Shallow, but accurate.

JOEL SELVIN Shallow but accurate was my brand.

SIDE TRIP

Why Do They Hate on the Hippie?

TERRY SOUTHERN, author of *Red Dirt Marijuana* It's 'cause a man see too much when he get high. I tell you there's a lotta trickin' an lyin' go on in the world. Well, a man get high . . . he see right through there into the truth of it!

ROLAND JACOPETTI, production It was possible to tune in to a station that was run by hippies, announced by hippies, supported by hippie advertisers, with music sung by hippies. It took me a while to get comfortable around all this, but eventually I was.

HOW WACHSPRESS, engineer Today I just vape cannabis oil. Talk about old-age laziness—I'm seventy-six—I just stick it in my mouth, suck on it, the heater goes on, and I'm in business. I go to one of the oldest dispensaries, near where I live on Polk Street. I still have my last California medical card. I carry it with me as a badge, because there's nothing like the sensation of twelve police officers with their guns out, looking for an excuse to shoot you. That was back when the whole attitude was stupid, and I was witness to the dark side. Falsely arrested, I went through the whole system, and finally they threw the case out.

I didn't have any; it was a felony bust. Today it's all legalized, homogenized, sanitized. People take a weekend workshop on ayahuasca. I have no interest. Having a little ganja makes me an old fart.

STEPHEN GASKIN Like the Rastafarians say, you don't need acid, because dynamite reefer makes you trip. My first hallucination was with Acapulco Gold.

ROGER STEFFENS Imagine dropping acid in Nam. We'd bring the guard at the Armed Forces Vietnam Network bottles of Ba Moui Ba beer or a pack of Park Lane joints, and he'd let us climb to the peak of their three-hundred-foot tower for a full 360. A light show way beyond anything the Fillmore ever attempted! One day around noon, I was on my way to the adjoining Vietnamese TV headquarters; a few moments before I arrived, a rocket landed on it. There was no safe place in Nam. The war was 24/7. But I never fired a single shot in twenty-six months in-country at the height of the war. *Hoa Binh!*

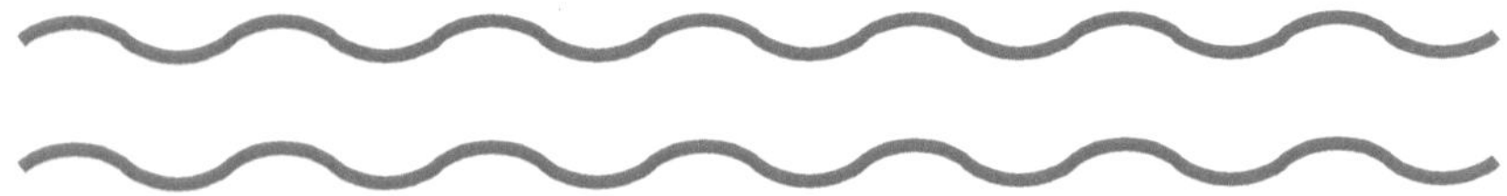

SIDE TRIP

The Bobby Dale Experience

https://www.youtube.com/watch?v=tfWps6RS8oY
Bobby Dale on KSFO, rapping about KSAN friends. 1972, 2 minutes.

Karma police
arrest this man,
he talks in maths,
he buzzes like a fridge,
he's like a detuned radio.

—Radiohead, "Karma Police"

Howard Hesseman, one of KMPX's original heads in '67, found a job in '78 starring in a sitcom about a radio station, *WKRP Cincinnati*.

HOWARD HESSEMAN Bobby Dale was one of the sources I drew on for my character, Johnny Fever. Bobby Dale and Bob McClay. And Tom, of course. I went in thinking, *I know who this guy is*. He's been around radio for a long time, and it's been shit radio. He's been given a chance to turn the station around. And like Bobby Dale, Fever had been on the air as an announcer all over the States.

> *BOBBY DALE*
>
> *That's B. B. King. Before that, really strange, unbelievable if you believe the liner notes: blues singer by the name of Rubber Legs Williams. Along with Charles Parker and "That's the Blues." [laughs] And I like to believe these things, man. Makes life more enjoyable. Could happen to me! How the combination ever got together at the time of the session with Rubber Legs, Charlie Parker, and a whole lotta heavy jazz cats. And Parker put around eight bennies in Rubber Legs' coffee [laughs] and that was it, man [whistles]. You know, they had him tied down. [barbaric yawp!] "That's the Blues." And before that, Otis Spann with Fleetwood Mac, and never heard Peter Green sound . . . quite so hot. And Josh White on a very early Electra album with one of those things on the back that says: "Should you purchase a stereo set, this hi-fidelity recording will never become obsolete, and neither will I, Jack Holtzman." Owner and whatever, and . . . was that it? God love ya, kid! Really nice to work with a really quick helper. Such is Carmelita. [Bobby's wife, Norma, in the studio with him.] Stand up, honey. Bobby Dale until six o'clock in the morning. Beaver, Beverley Wilshire along at six . . . but actually doesn't go on the air with records until eight because at six,* The Unheard of Hour, *and Alan Watts at seven.*

NORMAN DAVIS Gee, so many drug mentions in there, Bobby. Eight bennies!

BOB MCCLAY Bobby Dale was the guy who taught me what every one of those words meant. A pioneer in more ways than one.

NORMAN DAVIS I hear you did just regular salads in the old days, Bobby.

BOBBY DALE Oh yeah. Clean living. I never inhaled anything stronger than a Kool regular until I was thirty-three and moved to the bay.

NORMAN DAVIS Bobby and Donahue had the thing where they would look out from the Columbus flatiron building. From Tempo Records. They're up there with binoculars, looking right up Montgomery into Enrico's. And there was a guy in there they didn't like. So they go up and order all this food and force the guy—political guy, you remember that—forcing the guy to pay the tab.

BOBBY DALE I first ran into Tom Donahue when we were both strictly Top 40 jocks. But that was the early years. I didn't smoke any grass; I was from Minneapolis! You know, I took Tom Donahue on his first trip. I'd only been there twice, so appointed myself an expert immediately. I said, I don't have to read about it, man. I know what I'm doing. Just call me Dr. Feelgood, and boom! That was it. Oh, he was tough to control. Voco called him "Tom Dominant." This is a Friday night in North Beach, it's 11:30, and Tom wants to go out. I said, "Well, Tom, no, you don't really want to go out there. Remember we've all been out there before, right?" He walks out, no shoes, down the alley to Grant Avenue, and we can hear all these bottles blasting and, "Same to you, motherfucker!" Every noise is magnified two hundred times. We immediately run back upstairs, man, back into the apartment. It wasn't much of a trip, but it was intense. By the next night he thought he'd found the answer to everything. I knew what he meant.

Bobby Dale's drink was Cutty Sark, and he had a rule: no drinking on the job. Everything else was okay. Some Saturdays at Voco's house, Bobby said they would fill the pipe, watch Chuck Jones cartoons, and "just laugh our asses off for an hour." The first time he tried a sugar cube of LSD, he found himself at Donahue's place.

BOBBY DALE Here was Tom, sitting on the couch, he had all these broken amyl nitrates around him, and he was smoking a joint. The first thing he said to me was, "Man, am I high." Jesus, that just cracked me up. I thought, *You think you're high. I can barely see you down there and you're four hundred fuckin' pounds.*

Bobby died at sixty-nine in 2001.

TERRY MCGOVERN Oh man, Bobby and Carmelita. . . . I had come to San Francisco, July of '69 from Pittsburgh, looking for a job at KSFO. Don

Sherwood ruled the airwaves from there like a czar. It's a source of great wonder how a thousand-watt nighttime radio station that doesn't even get across the Golden Gate Bridge could have the Giants, the 49ers, the Warriors. Every fucking team, KSFO AM had it. It was due in large part because everybody listened to Don Sherwood. Program director Al Newman takes me to Ondine in Sausalito, and very gently tells me he thinks I'm good, maybe in a few years blah blah blah blah. I'm already on KDKA and I think I'm hot shit . . . I was gonna get on a plane the next morning—which I did. But that night crossing the Golden Gate with Peter Scott—the assistant PD—he's taking me back to the Fairmont in San Francisco, and it's just a gorgeous fuckin' night. The ice cold fog is layin' on the bridge like meringue, we're in this little Volkswagen Bug, and Peter turns on KSFO. It's midnight; out of the speakers comes "Wade in the Water," by Ramsey Lewis, followed by "When You Wish Upon a Star," by Cliff Edwards, the voice of Pinocchio. Those two, back to back. Then the mic opens . . . and there is nothing. Then, I don't know you can hear something . . . somebody grunting or something? "Hand me that, Carmelita"—it's like listening to a guy waking up in the morning—"Oh hi, hey . . . Big O Tires . . . Big O Tires. . . ." Reading some copy, a 60 second commercial, he couldn't get through it, and finally, music started . . . and he was gone. Peter doesn't say anything. I'm looking at him out of the corner of my eye, finally I said, "That's your all-night man?" He said, "Not anymore." He drops me off at the Tonga Room there in the Fairmont on California Street—KSFO was on the mezzanine floor of the Fairmont Hotel—and I run up to my room, turn on my radio and Peter Scott is on the air. He had taken over and sent Bobby home. Bobby was on acid; he and Norma would drop acid, and sometimes he'd function and sometimes he wouldn't. But nobody would fire Bobby! He was a treasure! He was just a big, goofy, lovable, brilliant son of a bitch, who loved music more than anybody I've ever heard. And very eclectic taste. One of a kind. He really was.

BEN FONG-TORRES He was singular. Bobby had a jazz soul. Even at Top 40, he was always his own guy, totally improv and off the wall, doing W. C. Fields, Lord Buckley–inspired riffs, goofing with live spots, and being so unpredictable that programmer Chuck Blore once called him the worst DJ he'd ever heard. And then, hearing him months later, declared him one of the best. Don Sherwood called him "the disc jockey's disc jockey."

JOE CONRAD, DJ One night in '71 the hotline rang, and it was Bobby Dale. "Joe, do you know where I can score some acid? Roland Kirk is in town!" I just happened to have a little vial of Grateful Dead windowpane on me. I got off the air and went up to Enrico's. Bobby was on his regular stool at the end of the bar, sucking up drinks with Richard Brautigan. I slipped him three hits. He said thanks and swallowed all three—roughly 450 mics—which stunned me because one hit was enough to destroy anybody for twelve hours. A few days later I ran into Bobby in North Beach. "How was Roland Kirk?" "Oh man. I never got to see him." "How come?" "Somehow I climbed up on my roof to see the stars and couldn't remember how to get back down."

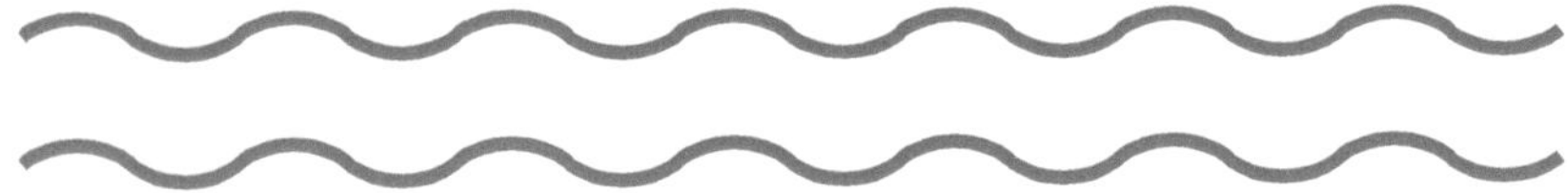

SIDE TRIP

Budd Stuntt, Blimp Pilot

https://www.youtube.com/watch?v=l4TIWkQ8UrU
TV promo with DJ Stephen Capen and Budd Stuntt's dog playing with KSAN's tenth-anniversary cake.

JOE LERER KSAN was the station I listened to when I worked at KFRC and KSFX. I joined the Jive 95 right after Tom died in 1975. I was so happy to be in sales at a much looser and more inclusive work environment. You could bring in ideas for programming—soon I was in the studio recording spots. Budd Stuntt came out of a collaboration with Terry McGovern. McGovern gets the credit. For three years, I called in as morning traffic and weather guy-in-the-sky in his blimp. I received a great lesson from the Committee Theatre, where I learned improv: it is always more interesting to "play against the obvious." A geezer in a blimp, on a totally hip FM station was so unhip—it was hip. *Who was this Stuntt guy* (two *d*'s, three *t*'s)*? Does he live in the blimp?* Live from the Jive LTA—lighter than air—95. Most endearing to listeners? My dog Bennet, who barked once for yes, twice for no. "Doggy, is it foggy up here?" "Arf!"

NORMAN DAVIS

KSAN's Guiding Light to a Better Beyond

Norman Davis began, he says, "back when Marconi was doing his thing," referring, of course, to Guglielmo Marconi, Nobel Prize winner in 1909 for inventing "a practical radio wave-based wireless telegraph system."

NORMAN DAVIS I got interested in Marconi's machine when I was a child in the 1940s in Idaho, because it was before television, and radio was *magic*. I think it was more powerful than a computer screen because your imagination is endless, and there were so many opportunities to use it. I had a very religious mom, so I had to pick when I could listen. I'd play sick and stay home when the kid serials were on: *Sky King*, *Captain Midnight*, *Tom Mix*, and the others.

His first radio job paid a dollar an hour. It took three months to get the dough. KGEM AM Boise. KSEI AM Pocatello. He had to cross state lines, use different names at different stations. Norman Davis was once "Lucky Logan."

NORMAN DAVIS I hated that.

Spokane, Denver, Kansas City, Pleasant Hill, Eugene, Portland. From San Rafael all the way to Santa Rosa, a Joseph Campbellian/Harry Chapinesque heroic trip into the mythical freaky DJ archetype: Norman Davis is coming to your town—hide your daughters!

CHAPTER 29

There goes the last DJ—Norman Davis in his 80s.
PHOTO BY SUSIE DAVIS

NORMAN DAVIS My only comment on that is—aside from your getting the order all wrong—at KYA I can claim credit for creating "Golden Gate Greats" and "Swingin' Sixty"—that's where we put sixty 45s into rotation instead of the usual forty. I met Tom Donahue there. He brought me to KSAN in the fall of '72, and I stayed until the summer of '78.

At KSAN, Norman (as one promo put it, "Radio's patron pervert and guiding light to a better beyond") played to the night people out there. Daughter Susie has her own rock 'n roll flare for living: she emceed a storytelling evening at Berkeley's Monkey House in '14 that inspired writer Jeff House to take notes for this book, and where filmmaker Jesse Block began shooting monologues for the KSAN film *Something's in the Air*. Susie has been a radio head, cherishing all things Jively.

SUSIE DAVIS The '70s KSAN was an amazing subculture. I was fourteen when my dad started working there, and I feel privileged to have been right in the middle of it. I was always observing, haunting the halls—nobody paying much attention to me—absorbing the music and all the brilliant craziness of the people there. They are like legends to me. Herewith, from the journal of an impressionable teenybopper: *This morning the station was all right: I did some coke and stayed up the whole night! Then Tom O'Hair and Dave McQueen came in about seven and smoked some pot, and that's what blew me away. You meet some heavy dopers around here. They were just starting the day out!*

NORMAN DAVIS In the six years that I was at KSAN, I was only talked to twice about my programming and behavior. Once, at a staff meeting, Tom said, "Norman, would you please not play 'Starfucker' anymore?" Remember that Rolling Stones record? That's the only thing he ever asked me to do on the air. And one time some really powerful mushrooms had come around—I had been getting into them for about a month, I guess—and Thom O'Hair, program director, said, "Norman, some of us are a little concerned you might be dipping into the mushroom bag a little too much." I don't know what it was that caused him to say that.

SUSIE DAVIS The type of adult I wanted to grow up to be was a combination of Mountain Girl from *The Electric Kool-Aid Acid Test*, the protagonists in *Fear and Loathing in Las Vegas*, and Dusty Street. She took me under her wing and turned me on to tons of cool music—and a ten-thousand-miles-an-hour lifestyle. The Queen. She said I reminded her of Dad because I spaced out like him. True.

Santana

The supergroup Santana had that "shock of the new" effect on the youth quake around the bay. Carlos Santana became a guitar god. He was so far out, he was transplendent; he didn't believe in time or gravity. Nearly sixty years on now, Santana still tours!

NORMAN DAVIS Santana's congas and timbales were inspired by groups like Olatunji and Willie Bobo. He adopted their driving rhythms, which became the hallmark of his sound.

CARLOS SANTANA KSAN was the first one I heard playing the long songs. The long versions. All of the music straight radio wouldn't play.

JOEL SELVIN One Sunday night at the Fillmore Auditorium, 1971, Santana was about to go out live on KSAN. Their ever-vigilant road manager Herbie Herbert reminded Donahue that there was a *broadcast ban* on Santana sets; they were concerned that music live on the radio took away album sales because bootlegs would circulate. When Herbert discovered that the station was going ahead with the broadcast, he picked up a hatchet from the band's toolbox and went to work on the phone lines. Hacking away, Herbie felt somebody jumping on his back. Turning to deliver a roundhouse blow, he knocked out KSAN's top female DJ. Then he turned back around and finished chopping up the phone lines feeding the broadcast back to KSAN.

PAUL "LOBSTER" WELLS, DJ Some things are said to embellish stories, and some memories are unclear. Joel's book, *Summer of Love*, clearly indicated that Big Daddy had been reminded of the band's wishes. I wasn't there. Everyone was pissed. No one expected Herbie to chop the lines, but if Santana didn't want it, Herbie was doing his job. Good thing he didn't use the hatchet on whoever tried to stop him.

BONNIE SIMMONS Herbie has fantastic stories and great flair in telling them. His penchant for hyperbole only enhanced them, for the most part.

KENNY WARDELL I was at this show. I seem to remember Dusty going nuts because KSAN had been broadcasting most of the sets all week. It was the last night during the closing week of the Fillmore, and Carlos was the star. And Herbie cut the wires to the stage, which was total chaos for us radio folks. He pulled the plug! I thought it was a very thug-like thing to do—KSAN Jive 95 had dead air that night.

SIDE TRIP

The Legendary O'Hair

DJ, program director, station manager, FM consultant—Thom O'Hair's real name was Gubbins, and his radio IQ was off the charts. Here's a "Metromedia radio memorandum," which O'Hair sent to corporate and affiliates down the line after a minor remodeling.

Well, we finally purged ourselves of October's flu, ingrown toenails, toothaches, and insecticide poisoning. A tip to all you Metromedia program directors: to ward away sickness, stand on your desk clad only in your shorts with a Roman candle in each hand, chanting "Eighteen Hammers" and

McQueen & O'Hair's morning show often started on time.
COURTESY DAVE MCQUEEN

"Oh, Susannah" four times, put an APC tablet under each turntable, and stay away from all contact sports for twenty-four hours.

JOHNNIE WALKER O'Hair was a tough biker sort, a very cool guy with a renegade mustache, long hair, and cowboy boots. He became the first guy I ever heard order a "JD on the rocks." We hit it off straightaway.

JOHN GRIVAS, DJ Thom O'Hair was an adventure. When he was a partier, it would be like getting on an elevator. He couldn't stop at the second or third floor. He had to go all the way to the penthouse. I could be like that too, so I always had to get off before him.

DAVE MCQUEEN, Gnus Thom was a storyteller. A fabulist. Which makes it difficult sometimes to sort out what actually happened from what Tom said happened. But he was a good disc jockey because of that ability to tell stories—an essential trait that any good jock has to have: the ability to tell stories quickly. Short.

JOHN GRIVAS I really admired his on-air delivery; hip, tight, and naturally funny. When he interacted with Dave McQueen, it was pure radio magic.

THOM O'HAIR In 1967, I'd drive down on weekends from my job in Oregon—as a disc jockey, you always had bald tires, one gauge on the dash was heading for E, and the other headed for H—white-knuckle all the way from Roseburg to San Francisco. I went to visit with Bob McClay, feeling fortunate enough to be the kid that kind of hung out at KMPX. After driving all night into a typical San Francisco day—cold and rainy—I went out to the Haight. It's probably around eight in the morning, and there's a line on Haight Street of long-haired types outside a store. I immediately pull over and go get in line, "Brothers, what's going on?" Pacific Stereo had gotten a shipment of FM radios in—so the rumor had it. The thing opened at, like, ten in the morning, and here were eighteen people in line, in this crummy weather, waiting to go in and spend *four hundred dollars* on a KLH Model 20 or something. A turntable with speakers in the lid. And an FM radio. To put that four hundred dollars in a little perspective: a normal disc jockey made about that a month. So you had to invest in order to hear what the hell was going on in FM! I knew on the drive back to this thousand-watt AM in Eugene that its days were numbered, that stereo had made a difference in this world. One thing Tom and I would talk about was how playing music for each other was a passion. Everyone in radio did it. It was the height of radio coolness to have the gear in your home to mix music.

JOHNNIE WALKER Thom O'Hair's first job as a teenager had been in a mechanic's shop, where he said he kept the guys entertained by picking records to play on their hi-fi.

GLENN LAMBERT, DJ In 1971, I became program director for WGRG, a free-form hippy-dippy radio station in the Berkshire Mountains of Massachusetts. That December I was in San Francisco, where I'd lived briefly and been a devoted KSAN listener. Somehow I arranged a lunch with Tom Donahue. The first person I met was Thom O'Hair, who looked me over with the O'Hairy eyeball. "Why are *you* here?" he asked. Blah-blah, I answered, dropped a name or two, mentioned Donahue. "You want a job, don't you?" "No," I told him, adding how I already had a job; I just wanted to visit radio mecca. "Bullshit! Of course you're looking for a job! That's the only reason anybody comes here. Well, let me tell you something"—his finger pointing this close to my face—"You can take any *asshole* off the street and put him behind a microphone and he *thinks* he's a *DJ*. But you know what he is? *Still* an *asshole*!" With that, he turned and exited, ending our warm one-minute relationship. I picked my jaw up off the floor.

Beginning in '76, Glenn occupied KSAN's 10 a.m. to 2 p.m. shift.

GLENN LAMBERT O'Hair was gone by then. But we did meet at a few reunion-type affairs over the years. Of course I told him the story. Of course he didn't remember.

JOANNE GREENE There was a mellow O'Hair, too, the opposite of that Alaskan brown bear that could make you feel pretty small. His piercing insights were not only original; they were spot on and just might work. His hilarious ones out of left field that often went up in smoke—you still wanted to remember them verbatim! Some of them. There was this day I recall from '79: Thom, afternoon jock, is with Chris Stanley, my Gnus partner and co-host on *The '80s*, our Sunday interview show. The two men are having two or four drinks with their acid across the street at the Financial Corner. On a tear about L. David Moorhead, the despised GM, whom Chris christened El Nuclear Warhead. The combination of acid and alcohol isn't new, but with O'Hair, results may vary. Walking into the studio for the 3 p.m. newscast, I notice his normal mischievous glint has gone into glaze mode. Maniacal. I hold my breath; the plan is to take over the microphone, do the newscast after this record, and leave without incident. As the song ends, I've got my stack of notes and miscellaneous wire copy, which

O'Hair grabs away, crunches up into a clump, flips his Bic—torches it. "*What the hell!*" I grab at the thing and blow out the fire, catching O'Hair exiting the studio with his triumphant laugh. Hardy-har-har. I collect myself and deliver what I hoped might sound like a semi-coherent newscast. Of course that part I don't remember anything of. I must have just kept talking.

JOHN GRIVAS In 1973, I sent Thom O'Hair air checks, and he wrote back, "We don't have any openings now, but if you are ever in the area, drop in." Now, when you are twenty-two and working for a station in Racine, Wisconsin—that seems like a *let's see if I can get a meeting and a job* invitation. My twenty-year-old bride and I loaded up the red '67 Beetle with all our worldly possessions. (Ah, to be young again!) Two thousand miles, one blown transmission, a couple of long-haired freaky people stranded outside Salt Lake City. Finally, the Bug attached to an eighteen-foot U-Haul, we lumbered into San Francisco. The car radio was blasting "Fresh Air" by Quicksilver as I parallel parked—found a space on Bush Street! Found a fleabag apartment house near Chinatown, and the next day I went to KSAN. For some reason O'Hair seemed a bit shocked. "Well, let's go for a ride." He took me in a cab to a house out by Golden Gate Park that he said was the Jefferson Airplane's house. Current home of Grunt Records. We played some pool with Papa John Creach. Had refreshments (he said he was a bit bummed someone made off with his stash)—a few refreshments. Thom left. I didn't realize the trip was my job interview. I walked all the way back downtown, bouncing off walls and doorways to that fleabag on Bush. Happiness! Definitely a wonderful stroll.

NORMAN DAVIS In the late '80s, Thom won a contract dispute with KOFY in San Francisco and was able to buy a house on the southern Oregon coast where he built his state-of-the-art studio. Then the IRS showed up and said he owed them fifty thousand dollars, and he had no other option but to sell his home. He rented a place, worked on some of his million ideas—like "RadiObits," which was a database of the famous, so you could read obituaries on the air right after they died. In '94, I got married and he came up to visit, and that was the last time I saw Thom. He had been a three-pack-a-day smoker, so the news of his heart attack was not a big surprise. Then I got the news of his second attack, and then the news he had expired.

We were about 150 strong at Thom's wake, held at the Firehouse on the Fort Mason Pier. His son and friends wired the event, so every tale told about O'Hair also aired from 88.3 FM to the universe—or to anyone tuned

in near that part of San Francisco. At sunset we walked out and stood at the edge of the water. His ashes were rocketed above the bay . . . a parachute bringing them back down into the deep. What a sendoff! O'Hair's legacy also included "Hog Ranch Radio": a signal he wired up at the Strawberry Music Festival, so folks in their tents could catch jam sessions and shows they weren't able to get up and boogie at. "Years ahead of wi-fi," he told us.

BONNIE SIMMONS Thom really put his heart into that Strawberry Music Festival. It was a weekend with wonderful bluegrass and great musicians from all over, held every summer near Yosemite National Park.

When I saw O'Hair in New York in 1980, he'd just come from a meeting with executives—he was a big-time media consultant by then—about a new venture starting up called MTV. I asked what he thought of a new music station that'll be on TV instead of FM radio. "Aw," he said, "it's the brotherhood of the beak over there." I didn't get it until he brushed an index finger a couple of times across his nose.

https://strawberrymusic.com/hog-ranch-radio
With O'Hair's report on the '96 fire up there.

95
FM
SHERIDAN '74
KSAN
SAN FRANCISCO · A Metromedia Stereo Station

KSAN Ad, 1974.

30

LAST DANCE WITH WINTERLAND (HE'S AL FRANKEN)

https://www.youtube.com/watch?v=gER0LhISPt0
Final night at Winterland Ballroom, simulcast with KQED.
Highlights, 1978, 29 minutes.

New Year's Eve of '78, KSAN FM and KQED TV simulcast the last rock 'n roll bash at the Winterland Ballroom. Featured on the air and on the screen were anchors Glenn Lambert and Norm Winer, and your roving floor reporter, Scoop Nisker.

NORM WINER The closing of the Winterland Ballroom after thirteen years was a phenomenal event—something that many people will never remember—so it's great there was technology to video it. Winterland and the Dead for New Year's figures prominently in the folklore surrounding *BGP: Bill Graham Presents*. It was always something people had to be part of.

BILL GRAHAM I always think of those Dead shows as "Timeout World." We'd do the shows from 9 p.m. to 9 a.m., and after the music we'd put on silent films, then turn the lights in Winterland up a bit and serve everybody breakfast.

Norm Winer came west from WBCN—the KSAN of Boston. He comes up big in Bill Lichtenstein's book, WBCN and the American Revolution. (The book and related documentary re BCN are definitely worth seeing.)

NORM WINER Planning this nine-hour simulcast with our friends from KQED—meaning, simultaneously televising on KQED while KSAN ran the audio in glamorous stereo—the public TV crew were talking camera positions, sequence flow. Now, having done a number of Deadcasts, I offered a suggestion to these professionals: "Whatever you do, do not eat, do not drink, anything backstage. It might look like a fabulous piece of fruit or a harmless can of soda, but it's not something to be drunk if you find it backstage." When you're talking about a Grateful Dead event, you have to talk slowly and repeat yourself. Finally, New Year's Eve arrived: around eleven o'clock, some cameramen went down. They would not be available for the duration, incapacitated because they overlooked words of warning. That was how the Dead entertained themselves and their coterie in those days. Tonight with them were the Blues Brothers, a novelty act based on a sketch on *Saturday Night Live*, only a couple of years old at that point. Because it was a hiatus for the show, Bill Murray joined John Belushi and Dan Aykroyd. Laraine Newman was there too, with two other *SNL* greats, the comedy duo of Al Franken and Tom Davis.

Norm and Glenn fill forty-five minutes at a time—breaks between sets. There's Glenn in a wacky '70s headset, on-camera bumping into a local celebrity, none other than the famous thousand-words-a-day/six-days-a-week *Chronicle* newspaper scribe from the colorful days of three-dot Big City journalism; a crushing wit, who coined *beatnik* and *Bagdad by the Bay*; this man dances to Jefferson Airplane in a tux! He dined out with others every night until he died in 1997. He's been called the Bay Godfather of the tweet, and "Mr. San Francisco" ("Don't Call it Frisco") . . . a chronicler since 1938 . . . Herb Caen!

GLENN LAMBERT Sir, how do you do? Herb, I'm Glenn Lambert, I'm from KSAN.

HERB CAEN I thought you were Werner Erhard!

GLENN LAMBERT Oh God, please.

HERB CAEN E-S-T is probably the way to go, huh? Well, Happy New Year!

GLENN LAMBERT Happy New Year to you; what is it, about 20 minutes or so?

HERB CAEN Well, I can't tell by my watch, because I'm on the wrong batteries. I'm connected to my pacemaker.

GLENN LAMBERT Is it a tradition with you, to come to Grateful Dead concerts New Year's Eve at Winterland?

HERB CAEN Not lately. Because the feet go first. This isn't on the air is it?

GLENN LAMBERT Yeah, I think we are. That shadowy form there is a camera.

HERB CAEN Why do you have to have all the lights? You're on radio!

GLENN LAMBERT This is TV as well.

HERB CAEN Channel 32?

GLENN LAMBERT That's right.

HERB CAEN I've contributed thousands of dollars to that station.

GLENN LAMBERT We have about fifty-four hundred people here; that's the official estimate.

HERB CAEN I don't feel as sentimental about this place as I do about the old Fillmore.

GLENN LAMBERT It's not the kind of place that has a history from another time.

HERB CAEN This place makes me think of the Ice Follies.

GLENN LAMBERT Were you here when the Ice Follies went on?

HERB CAEN Yeah. And what an improvement this is over the Ice Follies.

GLENN LAMBERT I learned this afternoon that there used to be an iceberg up in the balcony. Do you remember that?

HERB CAEN Yes I do. I think I married her. My second wife. We didn't really make it.

GLENN LAMBERT Well, thank you, Herb. We'll talk about that another time. They're signaling me to wrap up.

HERB CAEN Happy New Year to everybody.

GLENN LAMBERT Happy New Year to you!

HERB CAEN And buy the *Chronicle*; we really need the business.

NORM WINER Adding another level of excitement to the event, the Dead had recently played at the pyramids in Egypt. They were joined by an all-star cast—now tripping their brains out. I was a fan of Al Franken's and fortunate to run into him backstage. I asked him what he thought about the Winterland show. Franken believed he was at the 1968 Democratic Convention in Chicago. Because I was so youthful, I was experienced at interviewing people who were on acid when they were talking to a DJ, so I just went with him. He talked about Hubert Humphrey, he talked about the Chicago police riots, and chaos, and so on.

AL FRANKEN to Norm It's terrible what's happening in the streets. I just can't believe it.

Franken mentions Dan Rather, Abraham Ribicoff, someone funny in the Nebraska delegation, and Adlai Stevenson the Second, "who was quite a wit."

AL FRANKEN Morris Udall, who's down on the floor, I believe knows more Adlai Stevenson stories than practically anyone, so if we could just cut to Morris on the floor. There he is. Morris, of course, is the type of candidate who I think, in 1976, will have a lot to say about backpacking and solar energy.

Later, Al admitted he was just joking. He knew he was at Winterland on acid. He finished with a history lesson from 1924, an era when radio was the go-to for conventions. He said Al Smith's nomination took thirty ballots. And as the announcers talked on and on to kill time, "people turned off their radios."

31

ELVIS COSTELLO, WARREN ZEVON, AND SEX PISTOLS

Wonderful radio,
Marvelous radio.

—Elvis Costello, "Radio Radio"

When "(What's So Funny 'Bout) Peace, Love, and Understanding?" hit the station, everyone donned white buttons that said, "What's so funny?" Elvis Costello would have called us "tragically hip." He met Bonnie Simmons in '77 when she fetched Elvis Costello & The Attractions from SFO. The band brought her a pair of Doc Martens, which you couldn't get in the States then.

BONNIE SIMMONS All the jocks were excited by the music. I think Richard Gossett and I did the early beating of the drum. We started playing some Elvis singles way before the first album was released—"Radio Sweetheart," for one.

ELVIS COSTELLO KSAN probably spoiled me for everything else because there was nothing, of course, quite like it.

BONNIE SIMMONS Getting a record going—with no internet, no way to stream some radio station from somewhere else—took transferring the first station's excitement. If you loved something, you told other radio people in your city, your press contacts, neighbors, everyone!

ELVIS COSTELLO San Francisco was the first place I set foot in America, and Bonnie allowed me to run riot at KSAN. Years later, I found that first playlist I picked, written on KSAN notepaper and tucked in an old address book. It was like a blueprint: Iggy's "Search and Destroy," followed by the Searchers, "When You Walk in the Room"; Aretha's "Never Loved a Man"—I played NRBQ, Andy Williams, and the Mothers of Invention's "Who Needs the Peace Corps?" By my second visit, Bonnie let me ransack the record library. "Homework" by the J. Geils Band into Groucho Marx singing "Lydia the Tattooed Lady," into "Big Eyed Beans from Venus" by Captain Beefheart. We stayed on the air so long chatting that people thought we were stoned or in love.

https://soundcloud.com/dwingate/sets/elvis-costellos-first-radio-interview-on-ksan-sf-111517-wbonnie-simmons Elvis Costello's first radio interview in the United States, 1977. 60 minutes, also available on Jive 95 site.

I saw those werewolves walking up Nob Hill
Doing the Werewolves of K-SAN
I saw Bonnie Simmons walking and talking to the queen
Doing the Werewolves of K-SAN

—Warren Zevon at studio piano, 1978

In '78, Costello said, "My ultimate vocation in life is to be an irritant. Not something actively destructive, but someone who disorientates, who disrupts the daily drag of life just enough to leave the victim thinking there's maybe more to it than the mere humdrum quality of existence." An even faster-acting irritant arrived that year.

https://www.youtube.com/watch?v=USPEfbAiShM&t=86s Norman Davis, host of *The Outcastes Show*, tries to keep two Sex Pistols to a dozen dirty words on air in 1978. 53 minutes.

Rick Sadle interviews at Talking Heads concert, UC Berkeley, 1978.
PHOTO BY RICHARDMCCAFFREY.NET

JIM DRAPER On January 14, 1978, KSAN broadcast the Sex Pistols from Winterland. I was there with the Live-Jive crew to set up; we had audio equipment galore. Pulling up to the stage door two hours late, Sid Vicious walked out of the bus and put his cigarette out on the lens of my Polaroid. (I was able to snap four shots during the sound check and eight at the show—only a dozen to a Polaroid roll!) As their sound check began, I pressed a cassette into the deck, little realizing that this was the final Sex Pistols show, ever. I hit record.

https://www.youtube.com/watch?v=_GX-PZNig70
Sex Pistols sound check, Winterland, 20 min. Author Greil Marcus, at the show that night,wrote in his book, *Lipstick Traces: A Secret History of the Twentieth Century*: "They used rock & roll as a weapon against itself . . . stripping it down to essentials of speed, noise, fury, and manic glee no one had touched before."

BONNIE SIMMONS KSAN was the only place that would even imagine carrying the Pistols live. We'd been playing their records for a year; they weren't an oddity to us.

JOHNNIE WALKER The atmosphere at Winterland was almost on par with the Beatles' gig in Birmingham I saw so many years ago. Yes, they could play: Steve Jones knew his way round a guitar. Paul Cook kept it all hammering away at the back, and Johnny Rotten prowled and scowled his way round the stage hurling insults. Sid Vicious stood full on and faced the huge crowd—*come and get me if you dare*. He was so out of it, I expected him to fall off the stage at any moment. Complete mayhem, but I loved all of it.

NORM WINER I will always remember where I was sitting for the Sex Pistols, my vantage point watching the show unfold. They played their asses off. It was a phenomenal rock concert, and even if punk was not your bag, it was such a part of history KSAN brought to its listeners.

BONNIE SIMMONS A classic show. I was emcee, and Norman Davis was backstage broadcasting. As they came on stage, people started hurling everything they had onto the stage. Shoes, money—somebody threw their camera up there. Bill Graham reached out to pull me behind one of speakers. He wanted to get as many targets off stage as possible.

JOHNNIE WALKER The crowd and band, one heaving mass of glorious rock 'n roll rebellion. And like the Beatles at Candlestick Park before them, the Sex Pistols played their last ever gig, in San Francisco. Malcolm McLaren had manipulated the whole thing, the great rock 'n roll swindle, indeed. It had been a fun ride, but it was all over. They broke up the next day.

NORM WINER General manager Jerry Graham told us the morning after the Sex Pistols broadcast, "This never existed." Like, *this conversation never happened*. Asking us to delete from our minds any memory of the event. *This cultural touchstone never happened.*

JOHNNIE WALKER Jerry Graham was a bookish intellectual who liked his life, hosting dinner parties in the Berkeley hills, singer-songwriter LPs playing softly in the background. Jerry hated punk rock; so did Metromedia. *Get that damned punk rock off the air*. Some jocks—Richard Gossett, Beverley Wilshire, Sean Donahue, Vicenta Licata—loved the English "don't give a fuck, let's have a laugh" attitude. Freedom and anarchy and stirring things up were part of what KSAN was all about. They knew what *wanker* was about. Management and most of the audience didn't. Wankers!

JOEL SELVIN It was this bad moment when new wave emerged, because it created an immediate dichotomy in the staff. KSAN was sort of perched on this teetering point of, are we this, or are we that?

BONNIE SIMMONS We were going through a transition: playing highly produced music like the Eagles and Fleetwood Mac. But that came at a time when alternative and punk sounded extremely fresh and politically fit the time for us.

DAVE MCQUEEN Along came a new generation who didn't want to hear the same radio station with the music their older brothers and sisters had. KSAN got way too invested in punk music, which, let's face it, is not audience friendly.

DUSTY STREET Our audience rebelled. The generation that had listened to us coming up were in their late thirties, starting to have more "normal lives." They didn't want to hear about Talking Heads. And they sure didn't want to hear about Sex Pistols. They weren't angry anymore; they had nice jobs, probably 1.5 kids, and still wanted to hear Led Zeppelin and Tom Petty, and that. That's part of the reason I ended up going to LA, to become part of the first punk and new wave radio station, KROQ. I think that's why radio stations are successful for a short time. I think Bonnie Simmons said it best: "There's a shelf life to that kind of art."

BEN FONG-TORRES KSAN DJs being able to choose their own music had begun to backfire. The sound, to put it simply, became inconsistent. As FM rock became a moneymaker, KSAN drew increasingly powerful competition, and the booming record industry began to fragment into disco, punk, funk, and other responses to what was being called "corporate rock."

TRISH ROBBINS I wish we could've commercialized it in a way that worked for both sides of the argument: commercial *and* new.

DAVE MCQUEEN KMEL ["Camel"] came along, and a lot of our once-audience went over there. KSAN couldn't make it work: how to keep old listeners or pick up new listeners. And this is after we'd been on top for a *dozen years*.

JOEL SELVIN The San Francisco market's a little weird. You have this, like, hip enclave in San Francisco and Berkeley, but ratings were based on the nine neighboring counties, Contra Costa, Solano, San Mateo, San Jose—KMEL was making inroads in the suburbs.

KSAN AIR SCHEDULE FOR JANUARY 1979

MONDAY - FRIDAY

6AM-10AM----NORM WINER
10AM-2PM----GLENN LAMBERT
2PM-6PM-----BEVERLEY WILSHIRE
6PM-10PM----TONY KILBERT
10PM-2AM----RICHARD GOSSETT
2AM-6AM-----SEAN DONAHUE

SATURDAY

6AM-11AM---FRED GREENE
11AM-4PM---RON MIDDAG
4PM-9PM----JAY HANSEN
9PM-2AM----NANCY NEWHOUSE

SUNDAY

2AM-7AM---VINCENTA LICATA
7AM-8AM---ALAN WATTS
8AM-9AM---MS DEMEANORS &/or BEHIND THE GREEN ROOM
9AM-12N---TALKIES
12N-4PM---BEN FONG-TORRES
4PM-9PM---JAY HANSEN
9PM-12M---SUNDAY NITE LIVE
9PM-1AM---NANCY NEWHOUSE
1AM-6AM---TRISH ROBBINS

REGULAR FEATURES

ALAN WATTS	SUNDAY-7am; repeat Monday 2am.
ASTROLOGY REPORT	MONDAY-FRIDAY; 7am,9am,4:55pm.
BEHIND THE GREEN ROOM	SUNDAY; 8am-9am; repeat Tuesday 1am, TWICE MONTHLY.
BUDD STUNTT	MONDAY-FRIDAY; 8:25am, 5:25pm
DRUG REPORT	FRIDAY; 5:55pm.
HERETICS HOUR	SATURDAY; 2-4am.
LISTENER's PERSONALS	CALL-INS; 986-2825.
MS. DEMEANORS	SUNDAY; 8am-9am, repeat Tuesday 1am - ONCE A MONTH.
NEWSCASTS	MONDAY-FRIDAY; 7:30am, 8:30am, 9:30am, 12N, 4pm, 5:45pm.
PILEDRIVER	WEDNESDAYS; 2-4am.
SCOOP'S LAST NEWS SHOW	MONDAY-FRIDAY; 10am,10pm.
SNOW LINE	24 HOUR CALL-IN,982-2222.
SUNDAY NITE LIVE	SUNDAY; 9-12M.
TALKIES	SUNDAY; 9-12N.
WHAT'S HAPPENING	MONDAY-FRIDAY; 8am, 1pm, 6:30pm SATURDAY-SUNDAY; 9am, 1pm, 5pm.

1979 lineup.
COURTESY BOB SIMMONS

JOHNNIE WALKER Bonnie Simmons left, taking up an offer at Warner Brothers in LA. Jerry Graham put an ad in *Billboard*—the finest radio people in the States must have replied. Program director at KSAN? A high spot in anyone's career.

GLENN LAMBERT Norm Winer wanted it. Norm had years of experience at WXRT in Chicago and WBCN in Boston.

JOHNNIE WALKER Jerry hired his secretary. In terms of radio experience and musical knowledge, Abby Melamed had to have been the least qualified person for the job. Obviously Jerry wanted a yes-person.

GLENN LAMBERT Abby was installed to do what Metromedia and KMET wanted her to do. That was a real turning point. A downward turning point.

1980 Billboard.

PHOTO BY DAVE PATRICK / BERKELEY BARB, COURTESY OF RAQUEL SCHERR.

Lots of DJs play in rock & roll bands. Trish Robbins rocks here with Peterbilt & the Expressions at San Francisco's Mabuhay Gardens. The "Fab Mab" showcased Pearl Harbor & the Explosions (Trish sang backup) and Connie & the Cocksuckers et al. Dig that mullet! Trish the Dish!
COURTESY TRISH ROBBINS

THE END OF SOMETHING, 1978–1979

There is this thing called the mainstream media that is a giant corporate echo chamber that serves multinational corporations of billionaires and nobody else. It's destroying this country. It's destroying democracy.

—Thom Hartmann

KMPX DJs began at one extreme, introducing young Americans to psychedelic music from the Jefferson Airplane, and Country Joe & the Fish. KSAN DJs, introducing punk, tried to hear where their next wave of hip listeners were heading. "No future," spit the Pistols that final night in San Francisco.

GREIL MARCUS. author of *In the Fascist Bathroom: Punk in Pop Music, 1977-1992* While other FM outlets moved to the right in the face of punk challenge—Elvis Costello's "Radio Radio" tells the story—KSAN DJs Beverley Wilshire, Glenn Lambert, Richard Gossett, and Norm Winer sent probes to the left, opening the airwaves to outrage, farce, and surprise.

JOEL SELVIN Richard Gossett was playing "Money Changes Everything" by the Brains every night.

This is Kate Ingram, music director from July '78 to July '79.

KATE INGRAM I call that my "Year of Living Crazily." Metromedia fired Jerry and Abby and had L. David Moorhead—GM at KMET in LA—start commuting to San Francisco. That's when the bigger staff turnover happened.

GREIL MARCUS Metromedia deputized Moorhead to take care of business. Within little more than a month, every KSAN DJ was gone, and the music had turned to lead.

By November 1980, more than sixty employees had been canned.

FRED GREENE DJs who shaped their own shows became domesticated or unemployed. The corporatocracy won.

JOE LERER After nearly three years of reporting from my blimp, Budd Stuntt was let go by this bad-cologne-scented "rescue GM" sent up from LA to get rid of our culture. L. David play-the-top-two-hits Moorhead. He showed me a letter from the Metro lawyers saying that we were misleading the public by saying we had a reporter in a blimp. Really? I left my sales job and my daily broadcast buddies the next day. Like Budd said at the end of his reports: "I'm over, and now I'm out."

Joanne Green was horrified at what was happening in the Gnus department. Her co-anchor Chris Stanley was beyond the beyond by then; he'd been up a couple of days, saw the GM stalking the hallway, went up and slugged him. L. Nuclear Warhead went off. Then, like Chris always signed his letters, it was "Adios."

JOANNE GREENE I couldn't take it—I was getting hate mail from every hippie in San Francisco because they had no one to complain to now that Scoop and Larry Bensky were gone.

GREIL MARCUS The pods had seized control. On the eve of the purge, Moorhead held a press conference. It was sickening to watch his attempts to exploit San Francisco's famous superiority complex. Oh no, he said to the assembled writers, he would *never* try to impose his successful KMET format on KSAN; San Francisco was much more sophisticated than *Los Angeles.* New personnel would have close ties to "the City." Moorhead brought in a new program director, Jackie McCauley, and a new music director, KMET's David Perry: people well socialized in the values of the music industry. Disc jockeys who were committed to much that was adventurous in late-'70s rock were replaced by those willing to submit to all that was fraudulent. ("I hate the term 'disc jockey,'" Moorhead said; "I prefer 'air personality.'")

Some DJs held out as long as they could.

STEPHEN (JAY) HANSEN It seemed like half the songs played were message songs from staff to management. Every time I hear Rockpile's "Crawling from the Wreckage," I'm thrust back to that time.

GREIL MARCUS Glenn Lambert responded to word of Jackie McCauley's imminent arrival from LA with a thrown-away reference to "our new program director, the Ayatollah Khomeini" (this a week after Khomeini banned music on Iranian radio). He took his leave with a historic segue of Bob Dylan's "Man Gave Names to All the Animals" straight into the "The Teddy Bears' Picnic." For weeks, Beverley Wilshire closed her show with warnings: Peter Gabriel's "Here Comes the Flood," or "Radio Radio."

> *You're either shut up or get cut off*
> *they don't wanna hear about it's*
> *only inches on the reel-to-reel*
> *And the radio is in the hands*
> *of such a lot of fools trying to*
> *anesthetize the way that you feel.*
>
> —Elvis Costello, "Radio Radio"

GREIL MARCUS The new air staff spoke in professional voices and betrayed no personal taste: they played what the computers told their bosses to tell them to play. The result was an almost unrelieved diet of rock 'n roll that claims its listeners not through imagination and style but by going through the motions: Van Halen, ELO, Styx, Foreigner, Journey, the Knack.

NORM WINER Here's an anecdote about my final show in 1979 that figuratively, symbolically, and otherwise really seals for me the KSAN story. Among the first things Moorhead did was put a bunch of records in our studio in a bin,

Fred Greene & Norm Winer, 2021/1979.
PHOTO BY FRED GREENE / GREENECREATIVE.COM

like you'd find in record stores. Remember record bins? Those were the ones we'd be mandated to play for listeners. Suddenly it became Ted Nugent and Billy Joel records, which had no place being on KSAN. Here was this Giant Beautiful Record Library directly opposite the air studio—something that provoked awe in the press people who saw the scope of it. Every style of music, vintage LPs going back into the '40s and '50s. It. Was. Phenomenal! So now, on my final day on KSAN, I saw the carpenters building doors to our record library—I could see from the studio directly across the hall, these wooden doors. As my show continued, I watched as they put a padlock on the door, locked the padlock—entrance to that room was henceforth forbidden. How did a radio station broadcast the Sex Pistols' final performance and suddenly go to playing a mandated selection of records that had no place being on KSAN at the time—from a bin like you'd find in record stores, destroying for all intents and purposes the station and what it meant to so many loyal listeners, ending up in going country-western? My final words on the air as the KSAN morning DJ were, "To the people of San Francisco: you deserve better."

Chris Stanley and Steve Capen in the middle of everything—as usual—interview Fred and Joanne Green at their wedding.
PHOTO BY FRED GREENE / GREENECREATIVE.COM

1980 MediaFile

For whom the wedding bells toll: Last month we told you that **Joanne Rosenzweig** and **Fred Greene** were married. That's not the item this month. This month's news is that they were both fired (she from **KSAN** and he from **KSJO**) while away on their honeymoon! Fred's fall came in a station shakeup which eliminated three positions, including Fred's spot, creative director. Joanne's canning climaxed the problems she's been having with program director **Tom Yates**. (Also on the KSAN hit list last month were news writer **Hank Rosenfeld** and nighttime jock **Lobster**.) Yates found Joanne's approach to the news to be too "issue-oriented, and esoteric." Read not enough sex and drugs and rock and roll. Joanne's replacement is **Jack Popejoy**, who was flown up from L.A. But to avoid FCC flak, neither he nor **Marshall Phillips** has been made news director. With Joanne's ouster the KSAN management team is comprised totally of white males. On the bright side, Fred fell into a job jocking in the seven to midnight slot at **KRE** in Berkeley.

San Francisco Chronicle, *November 8, 1980.*
AUTHOR'S COLLECTION

In early 1980, Steve Chapple of the *Chronicle* wrote, "Crazed morning jock Stephen Capen restores some of the early KSAN spirit." When Stephen came in as "The Morning Product," we ran him for, candidate from the "This Ain't No Disco Party" (an excuse for us to play Talking Heads). Opening at the Boarding House on Bush Street one night for Dan Hicks & His Hot Licks, Capen gave a definitely twisted speech.

I was long gone, however, before my mentor did his last radio show on November 14. As was my Gnus boss, Joanne Greene. She was fired on her honeymoon. Jo Jo was in Maui with her husband Fred—a bunch of us danced at the wedding!—but after three nightmares, she phoned her pal Capen. That's how she found out they'd canned her. Metromedia's Moloch, Allen Ginsberg's destroyer-of-dreams, "whose soul is electricity and banks!" And warheads.

Capen's new Gnus foil was now Jack Popejoy. On the morning of the 14th, they played some old Donahue audio on the 8-track cart machine. The two radiomen thanked him, and then each another.

JACK POPEJOY Sixteen years I've been playing with records and microphones, and you're by far the best I've ever run into. Forever respected.

STEPHEN CAPEN It's been a real trip here. I don't think I've ever seen a radio station or a staff on a station, or people who listen to a radio station like KSAN. It's been amazing.

JACK POPEJOY It's what broadcasting is all about.

STEPHEN CAPEN Sure is.

JACK POPEJOY What living is all about. About humans being human.

STEPHEN CAPEN That's it. Thank you, Jack.

JACK POPEJOY Thank you. I appreciate it. Wanna go out for a little . . .

STEPHEN CAPEN Sure, I'd love a stiff one.

[Capen plays the Supremes, "Someday We'll Be Together."]

Another new guy at the station was Marshall Phillips.

MARSHALL PHILLIPS Tom Yates, the program director, handed me a script. "You're gonna read this." I went, "What?" I think I was one of the last hires. I felt like I was the "LA news guy," you know? And I got the horrible chance to read this:

> *KSAN was inaugurated in 1968 as the nation's first major underground rock 'n roll station. The man behind the format concept was Tom Donahue. KSAN now introduces its new sound of the '80s, on FM 95: stereo country.*

GREIL MARCUS For more than ten years, the station had been the heart of rock 'n roll in San Francisco; as the legatee of KMPX, the first non-Top 40 rock station in the country, it had in some ways been the heart of rock 'n roll radio in America.

JOEL SELVIN Underground radio was over. KSAN was dead, coffin nailed up, in the graveyard, toss some dirt on your way out.

33

TAILS OUT

KSAN Goes Country

New program director, Jackie McCauley, handling DJ duties spins a familiar tune from 1969's Nashville Skyline LP, "Lay Lady Lay." It's kind of a smooth way to segue from the old format into the new. When the song is over, McCauley turns on the microphone and announces, "That was Bob Dialin."

JOEL SELVIN Why did they go country? KMEL had handed them their ass in the ratings! The guys at Metromedia call me at the *Chronicle*, and they say, "We're turning this over to a country station, and we want some good will in the community." That's a big ask, you know? I mean, that's a news story, but I don't know about the good will thing. "Well, what can we do?" I said they needed to be conscious of the legacy, and they should turn the entire library over to the Bay Area Music Archives. "Okay, we'll do that." So I wrote a fairly positive article about the whole thing. And the night came, when a couple of friends and I went over to pack up the KSAN record collection. We're putting records in boxes. Jesse Rhodes is on the air, doing her country thing. And I hear alarm bells go off down the hall. I'm a newspaper guy—I know what that means—it's a flash transmission. I look up to see somebody go for it. I mean somebody's gotta go see *what the fuckin' thing is*, right? Nobody. Nobody even answers it. So I go to the wire machine to look at the teletype, and it says: "A man identified as John Lennon has been shot and taken to Bellevue Hospital." I rip into the library, pull a few Beatles records, a few Lennon records. I put the latest single on top, and into the booth. I show Jesse the wire and give her a stack of records. She breaks onto the air with the news, John Lennon has been shot, and plays "Yesterday." She got in Herb Caen thanks to me. I had complained to Herb, and in his column he wrote, "KSAN noted Lennon's death by DJ Jesse Rhodes spinning 'Yesterday,' one of the few Beatles songs upon which John Lennon didn't even appear." Yeah, talk about end of an era.

TIME IT WAS AND WHAT A TIME IT WAS A TIME OF

I was twenty-one years when I wrote this song.
I'm twenty-two now, but I won't be for long.

—Paul Simon

Before the little radio station that could (and did!) signs off, I asked folks to toast a quick-like, "fare-thee-well my honey," to what an old man with a Yiddish accent, in a Jive 95 promo, called, "the station of your wildest dreams."

BOB SIMMONS How did KSAN affect my life? I was happy to hop the train and be a part-time rider. I still have mixed feelings about the place. Some remember it as a kind of idyll. Me? Just like everything, you take the good with the bad. Roland Jacopetti and Paul Boucher were the first-string production cats. Roland was/is a great guy. Paul, RIP. My favorites were Sean, Raechel, Tom, both Larrys, Travus, Scoop, Rick, Ed Ely, Vicky, Phil Charles, Hadwig, Peter Laufer, McClay, Terry, Beverley, Ben, Willis, and a few others. It was a very interesting glob of people who served as the nucleus for a much larger community of listeners.

KATHY LERNER, engineer In '67, Howard [Hesseman] and I lived in a charmed fishing cottage, and we only had to hike down the Filbert steps to the radio station. We were married by a priest at the Zen Center. It was a new world of peace, love, and psychedelics giving fuel to the movement, a symbiotic relationship between music and the explorers of other realms. An amazing, idyllic life.

MICHAEL GOLDNER, listener The first time I ever took acid, someone was playing "Season of the Witch" by Donovan. The whole *Sunshine Superman* album, and *Surrealist Pillow* by Jefferson Airplane, that was KSAN. That and the Sandoz-quality LSD-25.

KATHY LERNER And I'll never forget seeing the Jimi Hendrix Experience with Tom and Rae up in the balcony of the Fillmore, snorting amyl nitrates.

TRISH ROBBINS I just remember feeling, *Oh God, I have found my home. I have found the place where I am supposed to be.* And obviously it was, because all I did was walk in and they gave me a job at the most famous radio station that ever was.

TERRY MCGOVERN I mean, I was fucking blessed. I don't take any credit—I had a talent, but I sure got more rewards out of it than I ever imagined. Donahue was a genius. He figured this out. He said, "How am I going to get people to listen to me?" By playing something nobody else on the planet plays.

BONNIE SIMMONS I think we knew that the real secret to keeping it successful was doing everything in the reverse from everyone around us. Tom told us: "Don't lie to them."

BEN FONG-TORRES In 1970, I got a call from the program director. "Ben, can you come over right away? We're doing our Christmas card shoot on Mount Tamalpais, and the whole gang is leaving the building. I'll teach you the ropes—three turntables, there's the board, the readings every hour for the FCC, this is the log, there's the phone, these are the cart machines, and you've got to write down what you're playing. We have a Kelly girl up front to answer the phone. Bye!" It was my first time on KSAN completely by myself; it was just that Kelly girl and me. And we did a three-hour show. Hey, it was the dream.

HANK ROSENFELD Speaking of the dream job, Ben—yes, for me, too! And now, after three years of discovering the ways that KMPX/KSAN was mythical, was a clique, was on a mission of bringing a community together with music and love—getting in touch with all of you and typing up whatever this all turned out to be—was another dream gig. That place taught me to keep dreaming.

JEFF NEMEROVSKI I was a teenager when I started there, filling the soda machine. I wore a tie and jacket—some of them suspected I was a narc. I worked my way into sales, where Bob Simmons said I could sell a refrigerator to an Eskimo. I was Captain Nemo on weekend shifts, from the bottom of the sea with songs of humpbacked whales in echo chambers around me. The happiest days of my life were spent at KSAN. We were in our twenties and owned the world.

SCOOP NISKER It's too bad we weren't taken more seriously. That's partly because we insisted that folk-rock music and revelry went with protest. We were drawing on the honorable tradition of jesters with our colorful clothes, pranks, and street theater challenging authority. There should be a statue of "the unknown hippie" on the DC mall and people could leave behind buttons and roaches.

BEN FONG-TORRES If there's one song that really captures the time that we lived in, something that was threaded through millions of us, it was Buffalo Springfield's, "For What It's Worth."

TONY PIGG, DJ We thought we were great; we felt we were into something that was really heavy. But it was a struggle to remain heavy.

THOM O'HAIR People forget, the front office of Metromedia was as important to the success of this form of radio as anybody. At the time I didn't feel that way. Like others, I thought they were just a bunch of old men interfering with us young Turks down in the radio trenches. But I learned after working for scared little ass bites over the years. I can't sufficiently express my respect for the people who ran the place. They gave us the sacred space necessary for flight.

TRISH ROBBINS I think we all thought it was going to keep on flying.

JOHN GRIVAS We were the proverbial tribal drum that kept the campfire going. But then the subculture became the mainstream culture, and everybody was banging on a drum and nobody could hear anymore because there were too many drums banging in the wind. Somehow those of us on the radio, and those of us listening to the radio, let this get away from us.

EDWARD BEAR We were generating light and love from listener ideas, the literature, the posters, the light shows, the clothing, and the fiber art, the healthier kitchens, and sexier bedrooms. Now I feel like an elder.

JOHN DENSMORE, drummer, the Doors I think of an elder as someone who cares about coming generations. If you don't feel longing about passing down some of the gems to your community, you're an *older*, not an elder. Politicians are olders. The job was to take the good intentions of places like KSAN and keep moving them into the power areas.

STEPHEN GASKIN The funny thing is, there was a reversal. John Mitchell, attorney general for Nixon, said, "This country's going to go so right wing you wouldn't recognize it."

BONNIE SIMMONS When you put this up against time clocks and against all the ratings books in the world and all the different focus groups in the world, it worked. And I know this is going to sound sappy—I like to think that in the end the good guys always win. Why else would we keep doing this if we didn't think it was worth it?

TRISH ROBBINS We need a Tom Donahue, a visionary, because the only way to bring back radio is to flip the switch, do what Tom did going from AM to FM. Go from FM to AM! Nobody cares about it; let's play! Tom would be doing that. Many of these stations are underwater anyway. If you did something crazy enough, I think people would listen. Get some characters back on the radio, people with musical knowledge, with stories!

BOB SIMMONS You know, radio is not like sculpture, and it's not like writing a book. You do a great show, you walk into the backyard, and throw it down in a well—you're creating something that's totally impermanent.

EDWARD BEAR I sometimes think that some of what we sent out into the foggy airwaves over the bay is still floating around out there. You never know.

NORMAN DAVIS It was, after all, the most exciting, caring, delicious radio there ever was.

BUZZY DONAHUE For a while I was living on Maui and had all kinds of jobs that had nothing to do with radio: I was a scuba diver on a glass-bottom boat and fed fish for a living; I was on the mic, telling people about the fish and making them mai tais. Then I moved to Port Townsend, Washington, to keep an eye on my mother. A good community radio station started up here in 2011, but I didn't get involved until an old friend from San Francisco moved here. She said, "I came up here because you have this radio station." That was Kate Ingram from KSAN. Six months later, she was in charge. I realized it was in my blood and volunteered at KPTZ. I'm in my seventies now, and I love the idea that I can be part of a radio station my community feels is there to help them. A listener will come up and say, "What are you doing over there?" and I say, "We're saving the world, one person at a time!" We're all volunteers, and I feel very grateful, sharing my love for music. That's what my father gave me. I mean, he didn't leave me any money, but he left me something better.

JOEL SELVIN Tom saw the whole thing; he got it, he knew what the cosmic joke was. He knew what we were put on the earth to do. And he lived it out every day, man. Being in his presence was just always a fuckin' thrill. Because you knew that he's the captain of the ship. We were gonna be sailing the high seas, we were gonna have more than our share of grog, and we were gonna have adventure and take home booty.

And that's the way it was, and that's the way it is, and it's always changing, and it is always the same. How's that for psychedelic? This is Tom Donahue. Raechel and I have really been having fun tonight. I'd had plans to go over to see Stoneground tonight; they've still got another show to do at the Keystone in Berkeley. So if you happen to go over there, would you tell 'em, "I can't make it, Jim. I'm just not in condition!" That's all tonight. This is Tom Donahue inviting you to listen in in Los Angeles, if you live there, visiting there, at KMET at 94.7. In San Francisco–Oakland, it's KSAN, Metromedia Stereo 95. The Jive 95!

CHAPTER 34

Everything is everything, and vice versa.
Everything is everything for better or for worse-a.
And everything is sex drugs rock 'n roll, body and soul,
birth death, and all the rest.
Everything is perfect in its imperfection,
in all the ten directions.
Everything is a metaphor for everything else.
Everything is you, and you are the next verse:
you are the universe;
You are the everything that is everything is everything is
everything is ______
Go ahead, fill in the blank.

"All and Everything Else," by Scoop Nisker

BONUS!

Mentors/Maniacs/Mates: Chris Stanley and Stephen Capen

Chris always had a book in his hand. He was blunt, loud, in-your-face.

—Bill Vitka

Steve's unleashed personality was entertaining beyond the boundaries of most in radio.

—Paul Wells

No one here to raise a toast
to a rock 'n roll ghost.

—The Replacements, "Rock & Roll Ghost"

My main mentors, a Gnus guy and a DJ, were maniacal. I met Chris "CBS" Stanley and Steve "Coyote" Capen at KSAN in '79. In '89, Chris got Capen a gig in New York, and Cape brought me in to produce the *Stephen Capen Afternoon Episode*, aired 2 to 6, on "WXRK. 92.3 K-Rock. Where it doesn't have to be old to be classic. Classic rock. K-Rock." The belly of the beast, 600 Madison Avenue, Midtown Manhattan—the beast being the main suit in sales, Mel Karmazin, future Sirius XM mogul (see Capen resume in the bonus section). Howard Stern, jewel of Infinity Broadcasting, would take everything from the waist down, and Capen would go for the neck up. (Howard said he liked listening to Steve as a young jock.) Cape sometimes played it as Coyote, come to the big city from Bisbee, way west in "Arid Zone A" (Cape's actual Arizona hideout). Like Bear in '68 coming down from the mountains to KMPX. Only trippier. K-Rock wanted Capen as their afternoon acid burnout, a flip side of Stern. We did what we could there: Wannabe-Scoop collages; *Bushwinkle & Danny the Flying Quayle!* cartoons; dropping psychedelics like Kesey, Gravy, and Alan Watts in between records ("Lo and behold, I had what I simply could not deny being an experience of cosmic consciousness, the sense of complete fundamental unity, forever and ever with the whole universe. And not only that. But that what this thing was fundamentally—despite everything and every kind of appearance in ordinary life to the contrary—that the energy behind the world was ecstatic bliss and love"), on eight-track cartridges from KSAN (I just realized: we were trying to do the Jive 95 again!). Capen's guests were from Greenpeace, Sea Shepherds, Venceremos Radio. Robert Bly came by and recited Rumi.

We were blown out of there in a year.

KSAN DJ Stephen Capen and Chronicle columnist Joel Selvin.
(Capen after playing David Bowie, "Changes") I love that song.
I love David Bowie. I love everybody! I love you. I-I-I'm under attack!
Have we been under attack yet this morning?
How long have we been under attack this morning?!"
PHOTO BY FRED GREENE / GREENECREATIVE.COM

Stephen Capen was born in Rockland, Massachusetts, February 28, 1946, and died at fifty-nine in his sister's house in Scituate, Massachusetts, September 12, 2005. In spring of '05, he sent an e-mail to Ben Fong-Torres, who had his "Radio Waves" column in the San Francisco Chronicle. In the e-missive, Cape mentioned the Firesign Theater classic game show satire, "Beat The Reaper!" And a line from a favorite book, Sheltering Sky by Paul Bowles: ". . . wondering how many more full moons we'll live to see. We act like it's limitless." Stephen offered this rendering of his radio tour through thirty-four stations in thirty-five years. "Give or take."

MY BRILLIANT CAREEN: AN ANNOTATED RADIOMAN'S RESUME

Mama, don't let your children grow up to be deejays
Unless you want them to wake up one day
realizing that what they do for a living
is sit in a padded room
speaking into a lead pipe.

—Stephen Capen, "My Brilliant Careen"

WFST AM AND FM, CARIBOU, MAINE, 1965

Learned that everybody in radio does everything at the radio station that needs doing. I was trashman, lawnmower/snow-shovel man, on air eight hours a day, six days a week.

GM unloads twelve-gauge at wife and children in a drive-by, emphasizing need for a divorce. Am smitten with manager of Norge Village Laundro (new advertiser!)

WBZA AM & FM, GLENS FALLS, NEW YORK, 1965

Morning *and* afternoon drive, go figure

Traded airtime for meals, motel rooms upstate, oblivion

WAAB, WORCESTER, MA, MORNINGS, 1966–1967

First air name, "Stephen Kane."

Fifty dollars to play your record? Wow!

WHYN, SPRINGFIELD, MA, P.M. DRIVE, 1967

WDRC, HARTFORD, CT, STEPHEN KANE, MIDDAYS, 1969

PD named Charlie Parker; you'd think I might have a prayer, instead starting to feel like unraveling New England sweater.

Contest with radio original John Rode: who could get away with the bluest comment? Board tech Paul Gregory judged competition. Me: "That's 'Mony, Mony' by Tommy James and the Dildos." That was pretty much it. GM Mike Boudrew, lovable lummox, asked why I'd said that. Told him I didn't even know what the word meant. I was twenty-three, speaking truth to powers that were! First of countless suspensions over the decades. Sometimes felt here like WBZ, the "Spirit of New England," which I loved as kid growing up in Maine.

WCCC AM AND FM, HARTFORD, PROGRAM DIRECTOR, 1969

While hospitalized, owner pays visit, asks if I want to take it as vacation time.

GM: "Triple C!" must be repeated every five. If you can hear bass through wall, do not play it.

WBCN, BOSTON, MORNING NEWS, PRODUCTION DIRECTOR, 1969

Owner: "This is show business. When your tits sag, you're finished!"

WGLD, CHICAGO, IL, BOSTON HAROLD, AFTERNOONS, 1970–1971

General manager believed he was Elvis reincarnate.

Arriving from WBCN, where I had a friend, Massachusetts Fats, took name Boston Harold (my middle name) after local *Herald* newspaper.

Flower power didn't last that long. What a ride. Like trying to interpret the Firesign Theatre logically.

WDAI, CHICAGO, EVENINGS, 1971

Chicago was one of the reasons I got into radio! Especially song "Listen."

Robot radio, after end of dismal ABC Love Network FM concept.

CJOM, WINDSOR, ONTARIO, CANADA, EVENINGS, PROGRAM DIRECTOR, 1972–1973

Owner makes fortune skinning alligators in South America to finance radio empire.

Morning show co-host Larry Himmel went on to become Mr. San Diego Media. Calling the Windsor mayor cocksucker didn't help.

There's a problem in Canada with calling the mayor a cocksucker?

Program director was expat from U.S. avoiding the draft.

DJ Kokaine Karma is from the Rainbow/White Panther Party that John Sinclair organized. Always striving to test limits of the CCC (Canadian Communications Commission), fired en masse, locked out Thanksgiving for invoking rebellions and sometimes obscene spirit of Lenny Bruce!

KPRI, SAN DIEGO, CA, THE MORNING TEAM, 1973

So ill conceived, people overslept for days.

Doobie and Roach, the Baloney Brothers. Twenty years before Beavis and Butt-Head.

KGB AM AND FM, SAN DIEGO, EVENINGS?, 1973

Whatever went wrong in radio originated right here.

WHCN, HARTFORD, CT, EVENINGS, 1974

Prog rock . . . Hartford for the taking! Who cares, right?

WINZ-FM, ZETA IV, MIAMI, FL, EVENINGS, 1975

When I was able to make it in.

Fired after stealing PD's girlfriend.

WCOZ, BOSTON, MORNING DRIVE, 1976–1978

Front for a drug company.

WCOP, BOSTON, KEVIN O'CAPEN WEEKENDS, SOMETIME IN THE '70S

Is rock "lite" a thing?

WEEI-FM, BOSTON, SAME TIME, DIFFERENT STATION

WPIX, NEW YORK CITY, AFTERNOONS, 1978

If shuttle from Connecticut was on time.

Faux Oldies.

WCBS FM, NEW YORK CITY, JIMMY FOXX ON WEEKENDS, 1979

They lied. I left.

Last song played* before going country-fried: "Summertime Blues" by Blue Cheer, first power trio ever named after brand of Owsley acid. *Not by me, by Billy Juggs!

Jive 95 still happening in 1980. That's pretty late in the free-form game. KSAN opened the door to other morning shows in the SF where they gave me carte blanche, so pulled off some pretty outrageous theater. This was all pre–Morning Zoo crap.

KSAN, SAN FRANCISCO, CA, MORNING PRODUCT, 1980–1981

Broadcasting from the "Stephen Capen Building."

Baseball's great play-by-play man, Ernie Harwell, friend of my producer, Hank, recorded this ID, in his fine Georgia peach tone, when Harwell's Tigers came to play our Oakland A's: "Hi everybody, this is Ernie Harwell, voice of the Detroit Tigers. And whenever we're in the Bay Area, we always tune in to K-SAN, the Jive 95. The Tigers and everybody else!"

Last gasp of original progressive. Fights broke out over drugs in hallways.

Metromeaningless GM El Nuclear Warhead seduced department heads, beat them, or both.

Steve Chapple in the *Chronicle* wrote: "The death of KSAN is as unthinkable as the defection of the Giants to San Jose or the toppling of the Transamerica pyramid into the bay."

KFRC, SAN FRANCISCO, NEWS ANCHOR, MORNINGS, 1981

Joanne Newsenzweig is news director here!

Called it "K-Farsi" or "K-Farce." Another in series of suspensions.

With legendary scumbag moaning man, Dr. Don.

KSFX/KGO AM AND FM, SAN FRANCISCO, MORNING DRIVE, NEWSTALK, 1981–1982

https://archive.org/details/KSFX_San_Francisco_04-26-82 Air check from April 26, 1982, just before I close down another format.

You can teach monkeys to do this. Taking calls: "Hello, you're out of your mind and in everyone else's!"

KMEL, SAN FRANCISCO, MORNINGS, 1984–1985

All kinds of Jiver 95ers were on board for this Dance-Band-on-the-Titanic format.

KRQR, SAN FRANCISCO, 1987

A two-day stint filling in for Peter B. Collins. Canceled after one.

GM Mel Karmazin, pre-Mr. Sirius mogul, made radio's bad boy Howard Stern promise to never make fun of him. We get suspended for calling him "New York Mutts announcer and Snagglepuss Ice Cream salesman, Mel Karamel!"

Hank produced. Additional wizardry by Bill Kates, especially Coyote's trickster yips; he also played "Hacker," ahead-of-his-millennium computer nerd.

WXRK (K-ROCK), NEW YORK CITY, AFTERNOON EPISODE, 1988–1989

Pretty good run. Why was I fired again?

Lou, at the end of "Great American Whale" off that album: "Stick a fork in them. They're done."

PD Pat Evans, GM Cheech reprimand us for "too many Chernobyl and *Exxon Valdez* jokes. Remember, our audience is the eggheads." Oh, we thought *egghead* meant braniac! No, they mean listeners in Jersey.

Lou Reed comes in after release of *New York* album. Lou Reed *is* New York, splendid having him in studio, listeners can hear his leather jacket squeaking on mic.

—Lou, I guess Andy Warhol gave you some of your first venues.

He'd say (imitating Warhol), "How many songs did you write today, Lou?" Oh, I don't know, Andy, maybe two. "Why not four? Why not six?"

—A real fount.

"Lou, why don't you write a really mean song?" What do you mean, Andy? "Oh, 'Vicious, I hit you with a flower.'" He'd say, "Lou, why does a song have to end?" I said, how do you mean, Andy? We manipulated the vinyl so the song went, "I'll be your mir—, I'll be your mir—, I'll be your mir—." Unless you physically went over and lifted the needle, it never ended.

—Fantastic! What song should we play off *New York*?

"Busload of Faith." Play that, yeah.

[That song hadn't been approved. We were only allowed to play the single "Dirty Boulevard."] Suspended.

RJ Smith of the *Village Voice* wrote us up after Robert Bly interview; I slept at Bly's men's conference in an Ojai yurt; on the air he talked about rock 'n roll figures like Mick Jagger rebelling against their fathers. Abbie Hoffman called in about Salman Rushdie and free speech. Chris Stanley called to say Abbie Hoffman had died and gave us Wavy Gravy's number. "Good grief," Wavy told listeners. "Good grief." Quoted Abbie: "There are no isms anymore, there are only reactionaries and revolutionaries. Reactionaries want things to stay the same, revolutionaries want change." Central Park ranger tells us what natural delights to dig this weekend. Segment ends with Gary Snyder poem, "For All." *One ecosystem / under sun / in diversity / with joyous interpenetration for all!*

MISSING IN JOURNALISM, NEW YORK, 1990–1992

Investigative pieces on transnational malfeasance. Japanese company bioengineered a food supplement that people were using as a sleeping pill. After a friend was paralyzed and then killed by it, wrote it up for *Village Voice*. Hopeful. Pursued field, after contributing to *San Francisco Magazine* fluffy and unsatisfying. Wrote screenplay about Sterling Hayden.

KFOG, SAN FRANCISCO, GRAVEYARD WEEKENDS, 1992–1993

Something innocuous this way slogged.

KDBK, SAN FRANCISCO, NEWSFLAP, WEEKENDS, 1993–1994

Fired by Viacom thugs while booking guests on studio phone (the high price of call-waiting then).

"Anemic Pop."

KTID, SAN RAFAEL, CA, WEEKENDS, 1994

On the downside of forty. The voice is the last thing to go. First the knees, then up the skeletal structure—the stab in the back, the pain in the neck . . . the voice is the last to go. Still got it. Because radiomen "take the long way home!" (Still playing Supertramp.)

Pursuing satellite deal with Rupert Murdoch's Star system. Never heard back.

KUSF, SAN FRANCISCO, THE FUTURIST HALF-HOUR RADIO HOUR, 1995–1996

Kate Ingram and Ben Fong-Torres created *Jive Radio* show at University of San Francisco station. Old-and-in-the-way and elder Jivers on Saturdays for a couple of hours, spinning favorites, recollecting.

Left San Francisco to study Jungian psychology.

Perorations! What of it?

KVON/KVYN, NAPA, CA, NEWS FOR THE DUMBED DOWN, 1998–2000

Cracker management meets Aryan Church. No veritas anywhere in this wine!

Hog reports.

REFERENCES

STEPHEN CAPEN Do not bother anyone connected with radio stations where I have worked. As a kid I listened to the big Magnavox hi-fi in the corner of the living room. Above it were plastic instruments and musical notes my artsy mother, consummate hostess and performer, had decorated the wall with. I'd grab the plastic sax off the wall and wail. Caught up in the music where you can't sit down. Playing to an invisible audience. A quote in Greil Marcus's book, *Like a Rolling Stone*, which he dedicates "to the radio," goes: "When it comes to radio, it's a surprise. It breaks the day, it gives you a lift and, suddenly, 'Okay, I'm sticking with the story as long as it lasts.' It's a gift when it comes from the radio."

Chris Stanley was the other radio sweetheart of mine. He'd gotten Cape and me our NYC gig because he knew the program director; and, he brought me in at KNX 1070 News Radio in L.A. In the '70s, Chris and his friend, writer/reporter Bill Vitka invented *Direct News*, an audio magazine. Featuring countercultural interviews, arts, music, and news, *Direct News* was pressed on vinyl and sent via U.S. mail to progressive stations nationwide.

BILL VITKA Chris had a story for everyone. Here's one he never told. During the Vietnam war, he was assigned to air force intelligence. But when they found out about his politics, he was reassigned to supply. In Thailand at the same time our government was launching planes from there, conducting a secret bombing campaign in Laos, Chris sat behind a mic on Armed Forces Radio. God know what he played. One day, a returning bomber crashed at the base. Plowed directly into the radio station—a tent—and everybody was killed. Chris had called in sick that day.

I met Chris at 5 a.m. He was in the Gnus studio, prepping his first Jive 95 broadcast. I watched him snap open a black attache case and pull out a hairbrush, sweeping it down long, blonde locks. He shook that manly mane all over, letting his freak flag fly. He'd interviewed Kurt Vonnegut and Gore Vidal, Edward Albee and Abbie Hoffman—when Abbie was on the run from the FBI. *Is this the coolest news guy ever?*

Joanne Greene: "Chris's passion for news was unmatched. His moral code could get in the way, as he became so outraged at injustice in any form. He smacked El Nuclear Warhead (our despised general manager) with this hat, to no avail."
PHOTO BY FRED GREENE / GREENECREATIVE.COM

BILL VITKA Chris did stellar interviews. He had a good run at CBS [1982–1998]. He won Golden Mike awards, covered six political conventions. Rode the campaign bus with Pat Buchanan and came back telling us, "Ride to the sound of the guns!"

Chris took an anchor job at Fox radio. He had to end every newscast, "Fair and balanced." He told Vitka, he had to quit, "before I shiv Bill O'Reilly in the elevator."

BILL VITKA Now the plan was to get to October 27, 2012, the birthday he'd be sixty-five. But one day he missed a deadline. *Chris Stanley, missing a deadline?* In radio, that's when bells go off. Now he's with his gumba Capen in that Heavenly Radio Choir. I think Chris taught me about a world where when you had a story, you worked that story, at that hour, that afternoon, that night, all that day, and the next. That's a reporter.

To the end, he told me a ninety-second newscast could change the world, because he knew how much he could fit in a minute.

We used to go see matiness after work together on Geary Street out in the Avenues. Chris identified with Bill Murray as Hunter Thompson in *Where The Buffalo Roams;* Stephen fell for Tom Waits as DJ Lee Baby Sims in Jim Jarmusch's, *Down By Law.* After, Cape began repeating Waits' talk up about a record by Earl King, " . . . a little somethin' called . . . *Trick Baaag.*" For years, Stephen did it. "Trick baaaag!" He identified with any DJ who had gigs at "WWOZ, WHLO, WAKR. . . ."

I remember a cocaine night in the late '70s, at a KSAN gathering where I was sitting at Chris's feet; he and Stephen made me take notes on their latest revolutionary programming plans. Too burnt to ever get them on the air. One of our last trips together was a pilgrimage to the Humboldt County redwoods on California's Lost Coast, because Chris needed advice (now it was Bush-Cheney driving him mad) from his idol, the brilliant *Village Voice* and *Nation* columnist, Alexander Cockburn. Alas, "Dr. Pressclips" was not at home. We found rooms to crash in that night, and, after getting into it about politics on the drive back, ended up tackling each other (after a few silly slaps, the pull-in to a clinch) in the parking lot at the Larkspur ferry. (Waits and John Lurie did that in *Down By Law!)* Here's one more memory from the early '80s: We drive through the fog to the buffalo paddock deep in Golden Gate Park. Bison hanging out in the big City. We have a loaf of

sourdough and push chunks of it through a hole in the security fence. Thick grey tongues are taking in our San Francisco treat! *Wow, man.* Such gentle, mythical beasts in the fog. And huge. Almost as big as Donahue.

SUPPLEMENTARY READING

The Kesey Tapes!

Secret tapes are part of KSAN lore (see SLA Communiques). I was lucky to liberate a couple reels. (Allen Ginsberg said to "liberate" is to free, that it's not stealing because "things are common mythological property." You go, Ginsy!) For *What Was That?* (see *What Was That?: Ten Years After*), a 1976 special, Bob Simmons invited novelist and pioneer of consciousness, Ken Kesey, to look back at 1967 and what was it all about, Mr. Natural? Kesey sent down two reels from Pleasant Hill, Oregon—where the Kesey Farm is now an artists' retreat—but only fifteen of those ninety minutes made it into *What Was That?* I found the reels in the basement, literally underground—thanks Bob!—just before the end, when Kesey might've said, "So long, so long, so short!" The following excerpts also feature Ken Babbs and interviewer John Teton. Nearly fifty years old, but their words resonate in the twenty-first century, when the effectiveness of psychedelics as therapeutics appears promising.

KEN KESEY Anyway, what you want to do is introduce John Teton, who will be introducing us to the KSAN audience. Where's my little thing that shines a light in front of my face?

JOHN TETON That marvelous miner's hat.

KEN BABBS Well, without further ado, I will present you now with a guest artist here, conducting today's interview. None other than journalist John Teton.

TETON I'm here from San Francisco, as a loyal listener to KSAN radio, the Jive 95. And shucks, Mr. Babbs, I can't tell you how honored I am to be placed in this position of interviewing such notable gentlemen as you and Dr. Kesey.

A BRIEF ORIGIN STORY

BABBS The Merry Band of Pranksters went on the bus trip in '64 and later began to put on the shows called the Acid Test, and also, little known to most people, was an actual band. As they said at Lake Pontchartrain, "What are you, some kind of band or something?" We said, "Yeah, we're a band. We're the merry band of pranksters!" In '64, we actually did a trip on the bus where we burned our shirts and gave up our lives as Pranksters in search of the Cool Place, to go out and become our regular selves in the world.

HOW THE PRANKSTERS SUPPORTED PRESIDENT JOHNSON ON BROWNIES

TETON You pointed out yesterday that if you put bad vibes into somebody, it's going to come out somewhere else. And in the case of Nixon, it came out in Cambodia.

KESEY This is important in the philosophy, that as Pranksters, we at one time vowed, swore to, as strong as anybody would swear to, say, a marital vow, which is: You try to go with the person's trip that's in front of you. We would start it when we would spin the thing on the floor. It would turn to somebody, it would point to them, and that meant that everybody supported that person for three minutes. Whatever he did, whatever his face did, if he broke down and cried, if he jumped up and down, if he just sat there and sucked his thumb, if he beat off. Whatever it was, you withdrew judgment and looked at him new. And at a certain point, in '68, when things were getting worse and worse, and Lyndon Johnson was beginning to drop cards out of his sleeve, we realized that everybody had been sending into Johnson the double barrel of our coven, which is what we are. Which is a dumb thing to do, because it was coming through Johnson and going right out and hurting other people. So we decided, the next time we see Johnson on TV, let's get stoned, completely stoned, look at him, and support him as a soul, even though we know that his policies are full of shit. The next time he got on, we ate a bunch of hash brownies. Went over to Chuck's house. And he came on and he gave this long talk; it was about the mining of something . . . no, that was fucking Nixon. Anyway, Johnson came on, and we did this thing. Just the way we used to practice it, with that thing of supporting this human, dropping all the stuff that we're getting through the media, just supporting the guy. And all of a sudden, you could see him begin to split and crack and climb out through this media wrapper. And say, "Fellow Amuricans, look here at my scar. It runs all the way from Cambodia clear to my goddamned asshole! I can't make it. I gotta sit down. I'm cutting out. I'm a Texan, and I hate to say this, but fellow Amuricans, I know that what I'm doin' is the best for the country. And that's hard for a big ol' mean Texan to say." And he said it, and everybody's heart watching him went, "Atunga-tunga-tunga-tunga." And that is the way it's won.

DRUGS AND THE CIA, THE DIFFERENCE BETWEEN EAST AND WEST COAST HIPPIES

KESEY The various chemicals which were suddenly being discovered at the time on all fronts, mainly the *government* making these great amounts of chemicals that they were giving to us, trying to convince *us* that we had a conspiracy going! *The CIA was taking LSD* at the same time that "IF IF" and "IS IS" was also taking LSD, IT-290, and MP-14.

BABBS It was the détente of the day. Everybody has to keep up with everybody else, even if it's in milligrams, not megatons.

TETON Can you explain what "IF IF" and "IS IS" were?

BABBS "IF IF" being Internal Freedoms of something.

KESEY No, no, the "International Federation for Internal Freedom" was Millbrook [New York]. This was the [Tim] Leary group. Leary was working on one front, without us knowing each other. We were working on another front, without us knowing each other. [giggles] And we're gradually coming around to a meeting, after all these years. I spoke to Leary the other day, and Leary sits and talks and [Eldridge] Cleaver and him sit across the same table, type across the same table twelve hours at a stretch. I mean, who knows what karmic gears are grinding the juice out of this drama?

TETON And "IS IS"?

BABBS Internal Source of Infernal . . .

KESEY The Intrepid Search for Internal Space.

BABBS Inner Space.

KESEY Inner Space! That was what it was. "IF IF" was Millbrook and [Billy] Hitchcock and Leary and a lotta rich people who were going to Mexico, to Zihuatanejo, to seek out some kind of paradise down below the border and probe drugs *that way*. We were, all of us, too low rent and funky for that. We headed directly into the heart of the country, trying to find inner space *here*, instead of *there*. This has always been one of the philosophical differences between us.

THE NEON HANDSHAKE AND HOW MUHAMMAD ALI WAS LIKE PSYCHEDELICS

KESEY Having read these questions that were sent up here from KSAN, there was this whole other thing that took place between us that I think makes sense and has to do with what happened during KSAN's great befuddled summer of whatever it was, that was . . .

BABBS Lost.

KESEY We have an *umbrella*. We are not many. This umbrella was knitted together cleverly by people who have been in on this for a whole lot longer than we are. And, once a person is dead, or even if the person is not even in the same plane with you, he may be part of your umbrella enough that you *support* him and what he is doing, even when you can't understand it sometimes. You reach across and you make this handshake. And that begins to knit up over time, through time; time can't touch it, because it doesn't recognize the *Rolling Stone* deadline that it has to make. Or the fact that KSAN has to get this show on the air by a certain time. And during various acid trips these things were vowed amongst each other in unspoken, yet glyphic ways. You would see actual hands extend, drawn, neon from your heart, reach across, to hands drawn, neon from this other guy's heart, and lock in a handshake and say: "Okay let's work on this until we get the damn thing across because otherwise it's gonna sink. There are not many of us on board anyway. We can't go around backbiting each other. But you and I will make this pact across the ether, and we won't break it." And that's what all of this has been, between any of these people who have been involved in an outright brotherhood. They are lazy. They're worthless. They malinger, they drop out, they die. But *nobody quits the mob, man!* I mean, anybody, who has seen the vision of what has to be, knows that he either has to do, what has to be done, to bring about what has to be or, he is fucking off! [laughter]

Before it made that leap into Bill Graham's pocket, there was a lot of nimble, far-out stuff decided and worked out that has never gone away. It's not listed anywhere. But it was the foundation of some kind of government that still works. And it came down to: we knew that we had to take a lotta dope, to get our heads out of the place that got Ehrlichman and Haldeman and Spiro Agnew's brows in that shape. So that that clot that is in there, in their heads—the same thing that Muhammad Ali saw when he dropped that grid out of his head. When we watched Ron Lyle and Foreman fight today, what you realize is that they may beat Ali every so often. But they're not in the same league with Ali. His mind moves at a different crack. Ali was the first guy, nationally, to suddenly drop a whole bunch of grids out of his mind, to where he was operating without having to have to send his voice through that. The next bunch of guys to do it were the people that started taking psychedelics. It just happened that Cassady was not only already a speed freak, not just by taking speed, but by moving fast all the time. As a trip. In trying to keep up with words. It just happened that he already had a foundation under him. He was well built, he was strong, he was sturdy, he was good looking, he had everything going. When acid hit him, man, he *took off* and just left a comet trail across what they eventually called the Haight-Ashbury, as the sparks fell into the street. [laughter]

MARTIN BUBER AND THE PASSING OF SOULS THROUGH ETERNITY, ETC.

KESEY The KSAN question is about the [Prankster] bus movie, and how do I feel about doing it now as opposed to then. Um, I feel better about it, but I still don't know what it was. Like Buber says, "When you know something, you have two things that you have to do: you have to make a sacrifice and you have to take a risk." And the sacrifice that you take is the endless amount of possibilities that are offered up on the *altar of form*. Now Cassady, the '60s, all that stuff that was cooking and bubbling back then, once it is laid out really well, to where it sets like good candy, then you have made that sacrifice. That's the first thing, that in some way we have decided to do again. This KSAN interview, us going through all these old tapes, talking about all this old shit, taking the last remnants of the last of the chemicals made by the government, to try on people to see what would happen. By *our government*! Given to people at Stanford, the smartest, the highest, the ex-student body presidents. One dot off the end of a hardest leaded pencil, on the highest bond of paper, which could be seen with the finest Bausch & Lomb loupe, was enough to get this one guy high for so many days that they completely crossed him off the Stanford faculty list. They stopped paying him, he was high for so long.

BABBS He's still running around. They find him around the nuclear accelerator once in a while.

KESEY Accelerating and still accelerating. The hand that we're being dealt is no ordinary hand. And everybody knows it. Whether we're winning or losing isn't as important as that we're sitting at the table in *the big game*. And the people that are sitting at the table in the big game, whether it is Howard Hughes, Neal Cassady, or Marty Balin, or Ravi Shankar, or Yehudi Menuhin, or Joan Baez, or Jackson Pollock, or Bob Kaufman—these people all know it. They'll have arguments, but they will *always play fair*. These people won't cheat you, because they know how important the game is. It's what you sit down around the table to do. And the people that have sat around this table, and always will, because the revolution runs lateral and linearly.

BABBS And vertically.

KESEY And every which way, so that the same caveman who gets stoned by his buddies for asking a guy in who's hungry, and says, "Here, take a bite out of this bone," instead of beating the guy with the bone. . . . When the revolution is finished, he will be given the Congressional Medal of Honor, and he will walk through the gates there, alongside of Hitler, Douglas MacArthur, Buddha, and Charlie Manson. People will take a look at him, and they'll say, "Far out, far out. Right! Right!" And they'll give him a huge, huge hand. And when Cassady goes through, he'll get a hell of a hand. By everybody who was paying attention. I mean, he'll get a bigger hand than Hitler, than Kennedy. The only person I can think of offhand, that I have ever known, that might go through and get a bigger hand than Cassady, is part of family, and I can't be trusted to be sure that I can make proper judgment. Because you usually judge family out of a different consciousness. But he will get a huge hand. He'll take many bows.

TETON You better explain how Hitler got on that roster with these other folks.

KESEY You know that book, *The Best of Life*? By *Life* magazine? I've looked at that book a lot of times, and finally, every time I look, go through it, what I begin to notice, more than anything else, is that the feeling I have for these characters gradually becomes one of affection. I mean, Goebbels I still don't feel any affection for. Mussolini I feel much affection for. I look at him, I know the guy, I know how his mind works. He was wrong. He was bad. But I feel affection for him. And that is the way the revolution is being won. We will cut Nixon loose, we will know how to pass him in eternity, and hit him on the shoulder, and say, "What's happening, you old fuck? Man, was that a trip or not?" [laughter] And Nixon will blush, drop his eyes, and he will give you five, and you will give him five, because what is important, always, is the passage of souls through eternity. Not the judgment of souls. That is not our job.

VIOLENCE IN THE COUNTERCULTURE AND A MEETING IN MINOT, NORTH DAKOTA

TETON KSAN's staff was interested in your views on violence in the counterculture.

KESEY I've always been strongly against violence. I mean, I mean I'm fierce; don't mess with me. [laughter]

TETON How many of you out there in KSAN radio land realize that Ken Kesey is in the Oregon Wrestling Hall of Fame, as one of the top five in the history of Oregon collegiate wrestling, in terms of total wins and losses, a former contender for Olympic championship? This man is not afraid to rustle and tumble!

KESEY One at a time or all at once, makes me no difference, come on. [laughter]

BABBS Any of those violent guys come around here, we're gonna kick their asses!

KESEY One time I saw, we were there in Minot, North Dakota. Me and Wendell Berry and some people making a talk. We looked down the long hall of the airport. And down there, we saw coming the biggest guy I've ever seen in my life. He was absolutely enormous. He walked on, and the closer he got, the bigger he got. He walked into the bar. The bar tilted to let him in. I said gosh, that's Chris . . . Chris Taylor, the Olympic wrestling champion. And everybody knew it was him. Four hundred eighty pounds, with a red beard. He was beat by the Russian in a great suplex. Pitched him over backwards. We asked this guy to come sit with us. And he was glad to find that I knew wrestling and knew about him going to the Olympics, and the guy, God, his brow was as big as my forearm! His eyes were hid way back under these red lichens of eyebrows. He was so hideous that he had achieved some kind of beatitude. And when you sat near him, what you realized was, that of all the people at the bar, this guy, least of all, wanted violence. He knew that it doesn't make any difference how big you get. All it takes is some runty little weasel sticking his finger in your eye, and it *hurts.* So the bigger a guy is usually, the more he is actually putting out there for, "Take it easy, folks, take it easy. Don't anybody move too fast or jerk too hard. Because I've been hit, and I'm big. And I know that you think you're little. But I know that it hurts a big person just as much as it hurts a little person, to get stuck in the eye or kneed in the balls." That's what I feel about violence.

CHARDIN'S THEORY OF THE NOOSPHERE, ENTROPY BIND, AND MEATBALL!

KESEY At a certain point, the noosphere of this world suffered a *leap*, that we're still trying to get over. A lot of people came along and tried to help us make the leap. Like Cassady. A lot of people tried to prepare us a long time before the leap. Like Dylan Thomas. And during the leap, like Bob Dylan. But the leap went on. Not just in the mind. Chardin's theory of the noosphere, it means that when consciousness strikes, it doesn't just hit one person or one thing. It hits everything. That consciousness, itself, is a material substance that *slocks* ya. I always think of Bob Crumb's thing, "Meatball." *Meatball!* When meatball hit, everybody knew. Meatball! You were hit by the meatball, man. It not only hit the human beings and the hippies; it hit the truck drivers, it hit the plants. It hit Nixon, it hit Ehrlichman, it hit Haldeman, the meatball hit everybody.

BABBS Oh yeah, everybody's turned on now.

KESEY It wasn't acknowledged by most people, because there was no way to frame it. The people who were into dope, or into some kind of arcane study, who were into enlightenment, knew what the meatball was. The meatball was the jump in the noosphere. It came concurrent with the acid consciousness. I think, and so do a lot of people, that when these new things hit our heads, they spread out, and we saw a bunch of new ways to make connections. To solve problems. To get out of the entropy bind that we're in.

TETON A lot of people are hanging around, waiting for another meatball.

KESEY Only one meatball! And, "you gets no bread with one meatball," is I believe the way the song goes. You can get the bread anytime, but you give up the meatball. Far out. I think Slim Gaylord wrote that years before that came by, but that's the way the meatball works. It's like those Escher spheres that move one inside of the other. Every once in a while, three or four holes on those spheres line up. And they are the meatball holes. The meatball goes through—*zhoom!*—those three holes. Strikes you in the face.

BABBS Right in the forehead!

KESEY Glory Hallelujah! Hallelujah, Lord!

BABBS I have seen the light!

KESEY And the light is clear!

BABBS Here, take one of these clear light tabs! [laughter]

KESEY And we not only did, but a lot of people did. And nobody that ever took it ever got over it. We thought we could turn a lot of people on to it. And that would make a change. The noosphere doesn't work like the vote for student body president in high school. When the thing strikes, like the distillation of alcohol struck and went through the world within a very short time, everybody, everything knew about it.

BABBS Everybody was drunk.

KESEY Everybody was drunk for a century! It had never happened before. When it was time, it went. When acid happened, I remember listening to this guy interviewed over, probably KSAN . . . does KSAN go back that far?

BABBS Oh, KSAN's been around forever!

TETON The first one was KMPX, but KSAN has been around for quite a few years now as the major progressive FM underground.

KESEY Well, this was like, I think maybe one step below or above KSAN. It was this Lou Irwin type of character, and he said, [news voice] "And here we have one of these typical young people in the streets, sons and daughters of the middle-class wealthy, who have dropped out, and seem to be taking this acid. Let me ask this young man, why are you doing this?" [hippie voice] "Well, man, you know, like it's just . . . happenin'."

And it *was* at that time, happenin', and everybody that was in on it knew what it meant. It meant that there was a thing going on, and the consciousness was giving a leap. What we didn't know, is that it was happening *everywhere.* We assumed that it was just us, like Charlie Manson.

BABBS He thought he had all the marbles.

KESEY Then, finally we assumed it was just the humans, or just the Americans. Or just the young. But now, it's the plants. Everybody knows that the plants knew it when we knew it. That the rocks knew it when we knew it.

BABBS The animals.

KESEY Everything knew it when we knew it. We had the *flash.* Everything now is waiting for us to say, "Okay." The light came on for a second. We saw the door. We saw the way out.

BABBS Then it slammed in our faces.

KESEY Then the light went out! The door's still open; we just can't find it. We're groping around.

BABBS The light is so bright it blinded us. Whoops!

KESEY But it has happened. Time, you know, is—that's no big deal in eternity. Kali can shuffle the cards faster than we can, uh, dream up funerals. Around the great long dance of time and humanity, there's *plenty* of time. And when that shot of the noosphere hit, we are still under recoil from it. Everybody that we know is still reeling from this shot. I used to think of it like this: that there suddenly happened, in the middle of the earth, a vibration, that started from, like, one tune was hit with one rock. And a new vibe was started, and it went out from there, like a ripple in the stream.

EDGAR CAYCE, THE GRATEFUL DEAD VS. PAUL REVERE AND THE RAIDERS

TETON I'm sure KSAN listeners would like to hear more about this *vibe.*

BABBS I've always thought it came in from outer space.

KESEY This is a killing vibe that I'm talking about. The killing vibe spread out like a ringworm, and when it touched you, it shook you to pieces. It moved on out like a ringworm, and it touched everybody; it shook them to pieces. Their cells couldn't abide the change that went down, as all of this stuff went on. The people that were killed didn't exactly look dead, but you could tell they were. The people that weren't killed could easily tell they weren't. They could tell it in their eyes. They could tell it by the way their voices were picking the words out of the air. They began to grab phones and pencils and movie cameras and tapes and tried to send out word across this spreading ringworm line, of *how to survive it.*

TETON In the belief that that particular form of death, which had claimed all those people, was one from which one could be revived.

KESEY The point that Cayce makes, that right down at the bottom, all you have to do, no matter how bad you've been, no matter how many bad things you've done—that is what redemption is about. You can actually cross off the karma. You jump out of karma. At any point, that can happen to anybody. It's as simple as reaching over and flipping the switch from on to off. But to get back to this noosphere thing, about what happened to us. And why we're still reeling from it is, we knew something happened. A lot of us tried to frame it fast. Jerry Rubin, he wanted to put it in a brown khaki jacket and have it march all the way to Hoboken. And take over every schoolhouse. Everybody had their own fantasy, us just as much as they, of how we were going to run things.

BABBS To run the world, heh heh. After that, the universe!

KESEY The most successful people have been the people who have not—at least yet—sacrificed the revolution on the altar of form, as we were saying. The Grateful Dead are still a great musical group because they didn't bend over to pick up the Paul Revere and the Raiders card. In fact, they didn't imagine any such thing as the Rolling Stones card. They were high on acid, man. They were trying to keep it together. They were trying to keep from falling off the stage. They were trying to keep alive. They were trying to tell the difference between their fingers and the people's fingers out there in front of them. And at a certain point, Paul Revere and the Raiders fell into that thing. It becomes part of what we'd think of as a bummer. Like some acidhead young kid said one time, "You know, my folks' sexual fantasies are my acid bummers!" [laughs] I can't think of anybody that didn't have a real bummer. The massive bummers struck deep, deep, deep into the heart of the revolution. Hurt it deeply. I saw it coming, and so did a lot of people see it, at Woodstock. It had moved into the feedback blowout. It could not stop. It had to blow out.

FOUR THINGS TO DO ON THE PATH OF ENLIGHTENMENT

KESEY I got this little book that says there's four things you have to do before you can continue on the path of enlightenment. First, you've gotta give up ambition, yet work like a man that's ambitious. You've got to kill out desire. You've got to kill out the need for comfort. And lastly, you have to remove the wound from your voice. Because the master will not listen to the wound in your voice. And Cassady, over three or four acid tests, had beat on me like that . . . "Keep your mouth shut, until you're *healed.* Don't put your vibes out until they're good vibes."

THE DOORS, SATORI-PARANOIA, AND THE BLOOD SACRIFICE OF ALTAMONT

BABBS [futzing with a whirring tape recorder, rewinding, stopping, clicking forward, stopping] For KSAN listeners, this is an old acid test recording made down in LA one day.

KESEY At about 11:30 on these Saturday nights, by one means or another, nothing ever planned, but always it would start happening—whatever had been brought would begin to move out to the people. At these scenes. And Pigpen it was that would be able to carry through it because he usually didn't take anything. He'd just be drinking. So when it came to "Midnight Hour," he was singing, at which point everybody, with the exception of him, was peaking out. But this is where the Dead, and us, and a lotta people came into some kind of conjunction. As it is around the poker table that we were talking about, everybody is playing fair. That means that nobody who was part of this scene was doing it for any of a number of reasons that we have all drawn a line through, which is to advance oneself in certain ways. Or to do this, or to do that. Because when you're really, really loaded, you not only can't do it, but you know that all that you've ever done before was such a horrible mistake that you wish you'd never even thought of it! And when the Dead played, and we were out there working, we were trying to get it all together; everybody that was in that building at the time, including the hired cops, wanted the good vibes to come through . . . nobody wants any trouble. And they knew as long as it remained pure and innocent, which it did, for a long time. The notion of a bad trip was not the way it is now. Once the bad trip began to hit, in a large, *Steppenwolf* fashion, I knew it, particularly when I came back out of jail and went to see the Doors. Now this relates to the KSAN. This really relates to the KSAN, and I think what they're asking. I came back from Mexico. Bam! I'm in jail. I don't know anything about anything, but what's going on in jail, and coming over the FM radio that comes into jail. I get out of jail. I go to San Francisco. The only other contact I've had has been this funny graduation thing which I've been away from, so I don't know what went down there. Why the Dead couldn't show up, and why, suddenly, this guy Bill Graham, who I didn't know, had a piece of the action. Which I hadn't even thought of as *action* yet!

BABBS More like an ordeal than action.

KESEY Right. We never charged more than a buck and never planned to. We never planned to suddenly create an industry. Anyway, I went to see the Doors. Playing at Winterland. *Bill Graham Presents!* We went there; it was packed full. I took some acid. It was a mistake. It was tight. I went in there and I saw, and everybody saw, but they couldn't admit it, that it wasn't happening. And everybody else was acting like they had, but they hadn't. So everybody was looking at each other and smiling and saying, "Mmm, this must be the way you smile when you're enlightened. But the fact is [weeps] I'm the only one that isn't enlightened."

BABBS Oh no, you're not. I'm not enlightened, either.

KESEY Well, there was a whole Winterland full of people that were not enlightened. And they came out with these frozen, cheated smiles. And there was Terry the Tramp standing there. And I looked at him, and he knew that I knew that they had been cheated. "They don't understand," he says. "The Doors just aren't big enough." And it was exactly that. The Grateful Dead was big enough to do what it was in the original fantasy. They still are. They can still play the top of the pyramid and give this noosphere another jump. But the Doors just didn't understand what it was about. And so, for a long time we had a lot of paranoid people. And it was called, what was it, enlightenment-paranoia? *Satori-paranoia.* That's what it was. Everybody had paranoia that other people had satori, had achieved satori in one form or another. Except them. So they had to fake it. So everybody was faking it. So it went around with everybody, *paranoid as shit.* Except, always, for Cassady. Who would puncture it. Who had been way, way beyond.

BABBS Beyond satori-paranoia.

KESEY And it took, finally, blood, as it always does. Altamont was the blood. Everybody knows it. It was the blood sacrifice, the blood ending of our claim to innocence anymore. From here on out it meant, it's gonna be hard. Up to then, we coulda' got it easy. After Altamont, we knew, it was gonna be a bitch, man.

BABBS Well, what was there to do, but to go on to eating meat? Even raising our own animals for the slaughter.

KESEY So we've been up here, ever since. Tending our properties. And our tapes and our films. And trying to keep our head above the same water that's been trying to wash across everybody's mouth that doesn't want to breathe shit.

VIKING PRESS, DYLAN'S MISTAKE, MORE CASSADY, AND A MUSE-FILLED SKY

TETON Say something about this image you had of Roman riding. That is, trying to ride two horses at once, a leg on each. One being the horse of the explorer and revolutionary in the realm of consciousness. And the other being the artist, the prodigy, pride and joy of Viking Press.

KESEY Okay, this always brings to mind, to me, Dylan's mistake as I think of it.

BABBS Dylan Thomas?

KESEY Ol' Bob Dylan. His mistake was, "Something is happening, and you don't know what it is, do you, Mr. Jones?" When you did that, you create the dichotomy of the horses. It means that there is one horse over here that Mr. Jones knows about, and one that he doesn't. The Viking Press horse, that I proved that I could get up on and ride, no longer was steed enough for me, after I met Cassady and then saw other vistas. Not just Cassady, but read Kerouac, read more Joyce, had taken more dope. Had just learned more about what was going on. I wanted to do what everybody who has ever had a taste of this has wanted to do, is *have one foot on grace, to where the words tumble from a muse-filled sky, down through your mind, and off the tip of your quilled tongue.* [Teton and Babbs applaud, "Very good, very good!"] Right out to Viking Press and to the paperback markets! So what I find is that nobody, with the exception of Cassady, and only him briefly, when he was writing, was able to ride those Roman horses—one foot on New-York-publishing-world-and-the-Hollywood-way-of-understanding-*Cuckoo's-Nest.* And the other foot on another kind of consciousness entirely, which has to do with automatic writing, grace, and revolution, and relation, and Buber. Well, anyway, finally I have learned that you can ride one horse and lead the other. And then get off onto the other one, when the one you're on gets tired. You can ride the Cassady freewheeling horse and lead New York, and you can ride New York and lead Cassady. You just have to be respectful of both mounts.

TETON Didn't you say that you saw, some years ago, the limit? That there is some maximum, which you may even have already reached, to the extent to which you can be an avatar?

KESEY Yes, but I think that you ought to keep your chops up. In case it comes back again.

TETON All right! See, you were being too pessimistic the other night.

KESEY No, I'm just saying, that I don't think that you can ever expect for . . .

TETON You said that you *knew* the limit.

KESEY Well the limit is, not to expect it! Knowing your own limits means you know that you can't reach down in your pocket and come up with it.

TETON You said before, you didn't think that you were going to get farther than you'd already gotten.

KESEY No, no, that's not what I meant.

TETON Okay, good.

KESEY No, not at all. I meant that to imagine that you can go ahead—Cassady used to say the same thing. "I haven't had a new thought in twenty years." What you say what comes to you, what comes by you, you say it as well as you can. But no, I think you want to keep your chops up. In not just the writing form. This is the changes that we've made. We have up here, within a twenty-mile radius, most of the same people that were on the bus. Most of them now with children.

BABBS With their own buses! [laughter]

KESEY On their own buses! And we see each other, if not regularly, at least more than we'd like to. [laughs]

BABBS More than we can stand.

KESEY As much as we can stand. Exactly. We make no money.

BABBS We've accumulated huge debts.

KESEY We have an enormous pile of film and tape that we have tried to keep track of. And we've tried not to sell it off.

BABBS So, if you want one foot of original Prankster film . . .

KESEY If any tape freak is out there, this Cassady footage, and the Cassady tapeage, [laughs] is fantastic. And ought to be regarded sometimes. There's no way that these people can write these things about Lenny Bruce, without having tapes of Lenny Bruce. Those are, as Buber says, "contemptible."

BABBS Which?

KESEY The movies without as much real stuff as you can get. Contemptible.

TETON The KSAN people are titling the special, "What Was That? Suddenly Lost Summer."

KESEY [Cassady is rapping with jazz underneath] And the man that had his finger on it and that was lost with it, and why we lost him, was Neal Cassady, which you have to kind of pick up on like he's in a corner somewhere and you are not paying too much attention because he's got foam in the corners of his mouth. And you can see by the glitter all around the red rims of his eyes that he's been up maybe six days. He has finally worn everybody out, listening to everything he's had to say about fearlessness and fireworks. And finally there he is in the corner talking to himself, and you would realize that as you would end your speaking so would he, and you'd find that he was saying something somewhat in relation to what you were saying. He was like going and davening somewhere in a large cavern. The sound that came back from the end of the cavern was your own voice, coming back. Scared sometimes and crazy sometimes, but at least always snuffing like a hound towards one light. He could talk in rhyme, he could talk in italic hexameter. He could scan. There was a message in this. It has to do with light, mercy, the future, and mainly the *revolution* and the movement toward the revolution. If the Haight-Ashbury is to be dedicated to anybody at all, if it rose out of any consciousness, it came out of *On the Road*, which came out of Jack Kerouac, which came out of Dean Moriarty, which came out of Neal Cassady. He was the one.

LAST GO ROUND: TWO REVOLUTIONARY ANGELS AND FAREWELL TO KSAN

KESEY I think what is approaching is what is known as a *window* in the space world. There is a window, occasionally comes by, in which you can make leaps into gathering great-enlightenment-masses, like, Boardwalk of the Id. And I know it's the same two guys that came in here the other day, that are two revolutionary angels, and they want to hear why. Because they didn't get any of the original flash, or the original cream. They want enough of that cream to continue working. One guy says, "We gotta fight 'em man." And the other guy's a writer and an artist. He was saying, "No, it's done with poetry." And I was saying, it's done *both ways*. You bomb at night, but you do it creatively. You do something that's never been seen. That's what a prank is. Hey, listen, let me tell you what the problem is, though, with this, with the America. We got just enough time to do this. We'll sing our song. We saw it on a marquee: "God Will

Bless America Only When America Blesses God." Things are backwards. So you take it like this, you go [they sing], "America bless God . . . Deity we know."

TETON I return you gentlemen to the world of KSAN's radio listeners.

BABBS Hello, radio listeners!

KESEY Hello, radio listeners!

BABBS This hasn't been too confusing, has it, I hope?

TETON Before this very non-commercial message, you were talking about the two revolutionaries that approached the other day. One being . . .

BABBS Black!

TETON And the other being . . .

KESEY White!

BABBS They were almost opposites. One being explosive, the other being . . .

KESEY Sanpaku. The one being sanpaku was the explosive one. The poetical one was very merry-of-eye. The other one, the black of face one, had very sanpaku eyes. But the longer he sat there, and the higher he got, the narrower his eyes became.

BABBS And the lesser his snot!

[Kesey plays his plastic flute, they listen to their own voices on tape]

BABBS It may be time to turn the earth, as spring approaches and the grass seed must be planted. Boo for the CIA and all nefarious activities! Yay for Gerry! And yay for détente! Yay for Henry, and yay for China.

KESEY And Lee Harvey Oswald!

BABBS Well, my goodness gracious, let us not roll over any bones in the graves!

KESEY That's true. Sorry about that, Lee . . . uh . . . lay back!

BABBS Relax. You've done your bit.

KESEY Literally . . . though we will lay it on.

BABBS At the jai alai game! [laughter] In Honolulu. And as lastly and lustily I lay myself limpid on life's . . .

KESEY Damp shore . . . we will bid forever adieu to KSAN.

BABBS All you eager listeners, who wanted to know how this all came about!

KESEY Seven dollars to Pleasant Hill, Oregon, order *Spit in the Ocean*. First issue edited by me, hee hee heee.

BABBS Second issue edited by my! [laughter]

KESEY Third issue edited by, if you're not weary already, edited by Leary.

BABBS The girls from San Francisco who say, straight from the gut, we'll get it to you.

KESEY Straight from the gut, all women from San Francisco lay on their backs with your legs well spread!

BABBS Ooh, please do! Because we in Oregon are ready to come down there with our Douglas firs outstretched. [laughter]

KESEY Send seven fifty to Pleasant Hill.

BABBS When the spring comes, we get in our boats, or else sit on the roof. What do you do when the catastrophe strikes?

KESEY I try to blow it out! [giddiness abounding]

BABBS We cover the flood with humor. Otherwise life would be unbearable to those picking up in the mud. Good-bye, eager listeners. We don't have anything left. You got any more questions? Write 'em!

KESEY We'll see you in the next millennium. Good-bye, KSAN! Good-bye, San Francisco!

BIBLIOGRAPHY

Altman, Robert. Introduction by Ben Fong-Torres. *The Sixties.* Santa Monica Press, 2007.

Anthony, Gene. *The Summer of Love: Haight-Ashbury at Its Highest.* Celestial Arts, 1980.

Armstrong, David. *A Trumpet to Arms: Alternative Media in America.* J. P. Tarcher Inc., 1981.

Armstrong, Moe. *Memories of a War Vet: A Hope for Many.* Self-published, 2021.

Austerlitz, Saul. *Just a Shot Away: Peace, Love, and Tragedy with the Rolling Stones at Altamont.* St. Martin's, 2018.

Boal, Iain, Janferie Stone, Michael Watts, and Cal Winslow. *West of Eden.* PM Press, 2012.

Boyle, T. C. *Drop City.* Viking, 2003.

Cain, Nancy. *Video Days and What We Saw through the Viewfinder.* CreateSpace, 2012.

Carson, David A. *Grit Noise and Revolution: The Birth of Detroit Rock 'n' Roll.* University of Michigan Press, 2005.

Caute, David. *The Year of the Barricades: A Journey through 1968.* Harper and Row, 1988.

Coyote, Peter. *Sleeping Where I Fall.* Counterpoint, 1998.

Cutler, Sam. *You Can't Always Get What You Want.* ECW Press, 2010.

D'Allesandro, Jill, and Colleen Terry, with Victoria Binder, Dennis McNally, Joel Selvin, and Ben Van Meter. *Summer of Love.* Fine Arts Museums of San Francisco, University of California Press, 2017.

Dalzell, Tom. *The Battle for People's Park: Berkeley, 1969.* Heyday, 2019.

Densmore, John. *Riders on the Storm.* Dell, 1990.

Dreyer, Thorne Webb. *Making Waves: The Rag Radio Interviews.* University of Texas Press, 2022.

Echols, Alice. *Shaky Ground: The Sixties and Its Aftershocks.* Columbia University Press, 2002.

Egan, Jennifer. *The Invisible Circus.* Random House, 1995.

English, Ilene. *Hippie Chick.* She Writes Press, 2019.

Fisher, Marc. *Something in the Air: Radio, Rock, and the Revolution That Shaped a Generation.* Random House, 2007.

Fong-Torres, Ben. *The Hits Just Keep on Coming: The History of Top 40 Radio.* Backbeat Books, 1998.

Fong-Torres, Ben. *Not Fade Away.* Backbeat Books, 1999.

Fong-Torres, Ben. *The Rice Room.* Hyperion, 1994.

Fong-Torres, Ben, ed. *The Rolling Stone Rock 'n' Roll Reader.* Bantam Books, 1974.

Fornatale, Pete. *Back to the Garden: The Story of Woodstock.* Touchstone, 2009.

Gaskin, Stephen. *Haight Ashbury Flashbacks.* Ronin, 1990.

Gitlin, Todd. *The Sixties: Years of Hope, Days of Rage.* Bantam, 1987.

Goldberg, Danny. *In Search of the Lost Chord: 1967 and the Hippie Idea.* Akashic, 2017.

Goodman, Lizzy. *Meet Me in the Bathroom: Rebirth and Rock and Roll in New York City, 2001–2011.* HarperCollins, 2017.

Graham, Bill, and Robert Greenfield. *Bill Graham Presents: My Life inside Rock and Out.* Da Capo, 1992.

Gravy, Wavy. *Something Good for a Change: Random Notes on Peace thru Living.* St. Martin's, 1992.

Greenfield, Robert. *Dark Star: An Oral Biography of Jerry Garcia.* Harper, 1996.

Grissim, John. *We've Come for Your Daughters: What Went Down on the Medicine Ball Caravan.* William Morrow, 1972.

Grushkin, Paul. *The Art of Rock Posters from Presley to Punk.* Abbeville Press, 1987.

Harcourt, Nic. *Music Lust.* Sasquatch Books, 2005.

Hayden, Tom. *Long Sixties: From 1960 to Barack Obama.* Routledge, 2009.

Hicks, Dan. *I Scare Myself: A Memoir.* Jawbone Press, 2017.

Hill, Sarah. *San Francisco and the Long '60s.* Bloomsbury Academic, 2016.

Hopkins, Jerry. *The Hippie Papers: Trip-Taking, Mind-Quaking, Scene-Making Words from Where It's At.* Signet, 1968.

Hoskyns, Barney. *Small Town Talk.* Da Capo, 2016.

House, Jeff. *To Live Outside the Law You Must Be Honest.* Unpublished.

Hyden, Steven. *Twilight of the Gods: A Journey to the End of Classic Rock.* Dey Street, 2018.

Jarnow, Jesse. *Heads: A Biography of Psychedelic America.* Da Capo, 2016.

Kaliss, Jeff. *I Want to Take You Higher: The Life and Times of Sly & the Family Stone.* Backbeat Books, 2009.

Kassel, Michael. *America's Favorite Radio Station: WKRP in Cincinnati.* Popular Press, 2013.

Keith, Michael C. *Talking Radio: An Oral History of American Radio in the Television Age.* M. E. Sharpe, 2000.

Keith, Michael C. *Voices in the Purple Haze: Underground Radio and the Sixties*. Praeger, 1997.

Klosterman, Chuck. *Sex, Drugs, and Cocoa Puffs: A Low Culture Manifesto*. Scribner, 2003.

Kramer, Michael J. *The Republic of Rock: Music and Citizenship in the Sixties Counterculture*. Oxford University Press, 2013.

Krieger, Susan. *Hip Capitalism*. Sage, 1979.

Kubernik, Harvey. *1967: A Complete Rock Music History of the Summer of Love*. Sterling Publishing, 2017.

Laufer, Peter, ed. *Highlights of a Lowlife: The Autobiography of Milan Melvin*. Jorvik Press, 2016.

Laufer, Peter. *Inside Talk Radio: America's Voice or Just Hot Air?* Birch Lane Press, 1995.

Laufer, Peter. *Interviewing: The Oregon Method*. Oregon State University Press, 2014.

Laufer, Peter. *Mission Rejected: U.S. Soldiers Who Say No to Iraq*. Chelsea Green Publishing, 2006.

Laufer, Peter. *Slow News: A Manifesto for the Critical News Consumer*. Oregon State University Press, 2014.

Laufer, Peter, and Christian Ruggiero. *Radio Vox Populi: Talk Radio from the Romantic to the Anglo-Saxon*. Anthem Publishing, 2022.

Law, Lisa. *Interviews with Icons*. Lumen Books, 1999.

Lee, Hermione. *Tom Stoppard: A Life*. Knopf, 2021.

Leibovitz, Annie. *Annie Leibovitz at Work*. Phaidon Press, 2018.

Lesh, Phil. *Searching for the Sound: My Life with the Grateful Dead*. Back Bay Books, 2005.

Levin, Bob. *The Pirates and the Mouse: Disney's War against the Counterculture*. Fantagraphics Books, 2003.

Lichtenstein, Bill. *WBCN and the American Revolution*. MIT Press, 2021.

Marcus, Greil. *The Doors: A Lifetime of Listening to Five Mean Years*. Faber and Faber, 2012.

Marcus, Greil. *In the Fascist Bathroom: Punk in Pop Music, 1977–92*. Harvard University Press, 1999.

Marcus, Greil. *Lipstick Traces: A Secret History of the 20th Century*. Harvard University Press, 1989.

Marcus, Greil. *Mystery Train: Images of America in Rock 'n' Roll*. Plume, 1975.

Marshall, Jim. *The Haight. Love Rock and Revolution—The Photography of Jim Marshall*. Insight Editions, 2014.

McNally, Dennis. *A Long Strange Trip: The Inside History of the Grateful Dead*. Broadway Books, 2002.

McNally, Dennis. *Desolation Angel*. Bantam Doubleday, 1979.

Melvin, Milan. *Highlights of a Lowlife: The Autobiography of Milan Melvin*. Edited by Peter Laufer. Jorvik Press, 2016.

Myers, Marc. *Rock Concert: An Oral History*. Grove Press, 2021.

Neer, Richard. *FM: The Rise and Fall of Rock Radio*. Villard Books, 2001.

Nisker, Wes. "Scoop." *The Big Bang, the Buddha, and the Baby Boom*. HarperCollins, 2003.

Nisker, Wes. *You Are Not Your Fault and Other Revelations: The Collected Wit and Wisdom of Wes "Scoop" Nisker*. Soft Skull Press, 2016.

Oseary, Guy. *Jews Who Rock*. St. Martin's, 2001.

Palao, Alec. *Love Is But a Song We Sing: San Francisco Nuggets, 1965–1970*. Rhino Entertainment, 2007.

Peck, Abe. *Uncovering the Sixties: The Life and Times of the Underground Press*. New York: Pantheon, 1985.

Pierce, Dave. *Riding on the Ether Express: A Memoir of 1960s Los Angeles, the Rise of Freeform Underground Radio, and the Legendary KPPC-FM*. Center for Louisiana Studies, 2008.

Proctor, Phil, and Brad Schreiber. *I Never Got My Fortune Cookie*. Blurb, 2021.

Richardson, Peter. *No Simple Highway: A Cultural History of the Grateful Dead*. St. Martin's/Griffin Books, 2014.

Rohrer, Jake. *A Banquet of Consequences: True Life Adventures of Sex (Not Too Much), Drugs (Plenty), Rock & Roll (of Course), and the Feds (Who Invited Them?)*. Indy Pub, 2020.

Rorabaugh, J. *Berkeley at War: The 1960s*. Oxford University Press, 1989.

Santelli, Robert. *Aquarius Rising: The Rock Festival Years*. Dell, 1980.

Schoenfeld, Eugene. *Dear Dr. HipPocrates*. Penguin, 1973.

Schreiber, Brad. *Music Is Power: Popular Songs, Social Justice, and the Will to Change*. Rutgers University Press, 2019.

Schreiber, Brad. *Revolution's End: The Patty Hearst Kidnapping, Mind Control, and the Secret History of Donald Defreeze and the SLA*. Skyhorse, 2016.

Selvin, Joel. *Altamont: The Rolling Stones, the Hells Angels, and the Inside Story of Rock's Darkest Day*. Dey Street, 2016.

Selvin, Joel. *Hollywood Eden*. House of Anansi Press, 2021.

Selvin, Joel. *Smartass: The Music Journalism of Joel Selvin; California Rock and Roll*. SLG Books, 2010.

Selvin, Joel. *Summer of Love: The Inside Story of LSD, Rock & Roll, Free Love and High Times in the Wild West*. Dutton, 1994.

Shales, Tom, and James Andrew Miller. *Live from New York: An Uncensored History of Saturday Night Live*. Little, Brown, 2002.

Slick, Grace, with Andrea Cagana. *Somebody to Love?* Warner Books, 1998.

Springsteen, Bruce. *Born to Run*. Simon and Schuster, 2016.

Steffens, Roger. *So Much Things to Say: The Oral History of Bob Marley*. Norton, 2017.

Szatmary, David P. *Rockin' in Time*. Prentice Hall, 2000.

Talbot, David. *Season of the Witch*. Free Press, 2012.

Twain, Mark. *Roughing It*. Signet Classic, 1962.

Walker, Johnnie. *The Autobiography*. Penguin, 2008.

Ward, Ed, Geoffrey Stokes, and Ken Tucker. *Rock of Ages: Rolling Stone History of Rock & Roll.* Rolling Stone Press, 1986.

Waters, Lou. *Have I Got a Song for You: The Bobby Dale Story; From Juvenile Delinquent on the Streets to the Rock and Roll Hall of Fame.* Infinity Publishing, 2009.

Werner, Craig. *Up around the Bend: The Oral History of Creedence Clearwater Revival.* Harper Perennial, 1999.

Whitley, Sheila. *The Space between the Notes: Rock and the Counter-Culture.* Routledge, 1992.

Zane, Warren. *Petty: The Biography*. Henry Holt, 2015.

Zimmerman, Nadya. *Counterculture Kaleidoscope: Music and Cultural Perspectives on Late Sixties San Francisco.* University of Michigan Press, 2013.

ARTICLES

Hall, Stuart, and Julian Nagel, ed. "The Hippies: An American Moment." In *Student Power*. London: Merlin Press, 1969.

Kai, Suzanne Joe. *Like a Rolling Stone: The Life and Times of Ben Fong-Torres.* Documentary, 2021.

Marcus, Greil. "Dead Air." *New West*, October 22, 1979.

Steffens, Roger. "Nine Meditations on Jimi and Nam." In *Jimi Hendrix: The Ultimate Experience*, edited by Adrian Boot and Chris Salewicz. Box Tree Limited, 1995.

https://www.washingtonpost.com/outlook/2019/08/22/this-month-people-are-remembering-woodstock-long-forgotten-music-festival-had-more-impact.

http://lostlivedead.blogspot.com/2010/09/march-18-1968-pier-10-san-francisco.html, story of the Grateful Dead playing outside KMPX on the first night of the strike.

https://www.jstor.org/site/reveal-digital/independent-voices, underground press archives.

JIVE95.COM AND FURTHER LINKS TO JIVER HIJINKS

https://bayarearadio.org/audio/ksan_fm/1978/KSAN_10th-Anniv_1978_A.mp3 Tenth-anniversary performances on KSAN by the Stones, Who, Petty, Mac, Costello, Queen, and Randy Newman. 1978, 60 minutes.

https://bayarearadio.org/audio/ksan-fm Bob Postle's Bob Dylan (triple Gemini, like Voco, Donahue, and Thom O'Hair), featuring KSAN's Congress of Wonders original interpretation of "Gates of Eden," produced by Roland Jacopetti. 1969, 71 minutes.

https://sexyboomershow.libsyn.com/mr-reggae-vietnam-vet-and-psychonaut-roger-steffens Interview with the amazing Roger Steffens.

http://www.jive95.com/mp3s/01%20Track%201.mp3 Live from the Boarding House in San Francisco! "KSAN's Kollege of Knowledge" quiz show. Grand Prize: A Kenwood stereo system: KR 2400 AM-FM receiver, KD 2333 turntable, pair of LS 403 two-way speakers! Retail value $519.90! Questions include: "Of what three charges was John Mitchell convicted, in regard to the Watergate coverup?" Dave McQueen, "Conspiracy, perjury, obstruction of justice." Ding! Ding! Ding! Guilty! Guilty! Guilty! (shout-out, *Doonesbury*).

https://www.youtube.com/watch?v=h3J4KnY_ziE Congress of Wonders comedy sketches.

https://archive.org/details/RC0538/RC0538.mp3 "Ask the Manager," Bonnie Simmons takes listeners' comments, April 1977.

https://www.youtube.com/watch?v=_GX-PZNig70 Sex Pistols sound check at Winterland, January 14, 1978.

https://www.youtube.com/watch?v=gER0LhISPt0 Co-simulcast co-hosts, Glenn Lambert and Norm Winer; Scoop Nisker with Chet Helms and others at the closing of Winterland, December 31, 1978.

https://www.youtube.com/watch?v=WS9vStrE-QI A Scoop collage after the Kent State massacre, May 1970.

http://radiothrills.com/ndlovesradio.htm Norman Davis's treasure trove of radio thrills!

https://www.youtube.com/watch?v=Cznih-0eZgQ&t=6s Dave McQueen does San Francisco comedy on *Videowest* in late '70s.

http://traxandgrooves.blogspot.com/p/ksan.html KSAN pix and audio and links to other stations.

https://digitalcollections.library.ucsc.edu/catalog?utf8=%E2%9C%93&search_field=all_fields&q=ksan Two dozen interviews, many from the KSAN special *What Was That? Or, Suddenly Lost Summer*, courtesy of the University of California at Santa Cruz.

http://www.reddogsaloonfilm.com Documentary on how the whole scene got started in Virginia City, Nevada.

CD, *The Golden Age of Underground Radio*, with Tom Donahue (DCC Compact Classics, 2006). There are also two CD collections of music and air checks, numerous Facebook groups, the Jive site; why, you can listen on the road, in headphones, even on the grass with an old radio, like Wavy Gravy did to heal himself, balancing the little music and revolution box on his chest!

ACKNOWLEDGMENTS

The idea for this project began at a Jive 95 Reunion Concert at Yoshi's in San Francisco, 2014, bringing together fifty alumni and some bands of the KSAN era, including Big Brother and the Holding Company, Cold Blood with Lydia Pense, Rick Stevens from Tower of Power, members of Jefferson Starship, Country Joe McDonald, Sal Valentino, and Annie Sampson.

Thank you also to Dan Crist for his all-around mensch-ness (and twelve-room writing cabin in Shelton, Washington); the Dove Library in Carlsbad, California (free screen wipes!), Santa Monica Library, and Shelton Library; Penmar Golf Club, Kafe K, Papille Gustative, Pancho Lopez y ganga Fiesta Brava in Venice; the Museum of Performance + Design; San Francisco State archives; Foundsf.org; BAM Media; California Historical Radio Society (CHRS); and *San Francisco Chronicle*, *San Francisco Examiner*, *Washington Post*, *Rolling Stone*, *Village Voice*, *Berkeley Barb*, *Bay Guardian*, *San Francisco Express Times*, and *Good Times*.

Thank you, Jesse Block, director of the KSAN documentary, for enlightening interviews, without which this would have been woefully incomplete; to Jasper Loftus and Jud Nirenberg for transcriptions; and Ed Brouder for his interview with Steve Capen. To beloved friends: Marta Cupesok and Denise Tabor; and Miriam Ancis, Dr. Bob, Ami Capen, Charlie Capen, Ronnie D. Clemmer, Dan Cohen, Laurence Cohen, Shel Cohn (co-host of our radio station when we were twelve), Dick Dahl, Gerry Fialka, Victoria Figueroa, Rose Flashenfeld, Don Foster, John Gabree, Michael Goldner, Bill Goldstein, Steven Alan Green, Meg Griffin, Zulie Heneghan, Pam and Jon Kalish, Lisa Karrer, George Laney, Chuck Levin, Paul Lyons, Ilan Mandil, Parlan McGaw, Marybugs Menaker,

Lisa Napoli, Kent Olson, Tom O'Neill, Colleen Preston, John Rabe, Ann Randolph, Stephen Ringold, Lisa Robins, Flash Rosenberg, Donna and Tommy, Andy Ross, Liz Ryan, Michael Segel, Jeff Shames, David Simons, Joe Smurda, Peter Staloch, Julius Valiunas, Reb Venice, Suzy Williams, Jamie Willoughby, Meredith Zamsky, Stu Zamsky, Claire and Arne Zaslove, and Roy Zimmerman. And Kris Strobeck (digging this journey the most!); Nick O'Connor and Ridge Tolbert letting me send Jive; Lisa Fliegel (finishing *Bulletproof Therapist* memoir, she gives the best advice); Danny Mandil and his father Binyamino for teaching me how to write this some; Annie Cronmiller, who reeled in Little Rock on her AM transistor from Appleton like I did Wheeling from mine in Traverse City; and her husband Bob Rees (our silly sketches interrupted the records on our WESU show in Middletown—and to Ted Stevens and Jerry Caplin for taping them!); and Eric Roth, author/publisher of Chimayo Press, for kickass input and books given freely. To the essential crack KSAN research team: Eric Meyers, Jim "Drapes" Draper, the Greenes up in Novato (who know who they are), and Brenda and Darryl Henriques (who has a memoir TK; title also TK)!

Finally, all praises to Tom Donahue, without whom none of this would be remembered; and honorary Jivers contributing to this project: Phil Austin, Ken Babbs, Peter Bergman, Joanne Braheny, Craig Chaquico, Peter Coyote, John Cuthbertson, Sandy Darlington, John Densmore, Jeff Dowd, Tom DeVries, Marc Fisher, Stephen Gaskin, Ronald Glaze, Ralph J. Gleason, John Grissim, Chet Helms, Sarah Hill, Jack Hines, Jeff House, Kate Ingram, David Jensen, Earl Jive, Brooke Jones, Mark Karan, Michael C. Keith, Alton Kelley, Zane Kesey, Michael J. Kramer, Susan Krieger, Paul Lambert, Lisa Law, Liz Lufkin, Greil Marcus, Rosie McGee, Dennis McNally, Robin Menken, Sandra Lee Palmer, Kathleen Petersen, Eric Postel, Phil Proctor, David Ossman, Jake Rohrer, George Russell, Michael Simmons, Bobby Slayton, John Teton, Rainbow Valentine, Diane Vitalich, Bill Vitka, Lou Waters, Wavy Gravy, Gordon Whiting, and Reggie Williams.

Given the dozens of folks I corresponded with (the nature of oral history projects), I am sorry if I've left you out; and to those who didn't send a story: Godspeed wherever you are! And much appreciation ("I appreciate you!") KSAN and KMPX folks: Randy Alfred, Moe (Jim) Armstrong, Dave Artale, Tom Ballantyne, Edward Bear, Alan Beim, Larry Bensky, Danice Bordett, David Bramnick, Stephen Capen, Dan Carlisle, Mimi Chen, Eric Christensen, Vicky Cunningham, Bobby Dale, Norma Dale, Norman Davis, Susie Davis, Buzzy Donahue, Raechel Donahue, Willis Duff, Denise Dunne, Samanthe Elmore, Ed Ely, Ben Fong-Torres, Rick Gardner, Richard Gossett, Joanne and

Fred Greene, John Grivas, Steve Hanson, Whitney Harris, Howard Hesseman, Travus T. Hipp, Kate Ingram, Roland Jacopetti, Sue Kagan, Tony Kilbert, Howie Klein, Chris Knab, Paul Krassner, Glenn Lambert, Peter Laufer, Chan Laughlin, Larry Lee, Joe Lerer, Kathy Lerner, Vicenta Licata, Hank London, Cynthia Louie, Bob McClay, Terry McGovern, Dave McQueen, Milan Melvin, Eric Meyers, Ron Middag, Larry Miller, Earn Morgan (whose dreads clicked like songs), Jeff Nemerovski, Nancy Newhouse, Scoop Nisker, Dan O'Neill, Marshall Phillips, Stefan Ponek, Bob Postle, Trish Robbins, Cathy Roy, Rick Sadle, Laurie Sayers, Eugene Schoenfeld, Brad Schreiber, Harry Shearer, Bob Simmons, Bonnie Simmons, Chris Stanley, Dusty Street, Budd Stuntt, John Teton, Voco, How Wachspress, Johnnie Walker, Kenny Wardell, Paul Wells, Norm Winer, and Roland Young.

Much affection and appreciation to Bonnie Simmons, Giovanni Natale, Roger Steffens, and Ted Bonnitt (who connected me with Roger and brought Dewar's late-night radio confab nightcaps on the back deck during Covid); especially to journalist/authors Ben Fong-Torres and Joel Selvin (who knows how the bodies got to where they're buried; journalists have the best stories); tireless online KSAN researchers Eric Meyers and Jim Draper (one hand held across the Atlantic, the other across the Bay); Bob Simmons for lending so much fabled history; Peter Laufer for similar knowledge and lore (and meeting in Eugene to give the best insight on this whatever-this-is; Simmons and Laufer are friends and colleagues since KSAN—I sure was lucky to find these amazing guys' help); and to the intrepid David Tabatsky, author of two dozen books, who gave me so much of his time on the coast-to-coast proposal and introduced me to his agent, Nancy A. Rosenfeld. And, always, to my original rock 'n roll siblings, sisters Nancy Rosenfeld (coolest rocker I ever knew; cosmic agent connection) and Jill (they saw the Beatles at Cobo Hall!), and Evan, Jimmie, Peggy, Liz, Adam, Jordan, Benjamin, Harrison, Jud, Emmet J. Nirenberg (top-notch comic book comrade and storyteller), my dear Aunt Margie, and to Mom and Dad, who showed me how much they loved books. Finally, to Peter Bergman, Firesign Theatre genius (invented the term "love-in" at LA's Elysian Park!). When we both had dumbed-down newswriting gigs at the local CBS owned-and-operated, he explained: "Radio is breath, theater is church, cinema is art, and television is furniture." And Bergman loved radio best, "Because the pictures are better."

PHOTO BY RICHARDMCCAFFREY.NET

Some of my Jive 95 superheroes who appear in this book:

Big Daddy Tom Donahue
First Freak Larry Miller
The Legendary Tom O'Hair
The Sage Bonnie Simmons
The Seeker Scoop Nisker
Clean Up Bob Simmons
Utility Man Fred Greene
Bear Edward Bear
Coyote Steve Capen
The Man Milan Melvin
The Beeb Johnnie Walker
The Amazing Moe
The Amazing McClay
The Anarchist Chan Laughlin
Anarchist, the Sequel Travus T. Hipp
Author Author Larry Lee
Night Man Norman Davis
Mr. Radio Norm Winer
Mr. Zen Alan Watts
Mahdi (The Expected One) Voco
The Chief Ken Kesey
Clown Prince Wavy Gravy
Storyteller R. Donahue
Budd Stuntt Joe Lerer
Dr. Hip Eugene Schoenfeld
The Gnus Inventor Bob Postle
Groucho Glenn Lambert
The Revolutionary Roland Young
The Human Cartoon Dan O'Neill
The Dish Trish Robbins
Keeper of the Jive Jim Draper
Lefty Larry Bensky
The Voice Dave McQueen
Sui Generis Man Bobby Dale
The Producer Rick Sadle
The Professor Peter Laufer
The Punk Richard Gossett
The Manager Willis Duff
Fabulous Terry McGovern
Nemo Jeffmerovski
Waterbed Man Roland Jacopetti
Newsenzweig Joanne Greene
The Lobster Paul Wells
The Acolyte Eric Christensen
Bam Bam Kenny Wardell
The Midwesterner John Grivas
The Stone Ben Fong-Torres
Listener Whisperer Vicky Cunningham
Superchick Dusty Street
Tully Tom Ballantyne
CBS Chris Stanley
The Engineer Howard Wachspress
Swami from Miami D. Henriques
"Jay" Steve Hansen
The Zen Bastard Paul Krassner